access to history

France in Revolution

FOURTH EDITION

Dylan Rees and Duncan Townson

HODDER
EDUCATION
PART OF HACHETTE LIVRE UK

Study guides updated, 2008, by Sally Waller (AQA), Angela Leonard (Edexcel), Geoff Woodward (OCR A) and Martin Jones (OCR B).

The publishers would like to thank the following for permission to reproduce copyright illustrations: © Archivo Iconografico, S.A./Corbis, pages 112, 125; © Bettman/Corbis, pages 4, 36, 44, 82, 93, 109, 144 (top), 144 (bottom), 157; Bibliotheque Nationale, pages 10, 16, 59, 61, 66, 68, 91, 119, 128, 158, 168, 180; Bridgeman Art Library, page 32; © Burstein Collection/Corbis, page 205; © The Gallery Collection/Corbis, page 190; Getty Images, pages 29, 94; © Gianni Dagli Orti/Corbis, page 88.

The publishers would like to acknowledge use of the following extracts: Cambridge University Press for an extract from *The French Revolution: An Economic Interpretation* by F. Aftalion, 1990; Cambridge University Press for an extract from *The Jacobin Republic 1792–1794* by M. Bouloiseau, 1983; Catholic University of America Press for an extract from *Religion and Revolution in France 1780–1804* by N. Aston, 2004; Fontana Press for an extract from *France 1789–1815 Revolution and Counter-Revolution* by D. Sutherland, 1985; HarperCollins Publishers Ltd. for an extract from *The French Revolution* by A. Goodwin, 1966; Longman for extracts from *Longman Companion to the French Revolution* by C. Jones, 1988; Longman for an extract from *Revolution and Terror in France 1789–1795* by D.G. Wright, 1974; Oxford University Press for an extract from *The Oxford History of the French Revolution* by W. Doyle, 1989; Simon and Schuster for an extract from *The French Revolution Voices from a Momentous Epoch 1789–1795* by R. Cobb and C. Jones, 1988; Weidenfeld and Nicholson for an extract from *The French Revolution* by G. Rudé, 1988.

Every effort has been made to trace all copyright holders, but if any have been inadvertently overlooked the Publishers will be pleased to make the necessary arrangements at the first opportunity.

Although every effort has been made to ensure that website addresses are correct at time of going to press, Hodder Murray cannot be held responsible for the content of any website mentioned in this book. It is sometimes possible to find a relocated web page by typing in the address of the home page for a website in the URL window of your browser.

Orders: please contact Bookpoint Ltd, 130 Milton Park, Abingdon, Oxon OX14 4SB. Telephone: (44) 01235 827720. Fax: (44) 01235 400454. Lines are open 9.00–6.00, Monday to Saturday, with a 24-hour message answering service. Visit our website at www.hoddereducation.co.uk

© Dylan Rees and Duncan Townson 2008
Fourth Edition published in 2008 by
Hodder Education,
Part of Hachette Livre UK
338 Euston Road
London NW1 3BH

Impression number   5 4 3 2 1
Year   2012 2011 2010 2009 2008

Cover photo: print of 'Prise de la Bastille', © Gianni Dagli Orti/Corbis
Typeset in Baskerville 10/12pt and produced by Gray Publishing, Tunbridge Wells
Printed in Malta

A catalogue record for this title is available from the British Library

ISBN: 978 0 340 965856

Contents

Dedication

Keith Randell (1943–2002)

The *Access to History* series was conceived and developed by Keith, who created a series to 'cater for students as they are, not as we might wish them to be'. He leaves a living legacy of a series that for over 20 years has provided a trusted, stimulating and well-loved accompaniment to post-16 study. Our aim with these new editions is to continue to offer students the best possible support for their studies.

1

The Origins of the French Revolution

POINTS TO CONSIDER

The French Revolution was one of the most dramatic events in modern European History and also one of the most complex. The date frequently associated with the Revolution is 14 July 1789 when a notorious prison, the Bastille, was stormed in Paris. This date and event came to symbolise the downfall of the old order and the forced acceptance by the French monarchy of limited democracy. From that point onwards the pace of change increased and the French people and their institutions were subjected to enormous upheavals resulting in war, civil war, persecution, execution, dictatorship and economic chaos. The origin of the Revolution was due to a combination of political, economic and social factors. This chapter examines these factors as two main themes:

- Long-term causes of the French Revolution
- Short-term causes of the French Revolution

Key dates

1614	Last summoning of the Estates-General before 1789
1756–63	The Seven Years War
1774	Accession of Louis XVI
1778	France entered the American War of Independence
1781–7	Economic crisis
1788	Declaration of bankruptcy

1 | Long-term Causes of the French Revolution

During the *ancien régime* there were a number of deep-rooted problems that affected successive royal governments. These problems influenced:

- the way France was governed, particularly the taxation system
- the carefully ordered yet deeply divided structure of French society
- the gradual spread of ideas which started to challenge this structure.

Key term

Ancien régime
An expression that was commonly used during the 1790s to describe the French system of government, laws and institutions before the Revolution of 1789.

These deep-rooted problems can be seen as long-term causes of the French Revolution and in order to understand them fully it is necessary to understand the nature of French society before 1789, namely:

(a) the structure of royal government
(b) the taxation system
(c) the structure of French society
(d) the Enlightenment.

(a) Royal government

France before 1789 was an absolute monarchy ruled by the Bourbons. This meant that the authority of the French Crown was not limited by any representative body, such as an elected parliament. The King was responsible only to God and answerable to no one on Earth. This system of government is also known as absolutism. In such a system the personality and

Key question
What was the nature of royal power?

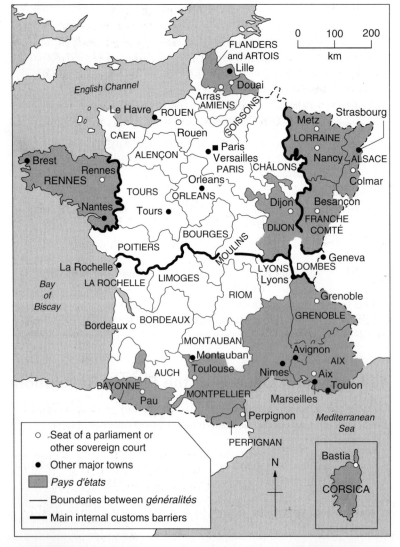

Figure 1.1:
Pre-revolutionary France's main administrative, judicial and financial sub-divisions

Key terms

Intendants
Officials appointed by and answerable to the Crown. They were responsible for police, justice and finance. They were also responsible for public works, communications, commerce and industry.

Généralités
34 areas into which France was divided for the purpose of collecting taxes and other administrative functions, and under the control of an *intendant*.

Key date

Accession of Louis XVI: 1774

Key question
Why was the unfairness of the taxation system an issue?

character of the ruler is very important as it sets the tone for the style of government.

In the century before the outbreak of the Revolution there were only three French Kings – Louis XIV, Louis XV and Louis XVI. Louis XV said in 1766 that 'sovereign power resides in my person alone ... the power of legislation belongs to me alone'.

Limitations to power

However, although their power was absolute, Kings were bound by the laws and customs of the kingdom. For example, there were many independent bodies such as the Assembly of the Clergy which had rights and privileges guaranteed by law. The King could not interfere with these.

The King also had to consult his council of ministers and advisers to make laws. This meant considerable power was in the hands of a small number of men. The most important of these was the Controller-General, who was in charge of royal finances. Each minister dealt with the King on an individual basis and did not form part of a cabinet system of government.

In the provinces the King's government was carried out by the *intendants* who had far-reaching powers in the *généralités*. In 1774 Louis XVI, the grandson of Louis XV, acceded to the French throne. The new King was well intentioned but never came to terms with the State's financial problems. In an absolutist system the monarch needed to be a strong figure with a dominant personality. Louis, although well intentioned, was rather weak and indecisive.

(b) The taxation system

Good government benefits greatly from an efficient taxation system that provides it with an adequate income. The taxation system in France was both chaotic and inefficient (see Table 1.1).

Table 1.1: The main taxes imposed during the *ancien régime*

Tax	Description	Indirect/ direct	Who was taxed?
Taille	Land tax	Direct	Third Estate
Vingtième	Five per cent tax on income	Direct	Third Estate
Capitation	Tax on people – poll tax	Direct	In theory Second and Third Estates
Gabelle	Salt tax	Indirect	Everyone
Aidas	Tax on food and drink	Indirect	Everyone
Octrois	Tax on goods entering a town	Indirect	Everyone

Direct taxes

The main direct tax before the Revolution was the *taille*. In theory this was payable by anyone who did not belong to one or other of the two privileged estates – the Church and the nobility (see pages 6–9). In reality, the inhabitants of some towns had been granted exemption by the Crown so the burden fell mainly on the peasantry. There was also the capitation (a tax on people frequently called a poll tax) and the *vingtième* (a five per cent levy on all incomes). However, not everyone was taxed equally and this unfairness created resentment. The Church did not pay them at all, and the nobles were exempt from the *taille*.

Profile: Louis XVI 1754–93

1754	– Born and christened Louis-Auguste, younger son of the dauphin Louis-Ferdinand (son and heir of Louis XV)
1765	– Following the death of his elder brother (1761) and the death of his father, Louis-Auguste becomes dauphin
1770	– Louis-Auguste marries Marie Antoinette, daughter of Empress Maria Theresa of Austria
1774	– Accession of Louis XVI following the death of his grandfather. Appoints Turgot as finance minister
1778	– French soldiers join American War of Independence
1781	– Publication by Necker of the *compte rendu* suggesting royal finances are in surplus
1785	– The Affair of the Diamond Necklace tarnished reputation of the royal family
1787	– Notables reject Louis' reform proposals
1788	– Louis sends the *Parlement* of Paris into exile causing popular disturbances
	– Agrees calls for summoning of Estates-General
1789	– May – Louis opens the Estates-General at Versailles
	– 14 July – Storming of the Bastille – Louis records in his diary the single word '*rien*' – nothing
	– October – Royal family brought forcibly to Paris
1791	– 20–21 June – 'flight to Varennes' Louis escapes from Paris
	– September – New Constitution agreed by Louis
	– November – Louis vetoes decrees against the *émigrés* and non-juring priests
1792	– 20 April – Declaration of war against Austria
	– 10 August – Storming of the Tuileries – overthrow of the monarchy
	– November – Discovery of the '*armoire de fer*' in the Tuileries
	– December – Trial of Louis
1793	– 21 January – Execution of the King

The character of Louis XVI is important in any analysis of the origins of the French Revolution because he was the absolute ruler of France. Previous views that he was unable to cope with the momentous events unfolding around him have recently been revised. While Louis had an excellent memory and took an interest in a range of intellectual subjects, he tended to lack self-confidence and appeared austere. Louis lacked the strength of character to combat the powerful factions in his court and failed at crucial times to give the necessary support to reforming ministers. In 1788 he was forced to summon the Estates-General.

Tax farming
A system where the government agrees a tax assessment figure for an area, which is then collected by a company that bids for the right to collect it.

Venality
A system whereby certain jobs could be bought and transferred on to descendants.

Philosophes
A group of writers and thinkers who formed the core of the French Enlightenment.

Guild
An organisation that tightly controls entry into a trade.

Corvée
Unpaid labour service to maintain roads, in many places money replaced the service.

Parlements
Consisted of 13 high courts of appeal. All edicts handed down by the Crown could not be enforced until registered by the *parlements*.

Indirect taxes

There was also a wide range of indirect taxes. These were levied on goods, not incomes. They proved to be a considerable burden to those on low incomes, but brought in a great deal of income to the Crown. Among the indirect taxes were the *gabelle* (a tax on salt), the *aidas* (tax on food and drink) and the *octrois* (this taxed goods entering a town).

Tax collection

Taxes were collected by a chaotic and inefficient system known as **tax farming**. The Farmers-General was a company that collected the indirect taxes for the government. They paid the State an agreed sum and kept for themselves anything collected above this figure. The French government consequently never received enough money from taxes to cover its expenditure, and so frequently had to borrow. Interest rate payments on the debt became an increasingly large part of government expenditure in the eighteenth century.

Many of the taxes were collected by officials who, under a system known as **venality**, had bought the right to hold their positions. They could not therefore be dismissed. Corruption and wastage was vast and this resulted in the Crown not receiving an adequate income while the tax-payers knew that much of the taxes they paid never reached the treasury.

On his accession in 1774 Louis XVI was aware of many of the problems affecting the finances of the State. He appointed Turgot as Controller-General. Turgot was influenced by the ideas of the *philosophes* and embarked on a reform programme. His attempts to abolish the trade **guilds** and the *corvée* and to reform the tax system provoked such a storm of protest from the *parlements* and other interested parties that Louis, for the sake of harmony, withdrew his support and Turgot left office.

The bulk of royal revenue was made up of taxation, yet because of the system of exemptions the Crown was denied an adequate income with which to govern the country. In order to meet the demands of war, the Crown was forced to borrow money. The tax collection system – 'tax farming' – meant that not all the revenue paid actually reached the treasury. The issue of taxation weakened the Crown and created resentment among the Third Estate. This was one of the most important of the long-term causes of the Revolution.

(c) French Society during the *ancien régime*

French society in the eighteenth century was divided into three orders known as the Estates of the Realm. The first two estates had many privileges that they frequently used to the disadvantage of the Third Estate. Over the course of the eighteenth century divisions appeared between the estates, and this became a long-term cause of the Revolution.

Figure 1.2: The structure of the *ancien régime c.* 1780

The First Estate

The First Estate was the clergy, which consisted of members of religious orders (monks and nuns) and clergy (parish priests). A number of issues contributed to the Church being unpopular with many people. These were:

- plurality and absenteeism
- tithes
- its exemption from taxes
- its power over the people.

Plurality and absenteeism

Many younger sons of noble families entered the Church and occupied its higher posts, such as bishops and archbishops, which provided large incomes. The Archbishop of Strasbourg received 400,000 **livres** per annum, which contrasted sharply with most parish priests (*curés*) who only who received between 700 and 1000 *livres* each year. Some bishops held more than one bishopric, which meant they were bishops of more than one **diocese**. This is called **plurality**. Many never visited their diocese, i.e. absenteeism. This made the Church very unpopular with many ordinary people who considered that bishops were more interested in wealth than the religious and spiritual needs of the people.

Tithes

The wealth of the Church came from the land it owned and the tithes paid to it. It was the largest single landowner in France, owning about 10 per cent of the land.

The tithe was a charge paid to the Church each year by landowners and was based on a proportion of the crops they

Key question
Why was the First Estate unpopular?

Key terms

Livres
The currency of France during the *ancien régime*. One *livre* was made up of 20 *sous*.

Diocese
An area served by a bishop. It is made up of a large number of parishes.

Plurality
The holding of more than one bishopric or parish by an individual.

produced. This charge varied widely. In Dauphine it amounted to about one-fiftieth of the crops produced, while in Brittany it was a quarter. In most parts of France it was about seven per cent of the crop. The income produced by the tithe provided the Church with 50 million *livres* each year.

Tithes were supposed to provide for parish priests, poor relief and the upkeep of Church buildings, but much of it went instead into the pockets of bishops and abbots. This was greatly resented by both the peasantry and the ordinary clergy and was one of the most common grievances made in their **cahiers** in 1788.

Tax exemption

The Church had many privileges apart from collecting the tithe. By far the most important of these was its exemption from taxation. This added to its unpopularity. Its income from property was immense: around 100 million *livres* per year in the closing years of the *ancien régime*. Instead of paying tax the Church agreed to make an annual payment, which it determined, known as the *don gratuit*. It was under five per cent of the Church's income and was much less than it could afford to pay.

Power over the people

France was a very religious country and Catholicism was the official state religion. The influence of the Church was considerable and touched many areas of people's lives.

It had wide-ranging powers of censorship over books which were critical of the Church, provided poor relief, hospitals and schools, and kept a list in the parish of all births, marriages and deaths. At a time when communication in general was very poor, the Church acted as a sort of Ministry of Information for the government, when parish priests informed their congregations about various policies and initiatives. The vast wealth of the Church and its resistance to new ideas made it unpopular with many people, which contributed to the long-term causes of the Revolution.

The Second Estate

Of the three estates, the nobility was the most powerful. Unlike the British nobility, which numbered hundreds, the French nobility numbered hundreds of thousands, although the exact numbers are disputed. Figures for the numbers of nobles by 1789 vary between 110,000 and 350,000. Within the nobility there were great variations in wealth and status.

- The most powerful were the 4000 court nobility, restricted in theory to those whose noble ancestry could be traced back to before 1400; in practice to those who could afford the high cost of living at **Versailles**.
- Second in importance were the *noblesse de robe* – legal and administrative nobles which included the 1200 magistrates of the *parlements*.
- The remainder of the nobility – the overwhelming majority – lived in the country in various states of prosperity. Under the

law of primogeniture, a landed estate was inherited by the eldest son. Younger sons were forced to fend for themselves and many joined the Church, the army or the administration.

The main source of income for the Second Estate was land, and they owned between a third and a quarter of France. Nearly all the main positions in the State were held by nobles – among them government ministers, *intendants* and upper ranks in the army.

Privileges

In addition to holding most of the top jobs in the State, the nobility had many privileges. They:

- were tried in special courts
- were exempt from military service
- were exempt from paying the *gabelle*
- were exempt from the *corvée* (forced labour on the roads)
- received a variety of **feudal** (also known as seigneurial) **dues**
- had exclusive rights to hunting and fishing
- in many areas had the monopoly right (known as banalities) to operate mills, ovens and winepresses.

Feudal dues
Either financial or work obligations imposed on the peasantry by landowners.

Key term

Perhaps their greatest privilege was exemption from taxation. Until 1695 they did not pay direct taxes at all. In that year the capitation was introduced and, in 1749, the *vingtième*. Even with these they managed to pay less than they could have done. They were generally exempt from the most onerous tax of all – the *taille*.

Provincial nobles were strongly attached to these privileges, which represented a significant part of their income. It was the less wealthy of the nobles who felt that if they were to lose their tax privileges and their seigneurial rights that they would face ruination. They were determined to oppose any changes that threatened their positions and undermined their privileges, as these were all they had to distinguish them from the commoners. The privileges relating to land ownership and tax exemption were resented by many ordinary people who saw the Second Estate as avoiding their share of the tax burdens borne by others. These issues contributed to the causes of the Revolution.

Joining the nobility

There were various ways of becoming a noble besides the obvious one of inheritance. One of the main ways of acquiring noble status was either by direct appointment from the King or by buying certain offices that carried hereditary titles. These were called venal offices and there were 12,000 of these in the service of the Crown. They carried titles that could be bought, sold or inherited like any other property.

Key question
How could an individual enter the nobility?

While gaining a title conveyed both status and benefits there were also limitations. Nobles were not in theory allowed to take part in industrial or commercial activities or they would suffer derogation (loss of their nobility). In reality many did, as the rule was not rigidly enforced. In Paris in 1749 nearly all the people with an income of over half a million *livres* were nobles. Even in industrial centres such as Lyon nobles were the wealthiest group. It has been estimated that during the eighteenth century between 30,000 and 50,000 people became nobles. Although the nobility formed a distinct and separate order it was not inaccessible to men of wealth and social ambition.

The Third Estate

In essence the Third Estate consisted of everyone who did not belong to one or other of the two privileged estates. There were enormous extremes of wealth within this estate.

The bourgeoisie

At the top end were the rich merchants, industrialist and business people. This group of rich commoners, who were not peasants or urban workers, is frequently referred to as the **bourgeoisie**.

Among the wealthiest of the bourgeoisie were the merchants and traders who made vast fortunes out of France's overseas trade. Others included financiers, landowners, members of the liberal professions (doctors and writers), lawyers and civil servants. Many were venal office-holders.

As a group the bourgeoisie were rising not only in wealth but also in numbers. There was a threefold increase in the number of bourgeoisie over the course of the eighteenth century to 2.3 million. Although the bourgeoisie was increasing in importance there was no real conflict between them and the nobility until at least the closing years of the *ancien régime*. They did, however, feel that their power and wealth should in some way be reflected in the political system as they bore such a substantial part of the tax revenue paid to the Crown. This slowly simmering resentment contributed to the long-term causes of the Revolution.

The peasantry

At the other extreme of the Third Estate from the bourgeoisie were the peasantry. They were by far the most numerous section of French society, comprising about 85 per cent of the population. This group, however, covered enormous variations in wealth and status.

At the top end was a small group of large farmers who owned their land, employed labourers and grew for the market. More numerous were the labourers who existed at, or near, subsistence levels. For much of the eighteenth century they, and the larger farmers, did well as agricultural conditions were favourable, particularly in the 1770s. Half of the peasants were share-croppers who did not own their land but farmed it and gave half of their crops to the landlords instead of rent. About a quarter of the peasants were landless labourers, who owned nothing but their house and garden.

In some parts of France **serfdom** continued to exist. There were a million serfs in the east, mainly in Franche Comté. They were at the bottom of the social structure and their children were unable to inherit even personal property without paying considerable dues to their lord. Poor peasants lived in state of chronic

Key question
Why did the Third Estate consider itself to be disadvantaged?

Key terms

Bourgeoisie
Usually translated as middle class. In the eighteenth century it carried a much less precise meaning and applied mainly to those who lived in towns and made a living through their intellectual skills or business practices.

Serfdom
Part of the feudal system where the inhabitants of the land are the property of the landowner.

A contemporary cartoon showing a peasant crushed by the weight of taxes and dues such as the *taille* and *corvée*, imposed by the privileged First and Second Estates

uncertainty. Bad weather or illness could push them into the ranks of the vagrants, who lived by begging, stealing and occasional employment.

Grievances

In many ways the peasants bore the burden of taxation and this made them extremely resentful. All peasants had to pay tithe to the Church, feudal dues to their lord and taxes to the State. Nearly all land was subject to feudal dues. These included the *corvée*, *champart* (a due paid in grain or other crops to the landlord which could vary from five to 33 per cent of the harvest) and *lods et ventes* (a payment to the *seigneur* when property changed hands).

A further grievance was that the peasant could be tried in the seigneurial court, where the lord acted as both judge and jury.

Taxes paid to the State included the *taille*, capitation and *gabelle*. All these increased enormously between 1749 and 1783 to pay for the various wars France was involved in. Taxes took between five and 10 per cent of the peasants' income. The heaviest burden on the peasantry was the rent they paid their landlords. This increased markedly during the second half of the eighteenth century as a result of the increase in population, which is estimated to have risen from 22.4 million in 1705 to

27.9 million in 1790. This increased the demand for farms, with the result that landlords could raise rents. The increasing financial burden placed on the peasantry along with growing resentment of the feudal system was an important long-term cause of the Revolution.

Key terms

Artisan
A skilled worker or craftsman.

Sans-culottes
Literally those who wear trousers (workers) and not knee-breaches (bourgeoisie) and has implications regarding social class. Used as a label to identify the more extreme urban revolutionaries of 1792–5.

Urban workers

The remaining part of the Third Estate was made up of urban workers. Small property owners and **artisans** in Paris were known as *sans-culottes*. The majority of workers in the towns lived in crowded insanitary housing blocks known as tenements. They were unskilled and poor.

On the other hand, skilled craftsmen were organised into guilds. In Paris in 1776, 100,000 workers – a third of the male population – belonged to guilds. The standard of living of wage-earners had slowly fallen in the eighteenth century, as prices had risen on average by 65 per cent between 1726 and 1789, but wages by only 22 per cent. In the years immediately preceding the Revolution the worsening economic situation caused considerable resentment among urban dwellers and contributed to the long-term causes of the Revolution. This helps explain their readiness to become involved in the popular demonstrations that helped bring about the overthrow of the *ancien régime*.

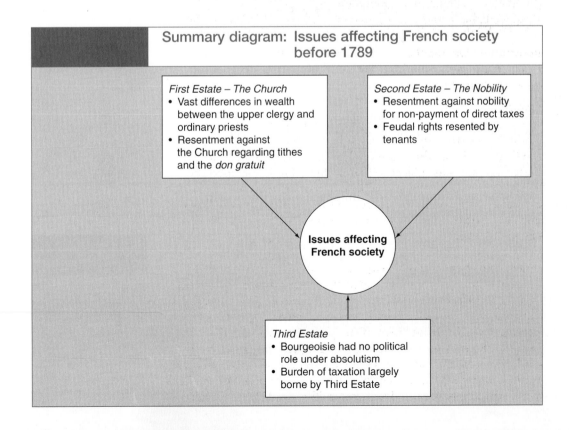

Summary diagram: Issues affecting French society before 1789

First Estate – The Church
- Vast differences in wealth between the upper clergy and ordinary priests
- Resentment against the Church regarding tithes and the *don gratuit*

Second Estate – The Nobility
- Resentment against nobility for non-payment of direct taxes
- Feudal rights resented by tenants

Issues affecting French society

Third Estate
- Bourgeoisie had no political role under absolutism
- Burden of taxation largely borne by Third Estate

(d) The Enlightenment

Key question
What role did the Enlightenment play in bringing about the Revolution?

During the course of the eighteenth century there emerged in Europe an intellectual movement of writers and thinkers known as the Enlightenment. The movement questioned and challenged a whole range of views and ideas that, at the time, were widely accepted – particularly relating to religion, nature and absolute monarchy. Their analysis of society was based on reason and rational thought, rather than superstition and tradition.

In France they were known as the *philosophes* and were writers rather than philosophers. The most famous were Voltaire, Montesqieu and Rousseau. They wrote on the problems of the day and attacked the prejudice and superstition they saw around them. Many of them contributed to the most important work of the French Enlightenment, *The Encyclopaedia* (edited by Diderot, the first volume appeared in 1752, the last of 35 in 1780).

Aims of the *philosophes*

The aim of the *philosophes* was to apply rational analysis to all activities. They were not prepared to accept tradition or revelation, as in the Bible, as a sufficient reason for doing anything. They were much more in favour of liberty – of the press, of speech, of trade, of freedom from arbitrary arrest – than of equality, although they did want equality before the law.

The main objects of their attack were the Church and despotic government. They did not accept the literal interpretation of the Bible and rejected anything that could not be explained by reason – miracles, for example – as superstitious. They condemned the Catholic Church because it was wealthy, corrupt and intolerant, and took up Voltaire's cry of '*Écrasez l'infâme*' ('crush the infamous' – meaning the Church).

The *philosophes*, while clearly critical of many aspects of the *ancien régime*, were not essentially opposed to the regime and they were not therefore revolutionary. Yet they did have an impact on the outbreak of the Revolution. Their ideas attacked all the assumptions on which the *ancien régime* was based. They challenged and helped undermine one of the key pillars of the old order, namely the position of the Church and the role of the King as God's servant. Although not revolutionary themselves their ideas and approaches did influence many who would become revolutionaries.

Summary diagram: Long-term causes of the French Revolution

Long-term causes

1. Problems of government and finance

2. Tensions in society – the Church, nobility, Third Estate

3. Impact of the Enlightenment

2 | Short-term Causes of the French Revolution

In the 10 years before the outbreak of the Revolution in 1789 a number of issues, crises and events contributed to the downfall of the *ancien régime* and should be viewed alongside the long-term causes. The main short-term causes were:

(a) foreign policy
(b) the financial crisis
(c) the economic crisis.

(a) Foreign policy

The Seven Years War

Key question
How did foreign policy contribute to the outbreak of the Revolution?

Since the fifteenth century France had more often than not had a hostile relationship with both Britain and Austria. Britain was viewed as France's only serious colonial rival and Austria was a rival for the dominance of mainland Europe. By the middle of the eighteenth century France and Austria had resolved their differences and were allies when the Seven Years War (1756–63) broke out in 1756. During the course of this war, French forces in India and North America suffered a series of crushing defeats at the hands of the British. Much of France's overseas territory was lost in 1763, although the profitable sugar-producing islands of Martinique and Guadeloupe, and some other lesser territories, were retained.

Key dates

France's defeat in the Seven Years War was sealed by the humiliating Peace of Paris, which resulted in the loss of significant parts of France's overseas empire. Britain took control of French territory in Canada and India, West Africa and a number of islands in the West Indies: 1763

France entered the American War of Independence: 1778

The American War of Independence

Following this humiliation at the hands of Britain and her ally Prussia, the French government dreamt of revenge. The opportunity came when Britain became involved in a bitter quarrel with her 13 North American colonies, who rebelled against British rule.

In the resulting American War of Independence (1776–83), France intervened on the side of the rebels, providing both financial and military support, including the Marquis de Lafayette (see profile on page 82). The intervention of France in 1778 was decisive and helped bring about the defeat of British forces and the creation of the United States of America.

Although France was unable to recover most of the territory lost during the Seven Years War, the Treaty of Versailles (1783) did satisfy French honour. Few at the time, however, could foresee what the real cost of the war would turn out to be – revolution in France. The war cost a great deal of money and in the short term worsened the already weak financial situation of the Crown. French soldiers who had fought in the war had been exposed to ideas such as liberty and democracy and many demanded similar rights for the people of France.

(b) The financial crisis

Key question
How significant was the financial crisis in bringing about the collapse of the monarchy?

The primary short-term cause of the French Revolution was the financial crisis. By far the most important aspect of this was the huge deficit that the government was building up. On 20 August 1786, Calonne, the Controller-General, told Louis XVI that the government was on the verge of bankruptcy. Revenue for 1786 would be 475 million *livres*, while expenditure would be 587 million *livres*, making a deficit of 112 million – almost a quarter of the total income. A much more detailed and alarming picture of the situation is provided in the Treasury account of 1788, which has been called the first and last budget of the monarchy (see Table 1.2).

The King is informed by his Controller-General that France is on the verge of bankruptcy: 20 August 1786

Key date

Table 1.2: Royal income and expenditure 1788 (millions of *livres*)

Royal income		Royal expenditure	
		Education and poor relief	(12)
		Court expenses	(36)
		Civil expenditure	145
		Military – Army and Navy	165
		Debt interest	318
Total	503	Total	629

The **deficit** had increased in two years to 126 million *livres* – 20 per cent of total expenditure. It was anticipated that for 1789, receipts would amount to only 325 million *livres* and that the interest payments on the deficit would amount to 62 per cent of the receipts.

Deficit
When expenditure is greater than income it results in a deficit.

Key term

There are two reasons to explain why there was a deficit and a financial crisis in France:

1. War
   Between 1740 and 1783, France was at war for 20 years, first in the War of Austrian Succession (1740–8), then the Seven Years War (1756–63) and finally the American War of Independence (1778–83). The cost of helping the American colonists defeat the British government was approximately 1066 million *livres*. This was mainly achieved through Necker's efforts in raising loans, rather than imposing any new taxes. While this did not directly lead to revolution, the lack of an elected parliament to guarantee loans, as in Britain, did not give lenders confidence.

2. Tax
   The Crown was not receiving much of the money collected in taxes (see page 5), and until it recovered control of its finances, no basic reforms could be carried out. The privileged classes, whose income from property had increased, were an untapped source of revenue that the Crown urgently needed to access. There would, however, be powerful resistance to any change in the taxation structure from those with vested interests in retaining the status quo.

Reform

Following Necker's dismissal in 1781 his successor Joly de Fleury discovered the true nature of France's finances. The Treasury was 160 million *livres* short for 1781 and 295 million *livres* short for 1782. To make good the shortfall Fleury and his successor, Calonne, undid much of Necker's work by resuming the practice

Key question
Why did the reform process fail and with what consequences?

Key date

Financial crisis:
1781–7

Key terms

Pays d'états
Areas that had local
representative
assemblies of the
three estates that
contributed to the
assessment and
collection of royal
taxes.

Estates-General
A body that, in
1789, contained
939 representatives
of all three estates
of the realm –
Church, nobility
and Third Estate. It
was only summoned
in times of extreme
national crisis, and
last met in 1614.

of selling offices (many of which Necker had abolished). They
both also borrowed much more heavily than Necker.

In 1786, with loans drying up, Calonne was forced to grasp the
nettle and embark upon a reform of the tax system, his plan
consisted of an ambitious three-part programme.

- The main proposal was to replace the capitation and the
  vingtième on landed property by a single land tax. It was to be a
  tax on the land and not on the person, and would therefore
  affect all landed proprietors – Church, noble and common alike
  – regardless of whether the lands were used for luxury purposes
  or crops. There were to be no exemptions, everyone including
  the nobles, the clergy and the **pays d'états** would pay.
- The second part of the programme was aimed at stimulating
  the economy to ensure that future tax revenues would increase.
  In order to try and achieve this Calonne proposed abandoning
  controls on the grain trade and abolishing internal customs
  barriers, which prevented the free movement of grain from one
  part of France to another.
- The final part of the programme was to try to restore national
  confidence so that new loans for the short term could be raised.
  By doing this Calonne hoped that the *parlements* would be less
  likely to oppose the registration of his measures. His plan was
  to achieve some display of national unity and consensus.

The failure of the reform process

The obvious body to summon to approve the reforms, that was
representative of the nation, was the **Estates-General**, but this was
rejected as being too unpredictable. Calonne and Louis XVI
opted instead for a handpicked Assembly of Notables. It was
anticipated that this would be a pliant body who would willingly
agree to rubberstamp the reform package.

The 144 members of the Assembly met in February 1787. It
included leading members of the *parlements*, princes, leading
nobles and important bishops. On examining the proposals it
became clear that they would not collaborate with Calonne and
Louis in agreeing the reforms. As representatives of the privileged
order they had the most to lose from them.

The Notables were not opposed to all change and agreed that
taxation should be extended to all. They claimed that the
approval of the nation was needed for Calonne's reforms and
urged the summoning of the Estates-General, which had last met
in 1614. Realising the strength of opposition to Calonne, Louis
dismissed him in April 1787.

Key question
What was the
significance of the
political crisis?

The political crisis 1787–8

Calonne was replaced by one of the Notables, Loménie de
Brienne, Archbishop of Toulouse, while another Notable,
Lamoignon, President of the *Parlement* of Paris, became head of
the Judiciary. The Assembly of Notables proved to be no more
co-operative with Brienne than it had been with Calonne.

Brienne retained Calonne's land tax and introduced a number
of new reforms following on from Necker's earlier plans. There

Contemporary French cartoon depicting the Assembly of Notables as birds. President Monkey (Calonne) addresses the Notables and asks them with which sauce they would like to be eaten. Animals were frequently used to depict people as they were considered to be much less intelligent than humans.

was to be an end to venal financial officials, a new central treasury established, laws codified in a printed form accessible to those who needed to consult them, the educational system reformed, religious toleration introduced and the army made more efficient and less expensive.

When Brienne presented his reforms to the *Parlement* of Paris for registration they refused and said that only the Estates-General who represented the whole nation could consent to any new taxes. Louis' reaction was to exile the *Parlement* to Troyes on 15 August.

Louis' action was considered to be high handed and the result was an aristocratic revolt, which proved to be the most violent opposition the government had yet faced. There were riots in some of the provincial capitals where the *parlements* met, such as Rennes in Brittany and Grenoble in Dauphine. In all parts of the country nobles met in unauthorised assemblies to discuss action in support of the *parlements*.

An assembly of the clergy also joined in on the side of the *parlements*, breaking its long tradition of loyalty to the Crown. It condemned the reforms and voted a *don gratuit* of less than a quarter the size requested by the Crown.

Although the opposition was fragmented and dispersed it continued because of the collapse of the government's finances. At the beginning of August 1788 the royal treasury was empty. Brienne agreed, with Louis' reluctant approval, to summon the Estates-General for 1 May 1789. On 16 August 1788, he suspended all payments from the royal treasury, in effect acknowledging that the Crown was bankrupt. The previous year, the then navy minister, the Marquis de Castries, had perceptively told the King, 'As a Frenchman I want the Estates-General, as a minister I am bound to tell you that they might destroy your authority'.

> French Crown is effectively bankrupt: 16 August 1788

Key date

In September 1788 Louis was forced to back down and allow the Paris *parlement* to return. Following the resignations of Brienne and Lamoignon, the King recalled Necker, in the belief that he was the only one who could restore the government's credit and raise new loans. Necker abandoned his predecessor's reform plans and, while indicating that he would try to raise new loans, stated that he would do nothing until the Estates-General had met.

The crisis had shown the limitations of royal power. Although Louis was in effect an Absolute ruler, in reality he was unable to impose his government's reforms on the State. The forces of opposition detected clear signs of weakness in the Crown. The failure to secure reform contributed to a paralysis of the government. In the short term this was very significant, particularly when linked to the economic crisis.

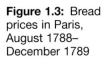

Key question
How did the economic crisis contribute to the outbreak of the Revolution?

(c) The economic crisis

In the years immediately preceding the outbreak of the Revolution in 1789 the French economy faced a number of crises. The economy was largely based on agriculture and this sector had grown steadily between the 1730s and 1770s. Good harvests had resulted in food surpluses, which in turn contributed to an increase in the population.

Bad harvests

During the 1780s the general agricultural prosperity came suddenly to an end. This was brought about in no small measure by a series of disastrous harvests in 1778–9, 1781–2, 1785–6 and 1787. In 1788 there was a major disaster. There was a very wet spring and freak hailstones in many areas in July resulting in a very poor harvest. This was particularly disastrous for peasants

Figure 1.3: Bread prices in Paris, August 1788–December 1789

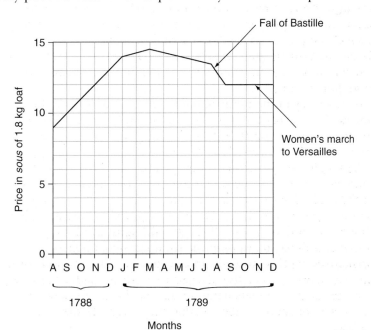

who produced wine as a cash crop. A bad harvest in a pre-industrial society always led to massive unemployment. The resulting rise in the price of food led to less demand for manufactured goods, at a time when both peasants and urban workers needed employment more than ever to cope with the higher prices. The impact on staple foods such as bread was significant. Over the period 1726 to 1789 wheat prices increased by about 60 per cent. In normal times it is estimated that about half a labourer's daily wage might be spent on bread. During the severe winter of 1788–9 this proportion was increased to 88 per cent.

The picture in other sectors of the economy was equally gloomy. Production and employment in the textile industries, which accounted for half of industrial production, fell by 50 per cent in 1789. The industry had been badly hit by the Eden Treaty of 1786. Textile production was largely carried out in rural cottages by women, and tended to supplement family incomes from agriculture. This further affected a group who were already suffering economic hardship. The market for wine was also very poor since rising bread prices meant that there was less money to spend on this and other goods. Unemployment was rising at the same time as the cost of living and, as production was either stagnant or falling, workers were unable to increase their wages.

The Eden Treaty: 1786

Allowed imports of English goods, including textiles, at reduced import duties (came into operation in May 1787).

Key date

Food shortage

Many ordinary people blamed tithe-owners and landowners for making the situation worse. They were accused of hoarding grain and speculating on prices rising during times of shortage, thereby contributing to the lack of food. In many areas there were food riots and disturbances as people attacked grain stores. These were most frequent in the spring and summer of 1789 when grain prices were at their peak, before the new harvest had been collected.

It was believed by many ordinary people in both rural and urban areas that the economic crisis was in part the fault of the nobility. Increasing disturbances against the nobility encouraged many ordinary people to take the first tentative steps towards direct political action. The **politicisation** of the majority of the Third Estate began as a result of the economic crisis. Louis' handling of the political crisis further exacerbated the situation in the eyes of ordinary people.

The deep-rooted long-term problems of the *ancien régime*, considered in the first part of this chapter, came to a head in the years immediately preceding 1789. Short-term causes such as poor harvests and rising bread prices helped to bring this about. The attempts at reform were an acknowledgement that changes were needed; the failure of the process showed the depth of the divisions within French society. When the French monarchy declared itself bankrupt and the Assembly of Notables refused to approve the reforms proposed by the King's ministers, the way was paved for the summoning of the Estates-General. Much was expected from this body by all parties. The next chapter will reveal how few could have anticipated the momentous consequences of the decision to summon it.

Politicisation
A process when people who were previously unconcerned with politics take an active interest in political issues which affect their daily lives.

Key term

Summary diagram: Short-term causes of the French Revolution

Foreign policy and the American War of Independence
• Government sought revenge against Britain following 1763
• Supporting American rebels against British 1778–83 results in:
  – massive additional debt (1000 million *livres*)
  – awareness of political liberty for USA while no political liberty in France

Financial crisis • Government on verge of bankruptcy • Seeks new measures to raise taxes
The failure of the reform process • Assembly of Notables refuses to back reform • Dismissal of Calonne
The political crisis 1787–8 • Louis' political weakness • Revolt of the Aristocracy
The economic crisis • Bad harvests – rising bread prices • Less consumption – unemployment • Grain and food riots

3 | The Key Debate

A wide variety of historians of sharply contrasting political and social viewpoints and at differing times have contributed to analysing the origins of the French Revolution. One of the main schools is the **Marxist interpretation**. Marxist historians see the Revolution as part of the class struggle prophesised in the mid-nineteenth century by the German-born philosopher and social economist Karl Marx (1818–83). More recently **Revisionist historians** have rejected this view in favour of different interpretations. The central issue, which historians seek to address, is:

Why did the French Revolution occur?

Georges Lefebvre and Albert Soboul

The dominant interpretation of the French Revolution for much of the last 100 years has been the Marxist interpretation. This was most clearly expressed by Georges Lefebvre and later by his disciple Albert Soboul. Lefebvre regarded the French Revolution as a bourgeois revolution. The commercial and industrial bourgeoisie had been growing in importance in the eighteenth century and had become stronger economically than the nobility. Yet they were kept out of positions of power by the privileged nobility. According to the Marxists a class struggle developed between the rising bourgeoisie and the declining aristocracy. The bourgeoisie won this struggle because the monarchy became bankrupt owing to the cost of the war in America. The French Revolution was, according to Lefebvre, a struggle for equal rights.

Key terms

Marxist interpretations
The interpretation of the Revolution as part of Karl Marx's analysis of history as a series of class-based struggles, resulting in the triumph of the proletariat.

Revisionist historians
Historians who reject the Marxist analysis of the French Revolution and provide a revised interpretation.

Alfred Cobban and François Furet

The Marxist account of the Revolution was generally accepted until the 1960s. It was challenged by a group of 'Revisionist' (anti-Marxist) historians. The first important critic was Alfred Cobban who questioned the validity of the **social interpretation** and also whether the Revolution was led by a rising bourgeoisie. The best known of the Revisionist historians is François Furet. He went beyond merely questioning the economic and social interpretations of the Revolution as a class-based struggle, favoured by the Marxists, to considering the intellectual and cultural background to 1789. According to Furet, the driving force for change was the advanced democratic ideas of the Enlightenment *philosophes* such as Rousseau.

> **Social interpretations** The emphasis on changes in society – population trends, social class – as having a significant impact upon the Revolution.
>
> Key term

J.H. Shennan

J.H. Shennan's analysis, based on much recent research, argues that the most likely cause of the Revolution is that long-term problems and resentments were brought to a head by events immediately preceding 1789. According to Professor Shennan the two most important areas in which deep-seated problems reached a critical point in the 1770s and 1780s were finance and government. Financial problems bought about by involvement in the American War of Independence were compounded by a series of bad harvests, which resulted in steep increases in the price of bread. Behind both of these factors lay the permanent problem posed by the conservative social and political order which prevented the rich land of France developing as it should, and the government constantly starved of income.

Gwynne Lewis

Gwynne Lewis attempts to synthesise the debate and seeks to reach some kind of post-Revisionist consensus. While Marxist historians stress the social and economic aspects of the origins such as rising prices and unemployment, Revisionists focus on political and cultural issues such as the nature of absolutism and the role of the Church. Lewis' main criticism of the Revisionist historians is the way in which they have tended to down-play the importance of social causes of the Revolution.

Some key books in the debate

Alfred Cobban, *The Social Interpretation of the French Revolution* (Cambridge University Press,1964).

François Furet, *Interpreting the French Revolution* (Cambridge University Press,1981).

George Lefebvre, *The Coming of the French Revolution* (Vintage Books,1947).

George Lefebvre, *The French Revolution* (Routledge, 2001).

Gwynne Lewis, *The French Revolution. Rethinking the Debate* (Routledge, 1993).

J.H. Shennan, *France before the Revolution* (Methuen, 1983).

Albert Soboul, *The French Revolution 1787–1799* (Unwin, 1989).

Study Guide: AS Questions

In the style of AQA

(a) Explain why the French monarchy experienced a mounting financial crisis in the 1770s. (12 marks)

(b) How important were the ideas of the Enlightenment in undermining the *ancien régime* in France by 1780?

(24 marks)

Exam tips

The cross-references are intended to take you straight to the material that will help you to answer the questions.

(a) To explain why something happens it is always helpful to think of long- and short-term factors. The long-term factors include: the inadequacy of the *ancien régime* to extract sufficient taxation (particularly because of tax farming, but also because of the inappropriateness of the taxes levied); the amassing of debt through war; and the failure of ministers to provide a solution other than borrowing. These should be balanced against the short-term factors which help explain 'why in the 1770s'. The short-term factors include: the impact of the American War of Independence (on top of the Seven Years' War); the demands of supporting an army and navy; the weaknesses of Louis XVI and the failures of his ministers, including Necker; excessive court expenditure and poor accounting; plus the need to repay interest on the royal debt. You should try to assess the relative importance of the points you mention and draw an appropriate and convincing conclusion identifying a main factor and/or showing how the factors interlink.

(b) It is important to be aware that a number of circumstances were helping to undermine the *ancien régime*. In this question you are asked to assess the importance of the Enlightenment, but you will need to balance its contribution against other factors in order to provide an informed judgement.

The views of the *philosophes* are explained on page 12. You should consider these in conjunction with the existing tensions in society – particular with regard to attitudes towards the Church and government. Other factors to be weighed against such ideas would include the structure of government, the King, the taxation system, the state of French society and financial concerns. Ensure that you argue a case throughout your answer and reach a well-supported conclusion.

In the style of OCR A

Study the four sources on the origins of the French Revolution and then answer **both** sub-questions. It is recommended that you spend two-thirds of your time in answering part **(b)**.

(a) Study Sources B and C.
Compare these sources as evidence of the influence of Queen Marie Antoinette on French politics before 1789. (30 marks)

(b) Study all the sources.
Use your own knowledge to assess how far the sources support the interpretation that the greatest challenge to the authority of the Crown came from the nobility. (70 marks)

Source A

From: a decree of Turgot abolishing the Corvée, *1776. Turgot was Louis XVI's first Controller-General of finances and, with the King's support, attempted to introduce a wide-reaching reform programme, which included abolishing the* Corvée *in 1776.*

We have noted with pain that works have been carried out, for the most part, by means of the *corvées** required of our subjects. They have been paid no wages for the time they are so employed. The weight of this obligation does not fall, nor can it ever fall, anywhere else than upon the poorest part of our subjects, upon those who have no property other than their hands and their industry, upon the peasants, the farmers. The landowners, almost all of whom are exempt, contribute but very little.

[* *Corvées* – this obligation required the peasants to provide free labour for public works or other tasks as directed by the nobility.]

Source B

From: Daniel Hales' letter to Lord Carmarthen, October 1786. There was concern in some sections of political life about the influence of Marie Antoinette and her circle. Daniel Hales was a British government representative based in the embassy in Paris.

The voice of the people is now and then faintly heard in the remonstrances* issued by the *parlement*. In general however access to the throne is very limited. I know it has been said that the extent of the influence of the Queen's party goes no further than to the disposal of certain places and pensions without interfering with the great line of public business, and particularly that of foreign affairs. But when they command the person who holds the purse of state, they necessarily have the greatest direct influence in all internal affairs and a considerable indirect share in foreign affairs.

[* Remonstrances – the practice of the *parlement* to urge the king to address abuses before they agreed to register laws.]

Source C

From: Countess d'Aldehamar's Memoirs, *published in 1836. The Countess d'Aldehamar was a close associate of the Queen and she comments on Marie Antoinette's frustrations at her inability to influence the King.*

We, the circle of friends of the Queen, never ceased repeating to the King that the Third Estate would wreck everything – and we were right. The King deceived by the Genevan Necker, paid no attention to the Queen's fears. This well-informed Princess knew all about the plots that were being woven, but her concerns appeared to have been largely ignored.

Source D

From: Calonne, a Memorandum to Louis XVI, August 1786. Calonne was Louis' Controller-General and as such was responsible for the government's finances. He was determined to try and reform these but was confronted by powerful opposition from the nobility.

An Assembly of Notables ought not to be confused with a meeting of the Estates-General. They are essentially different in every respect. In the first place members of the Estates-General were not chosen by the King but by each order of the three orders who chose their deputies, whereas with Assemblies of Notables the King individually summons those whom he sees fit. The difference is even more marked when it comes to the topics for discussion. In the Estates-General the three orders present the crown with cahiers containing their complaints. With the Assembly of Notables it is the King himself who decides the matters for discussion.

Exam tips

The cross-references are intended to take you straight to the material that will help you to answer the questions.

(a) Part **(a)** requires you to examine closely the content of the two sources and compare the way they show the influence of Marie Antoinette on French politics before 1789. Source B implies that the 'Queen's party' exerted considerable influence in the political life of France, while Source C effectively challenges this assertion. With this question the main focus of the response should be on the content of the two sources.

(b) You are expected for question **(b)** to examine all four sources together thematically and to introduce your own background knowledge. You should then come to a conclusion about whether you agree with the view or not.

Consider the following:
- Louis' handling of the financial reforms proposed by his ministers (page 15)
- the perceived influence of the Queen and her supporters – link this to Louis' own character (page 4)
- the ideas of the *philosophes* (page 12)
- the revolt of the nobility and influence of powerful vested interests in blocking the reform process (page 16).

In the style of OCR B

Answer **both** parts of the question.

(a) How is the calling of the Assembly of Notables in 1787 best explained?
[Explaining ideas, attitudes and beliefs.] (25 marks)
(b) How significant were bad harvests as a factor explaining the outbreak of revolution in 1789?
[Explaining events and circumstances.] (25 marks)

Exam tips

General Introduction

You will always be presented with two pairs of questions and you have to answer both parts of one pair. In your chosen pair, each question will be different so each needs full and separate treatment. Each question in your pair carries equal marks so spend equal time on each part. Both parts must be answered with an essay.

All questions in this exam paper require an answer that explains and makes sense of the past. Your task is to construct that historical explanation. The information in the square brackets below each question identifies for you the kind of explanation that you need to start off working with. To prepare a good answer for each essay, you have to work through four stages: (i) identify the relevant factors (ideas, actions and events) that explain the exam question; (ii) work out the role that each factor played; (iii) decide which factor or factors were more important than the others and explain why, with supporting evidence; (iv) work out how each significant part influenced other parts and/or was influenced by those, and show how this was the case, with supporting evidence to back up your claims. Explanation goes well beyond reciting the facts to weigh them up and offer judgements.

Work through each of these four steps in rough and you have got your essay plan. Write up each stage and you have got your essay: well structured and focused on the question. If you only complete step (i), your answer will be just a basic list of ideas, actions and events so it will not score well. If you complete steps (ii) and (iii), your answer will have arranged those ideas, actions and events according to their relative importance. That explanation of the issue set will be quite advanced so if you really have explained things carefully it will score in level 4 (16–20 marks). To reach the top (21–5 marks), you have to go one stage further and simultaneously explain the interaction of those component ideas, actions and events – not just putting them in rank order of importance but establishing cause and effect from one to another. Do all of that and you will have given an excellent answer and constructed a strong historical explanation that makes real sense of the past and shows that you don't merely know what happened but understand what was going on.

(a) The information in the square brackets is a prompt to get you to start with a focus on empathetic explanation. So start by explaining attitudes in France in 1787, including issues of monarchy and governance, the political situation, economic and social conditions and circumstances. In what ways did they relate to the financial crisis, Calonne's failure to fund the Treasury by loans and other 'traditional' means and his subsequent plans to reform the tax system? From there you can move into explaining events (causes) and actions (motives and intentions). Note the question: don't wander off into Brienne's plans, let alone why the Estates-General were called. Note you have two things to explain: why the Assembly was called and why it was called when it was. To explain the first, you must consider longer-term developments. To explain the second, you will have to assess the short-term and immediate causes.

(b) The prompt here tells you to start with a causal explanation so identify and explain the circumstances and events leading to the outbreak of revolution in 1789. Assessing the relative importance of causal factors must be central to your entire answer and you must give serious consideration to bad harvests (as the given factor in the question), even if you want to argue that other circumstances were more significant. Examine the degree to which bad harvests led to events such as the Storming of the Bastille and the Great Fear. Consider also the significance of more general economic problems in bringing about not just the popular unrest of July and August 1789, but also their impact in the October Days. Bring other points into your examination, e.g. religious divisions, the policy of the King and the Court (weak royal leadership, incompetence, indecision, reluctance to accept change). In doing so, you will develop your explanation by broadening its scope to include consideration of the intentions and motives of various key individuals and groups. And don't forget while you're doing that to examine the interaction between these various elements. Some influenced others and, in doing so, altered the course of events.

Study Guide: Advanced Level Question

In the style of Edexcel

'Louis XVI's failings as a monarch primarily account for the strength of the challenge to absolutism in France which existed by the beginning of May 1789.' How far do you agree with this view of the origins on the French revolution in the period before May 1789? (30 marks)

Exam tips

The cross-references are intended to take you straight to the material that will help you to answer the question.

To address this question you should plan to consider Louis' failings and also other factors that created a situation ripe for challenge to develop to the authority of the King in May 1789.

Louis' failings can be seen in his personality (page 4); poor handling of the failed financial reform process and weakness revealed during the political crises of 1787–8 (pages 13–17). You could also consider how far the decision to intervene in the American War of Independence was ill-judged in view of its effect in highlighting the lack of political liberty in France and in creating a massive additional debt (pages 13–14 and 19).

Other factors to take into account are:

- long-term problems and grievances of the peasantry and urban workers (pages 10–11)
- the influence of the ideas of the Enlightenment (page 12)
- the power of the privileged classes to resist reform (pages 7–8)
- the severity of the economic crisis and the failed harvest 1788 – and its role in politicising the Third Estate (pages 17–18).

It is clear that this an area where historians have placed different weight on the various contributory factors (pages 19–20). In asking for your overall conclusion, this question provides you with the opportunity to enter the debate.

2

1789: The End of the *Ancien Régime*

POINTS TO CONSIDER

The enormous problems that confronted Louis XVI compelled him to summon the Estates-General. This met in May 1789. A combination of Louis' attempts to control the situation and the determination of his opponents to resist, brought about a rapidly escalating crisis that resulted in the downfall of the *ancien régime*. The events of this momentous year are considered under five themes:

- The Estates-General – the early meetings and their consequences
- The revolt in Paris – storming of the Bastille and the popular movement
- The Revolution in the provinces
- The dismantling of the *ancien régime*
- The reaction of the monarchy

Key dates

1789		
	May 5	Estates-General met at Versailles
	June 17	National Assembly proclaimed
	June 20	Tennis Court Oath
	July 10	Formation of the citizens' militia
	July 14	The storming of the Bastille
	July 20	Start of the Great Fear
	August 4	Decrees dismantling feudalism passed
	August 26	Declaration of the Rights of Man and the Citizen
	October 5–6	'October Days'
	November 2	Church property nationalised

1789 is not only one of the most important years in French history, it is also central to the history of Europe. As events escalated out of Louis' control, resulting in the collapse of the *ancien régime* in France, new structures were created. The emergence of a more democratic system of government as a consequence of popular upheaval set a precedent for other downtrodden people in other countries.

1 | The Estates-General

As we saw in Chapter 1, by late 1788 the financial and political problems facing the Crown had forced Louis XVI to summon the Estates-General. This was the first time it had been summoned since 1614, and presented the government with a number of concerns.

- What method would the Estates-General use to vote on any issue presented to it – by head or by estate?
- Who would be elected as deputies to the Estates-General?
- To what extent should the grievances noted in the *cahiers* be addressed?

The method of voting

The recently restored Paris *parlement* (see page 17) declared that the Estates-General should meet as in 1614 and that voting should be by estate or order. This would favour the two privileged orders, who wished to protect their privileges and tended to act together. Up to this point the bourgeoisie had taken little part in political agitation. The bourgeoisie had tended to follow the lead given by the privileged classes (the nobles and the clergy) in the *parlements* and the Assembly of Notables.

In 1789 bourgeois leaders of the Third Estate began to suspect that the privileged orders who wanted **voting by order** had opposed the government because they wanted power for themselves and not because they wanted justice for the nation as a whole. The Third Estate now demanded twice the number of deputies (so that they would have as many deputies as the other two orders combined), and **voting by head** instead of voting by order. This form of voting would give them a majority, as many of the First Estate's deputies were poor parish priests who were likely to support the Third Estate.

In December 1788, the King's Council allowed the number of Third Estate deputies to be doubled. Nothing was said about voting by head. When the Estates-General met there was confusion. The Third Estate assumed that there would be voting by head (otherwise doubling served no purpose), while the first two Estates believed that this was not the case.

Electing the deputies

The government did not make any attempt to influence the elections to the Estates-General and had no candidates of its own. Yet it was to a degree concerned that the deputies who were chosen would in general be sympathetic to the dire economic circumstances it was in, and be supportive to any proposals made by the King.

For the First Estate, the clergy overwhelmingly elected parish priests to represent them: only 51 of the 291 deputies were bishops.

In the Second Estate, the majority of noble deputies were from old noble families in the provinces, many of them poor and

Key question
Why was the method of voting important?

Voting by order
Each estate votes separately on any issue. Any two estates together would outvote the third.

Voting by head
Decisions taken by the Estates-General would be agreed by a simple vote with a majority sufficient to agree any policy. This favoured the Third Estate, which had the most deputies.

Key terms

Key question
Who were the deputies elected to the Estates-General?

Profile: Abbé Emmanuel Sieyès 1748–1836

1748 – Born in Fréjus into a bourgeois family

1773 – Ordained as a priest

1787 – Elected as a clerical representative at the provincial Assembly of Orleans, where he was particularly interested in issues relating to taxation, agriculture and poor relief

1789 – Published a highly influential pamphlet *What is the Third Estate?* in which he argued that it was the most important part of the nation. Represented the Third Estate of Paris in the Estates-General. Drew up the Tennis Court Oath and contributed to the Declaration of the Rights of Man

1792 – Elected to the Convention and voted for the King's execution but took no active part in the Terror

1793 – Following Thermidor he served on the **Committee of Public Safety**

1794 – Elected to the Council of 500

1798 – Appointed ambassador to Berlin

1799 – Elected Director and plotted the *Coup* of Brumaire with Bonaparte. Left public office during the Napoleonic Empire and retired from public life

Sieyès was one of the main constitutional planners of the revolutionary period. When asked what he had done during the Terror he declared 'I survived'. He helped draw up the constitutions linked with the Revolution and was one of its most influential political thinkers.

Key term

Committee of Public Safety Effectively, the government of France during 1793–4 and one of the twin pillars of the Terror along with the CGS (see page 107).

Key terms

Conservatives Those who did not want any reforms. They were deeply suspicious and sceptical of the need for any social or political change.

Liberals Deputies who were far more tolerant of differing political views and who supported a measure of cautious reform.

conservative, but 90 out of the 282 could be classed as **liberals** and these were to play a leading role in the Estates-General.

The 580 deputies elected to represent the Third Estate were educated, articulate and almost entirely well-off, largely because deputies were expected to pay their own expenses. This was something peasants and artisans could not afford. Not a single peasant or urban worker was elected. The largest group of Third Estate deputies were venal office holders (43 per cent), followed by lawyers (35 per cent), although two-thirds of deputies had some legal qualification. Only 13 per cent were from trade and industry. This meant that the industrial middle class did not play a leading role in events leading to the Revolution or, indeed, in the Revolution itself.

All the adult male members of the two privileged orders had a vote for electing their deputies. The Third Estate however was to be chosen by a complicated system of indirect election. Frenchmen over the age of 25 were entitled to vote in a primary assembly, either of their parish or their urban guild, if they paid taxes. At these primary assemblies they would choose representatives who in turn elected the deputies.

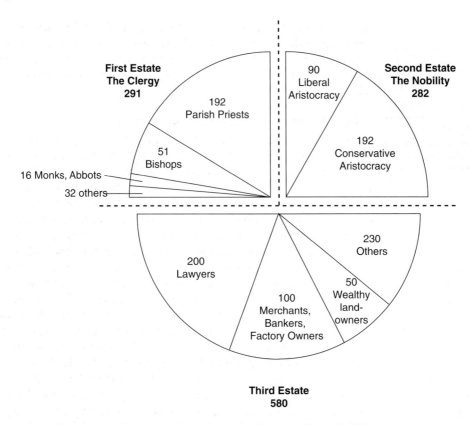

Figure 2.1: The composition of the deputies in the Estates-General 1789

Cahiers

Key question
What concerns were reflected in the *cahiers*?

Before the meeting of the Estates-General the electors of each of the three orders drew up *cahiers* – lists of grievances and suggestions for reform.

The *cahiers* of the First Estate reflected the interests of the parish clergy. They called for an end to bishops holding more than one diocese, and demanded that those who were not noble be able to become bishops. In return they were prepared to give up the financial privileges of the Church. They were not, however, prepared to give up the dominant position of the Church: Catholicism should remain the established religion and retain control of education. They did not intend to tolerate Protestantism.

The nobles' *cahiers* were surprisingly liberal – 89 per cent were prepared to give up their financial privileges and nearly 39 per cent supported voting by head, at least on matters of general interest. Instead of trying to preserve their own privileges, they showed a desire for change and were prepared to admit that merit rather than birth should be the key to high office. They attacked the government for its despotism, its inefficiency and its injustice. On many issues they were more liberal than the Third Estate.

The *cahiers* of all three orders had a great deal in common. All were against absolute royal power and all wanted a King whose powers would be limited by an elected assembly, which would have the right to vote taxes and pass laws. Only one major issue separated the Third Estate from the other two orders – voting by head. It was this that was to cause conflict when the Estates-General met.

The Meeting of the Estates-General

Key question
How did the demands of the Third Estate lead to the creation of a National Assembly?

When the Estates-General met on 5 May 1789 the government had the opportunity to take control of the situation. The Third Estate deputies, lacking experience and having no recognised leaders, would have supported the King if he had promised reforms, but the government did not take the initiative and put forward no programme. Necker talked about making taxation fairer but did not mention any other reform. Nothing was said about a new **constitution**, which all the *cahiers* had demanded.

Although the Estates-General met as three separate groups, the Third Estate insisted that the credentials (details relating to eligibility, status, etc.) of those who claimed to have been elected should be verified in a common session comprising the deputies of all three estates. This appeared a trivial matter but was seen by everyone as setting a precedent of deciding whether the Estates-General should meet as one body (and vote by head) when discussing all other matters. The nobles rejected the Third Estate's demand and declared themselves a separate order by 188 votes to 46, as did the clergy but with a slender majority of 19 (133 to 114). The Third Estate refused to do anything until the other two orders joined them, so weeks of inaction followed, with the government failing to provide any leadership.

Key terms

Constitution
The establishment of structures for governing a country. Among the most important of these are the making of laws, forming governments, conduct of elections, division of powers. The detail relating to these structures would be presented in the form of a written document.

Séance royale
Session of the Estates-General in the presence of the monarch.

The National Assembly

On 10 June, the deadlock was broken when the Third Estate passed a motion that it would begin verifying the deputies' credentials, even if the other two orders did not accept their invitation to join in. A trickle of priests joined the Third Estate in the following days. After a debate on 15 June the deputies of the Third Estate on 17 June voted by 490 to 90 to call themselves the National Assembly. The Third Estate was now claiming that, as it represented most of the nation, it had the right to manage its affairs and decide taxation. Events were rapidly moving out of the control of the government, especially when on 19 June the clergy voted to join the Third Estate.

The Tennis Court Oath

Key question
How did Louis react to actions of the Estates-General?

All of this was a direct challenge to the authority of the King, who was at last forced to act. On 23 June, he decided to hold a Royal Session known as a ***séance royale***, attended by all three Estates, when he would propose a series of reforms. On 20 June 1789 the deputies of the Third Estate found that the hall in which they met had been closed to prepare for the Royal Session. They had not been informed and were furious. They met instead on a tennis court nearby and took an oath, known as the Tennis Court Oath, not to disperse until they had given France a constitution, thus

A painting of the Tennis Court Oath by Jacques-Louis David. Look closely at the image. How does the artist seek to portray the great importance and drama of this occasion?

claiming that the King did not have the right to dissolve them. Only one member voted against the motion; since, only three days before, 90 had voted against a motion to call themselves the National Assembly, it was clear that the deputies were rapidly becoming more radical.

The response of the Crown

To restore a measure of royal authority, Necker advised the King to hold a *séance royale*. It was hoped that the King would ignore the events of 10–17 June and accept voting in common on all important matters. Louis, under pressure from the Queen and his brothers, ignored this advice and came down very firmly on the side of the privileged orders. When the *séance royale* met on the 23 June, Louis declared null and void the decisions taken by the deputies of the Third Estate on 17 June. He would not allow the privileges of the nobility and clergy to be discussed in common.

The King was however, prepared to accept considerable restrictions on his own power. No taxes would be imposed without

Key date

The Tennis Court Oath – deputies of the National Assembly meet at a tennis court in Versailles and swear that they will secure a constitution for France: 20 June 1789

Key term

Lettres de cachet
Sealed instructions
from the Crown
allowing detention
without trial of a
named individual.

the consent of the representatives of the nation, ***lettres de cachet***
would be abolished and freedom of the press introduced. Internal
customs barriers, and the *gabelle* and *corvée* were to be abolished.
If these reforms had been put forward in May, a majority of the
Third Estate would probably have been satisfied, but now they did
not go far enough. The King ended by ordering the deputies to
disperse and meet in their separate assemblies.

The next day, 24 June, 151 clergy joined the Third Estate. The
day after that, 47 nobles, including one of Louis' leading
opponents, the Duc d'Orléans, did the same. There were popular
demonstrations in Paris in favour of the Assembly. On 27 June,
the King gave way. He reversed his decision of 23 June and
ordered the nobles and clergy to join the Third Estate and vote
by head.

Louis was contemplating another strategy – military force. He
had ordered troops to be moved to Paris and Versailles on 22
June. By late June, nearly 4000 troops, including 2600 in foreign-
speaking units, were stationed round Paris. Many of these troops
were élite units of the army – the French guards, whose loyalty to
the Crown Louis believed to be certain. This caused alarm in the
capital. Government claims that they were there simply to
preserve order seemed to have been sincere – until the last week
in June. On 26 June, 4800 extra troops were ordered into the
Paris region and on 1 July, 11,500 more. In less than a week the
strength of army units called to Paris increased from 4000 to over
20,000. It was impossible to doubt any longer that the King and
his advisers had decided to dissolve the National Assembly, by
force if necessary. In this desperate situation the Assembly was
saved by the revolt of the people of Paris.

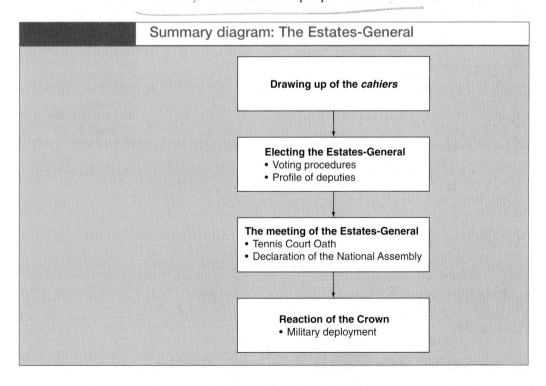

Summary diagram: The Estates-General

Drawing up of the *cahiers*

Electing the Estates-General
• Voting procedures
• Profile of deputies

The meeting of the Estates-General
• Tennis Court Oath
• Declaration of the National Assembly

Reaction of the Crown
• Military deployment

2 | The Revolt in Paris

In the spring and summer of 1789 the population of Paris was facing difficult times. The economic crisis (see page 17) was causing hardship, which led to anti-government feelings and fuelled the rise of the **popular movement**.

The economic crisis in Paris

In normal times a worker spent up to 50 per cent of his income on bread. In August 1788 the price of a 1.8 kg loaf was 9 *sous* (1 *livre* = 20 *sous* – a *livre* would be equivalent to about eight pence). By March 1789, it had risen to over 14 *sous* per loaf (see Figure 1.3, page 17). By the spring of 1789 a Parisian worker could be spending 88 per cent of his wages on bread. This caused hardship and unrest amongst the Parisian population. For example, on 28 April, the premises of a prosperous wallpaper manufacturer, Réveillon, were set on fire, following a rumour that he was going to reduce wages. But this riot was more a violent protest against the scarcity and high price of bread than a protest against wages. At least 50 people were killed or wounded by troops.

Thus the situation was very volatile when the Estates-General met. Economic issues (the price of bread and unemployment) were, for the first time, pushing France towards revolution. Falling living standards were creating dissatisfaction, which in turn led to discontent. Political opponents of the King were harnessing this discontent to bring crowds on to the streets to save the National Assembly. The economic crisis created a dangerously unstable situation and contributed to the emergence of a 'popular movement'. Protests among workers and small traders were directed against the government because of its inability to deal with the economic crisis.

The popular movement

In late June, journalists and politicians established a permanent headquarters in the Palais Royal in Paris, home of the Duc d'Orléans. Its central location (see map on page 35) made it a popular venue. Each night thousands of ordinary Parisians gathered to listen to revolutionary speakers such as Camille Desmoulins. The Palais Royal became the unofficial headquarters of the popular movement whose activities were directed through its speakers. By 11 July, Louis had about 25,000 troops in total located in the Paris-Versailles area. The King felt strong enough to dismiss Necker. Necker was at the height of his popularity and was considered as the only minister able to tackle the financial crisis. The deputies of the Estates-General expected Louis to use force to dissolve the Assembly and arrest its leading members.

News of Necker's dismissal reached Paris on 12 July, where it inspired large-scale popular demonstrations against the King. The population of Paris feared that this marked the start of Louis' attempt to restore his power by means of force. Parisians flocked to the Palais Royal, where speakers called on them to take up

Key question
What impact did the economic crisis have on the population of Paris?

Key term

Popular movement
Crowds of ordinary Parisians who became politically active as a consequence of the economic crisis. They demanded a political role as a means of improving their living standards.

Key question
How important was the popular movement in the outbreak of the Revolution?

Gardes-françaises
A royal infantry
regiment, many of
whom deserted to
opponents of the
King in July 1789.
They helped
capture the Bastille.

arms. A frantic search began for muskets and ammunition.
Gunsmith shops were looted and many ordinary people began
arming themselves. There were clashes with royal troops guarding
the Tuileries. When the **Gardes-françaises** were ordered to
withdraw from Paris many disobeyed their orders and deserted to
the representatives of the people of Paris. Discipline in this élite
unit was deteriorating rapidly. On the same day crowds of poor
Parisians attacked the hated customs posts that surrounded Paris
and imposed duties on goods, including food, entering the city.
Out of 54 posts, 40 were destroyed. Fearing an imminent attack
by royal forces, barricades were thrown up on 13 July across many
streets in Paris to impede the movement of royal troops.

The capture of the Bastille

Their search for weapons took the Parisian demonstrators to
Les Invalides, an old soldiers' retirement home that also served as
an arsenal, where they seized over 28,000 muskets and 20
cannon. They were still short of gunpowder and cartridges, so
they marched on the fortress of the Bastille. This imposing royal
prison was a permanent reminder of the power of the *ancien
régime*. News of the desertions among the *Gardes-françaises* led the
army commanders to advise the King that the reliability of the
troops to crush the rising could not be counted on.

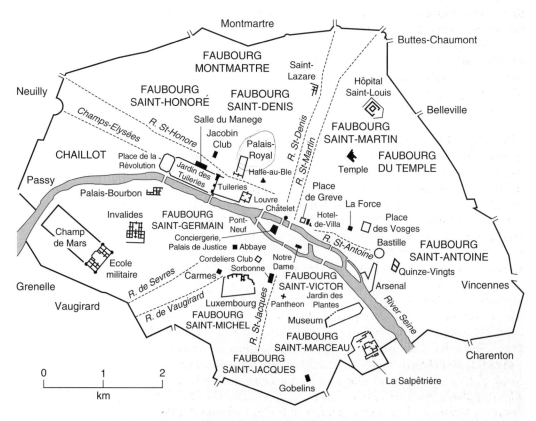

Figure 2.2: The main locations in revolutionary Paris

Throughout late June, many *Gardes-françaises*, who worked at various trades in Paris in their off-duty hours and mixed with the population, were being influenced by agitators at the Palais Royal. As early as 24 June, two companies had refused to go on duty. By 14 July 1789, five out of six battalions of *Gardes-françaises* had deserted and some joined the Parisians besieging the Bastille. There were 5000 other troops nearby, but the officers told their commander that they could not rely on their men. Troops were removed from the streets of Paris to the Champ de Mars, a wide-open area south of the river Seine, where they did nothing.

The crowd outside the Bastille were denied entry by the governor, de Launay, who also refused to hand over any gunpowder. There was no intention of storming the fortress, although a group managed to enter the inner courtyard. De Launay ordered his troops to open fire on them and 98 were killed. *Gardes-françaises* supporting the crowd, using cannon taken from *Les Invalides* that morning, overcame the defenders. De Launay was forced to surrender. He was murdered and decapitated by an enraged crowd.

Those who had taken part in the attack on the Bastille were not wealthy middle class but *sans-culottes*. At the height of the rebellion about a quarter of a million Parisians were under arms. This was the first and most famous of the ***journées***, which occurred at decisive moments during the course of the Revolution.

The establishment of the Commune of Paris

The popular disturbances in early July 1789 were not planned. They were the reaction of ordinary people to the actions of the King and his ministers. The respectable bourgeoisie of Paris were afraid that a breakdown of law and order was occurring, resulting in the destruction of property, looting and attacks on individuals and property. To regain control of the situation, and prevent the indiscriminate arming of the population, on 15 July the Paris

Key date
The date the Bastille was captured is commemorated annually as France's national day: 14 July 1789

Key term
Journée
Day of popular action and disturbance linked to great political change.

Key question
What was the significance of the setting up of the Paris Commune?

The Storming of the Bastille, 14 July 1789. What does this print suggest about the storming of the Bastille?

electors (representatives of the 60 electoral districts that had chosen the deputies to the Estates-General), set up a new body to govern the city. This was known as the Commune and it would be at the forefront of the clash between Parisians and the King. Sylvain Bailly was elected the mayor of Paris to carry out the Commune's policies.

Key date
Formation of the citizens' militia, which becomes the National Guard: 10 July 1789

On 10 July 1789, shortly before the formation of the Commune, the electors of Paris proposed forming a **citizens' militia** to defend the interests of property owners. It was envisaged that the militia would be predominantly bourgeois, and that the *sans-culottes* would be excluded from its ranks. It had the double purpose of protecting property against the attacks of the *menu peuple* and of defending Paris against any possible threat by royal troops. It was these electors and the supporters of the Duc d'Orléans who were to turn what had begun as spontaneous riots into a general rising. On 15 July the citizens' militia became the National Guard and Lafayette was appointed its commander.

The significance of the storming of the Bastille

The events in Paris on 14 July had far-reaching results:

Key question
Why was the storming of the Bastille important?

- The King had lost control of Paris, where the electors set up a Commune to run the city.
- Lafayette (see page 82) was appointed commander of the predominantly bourgeois National Guard.
- The Assembly (which on 9 July had taken the name of the National Constituent Assembly) prepared to draw up a constitution, no longer under threat of being dissolved by the King.
- Real power had passed from the King to the elected representatives of the people. Louis now had to share his power with the National Assembly.
- Louis was no longer in a position to dictate to the Assembly, because he could not rely upon the army.
- News of the fall of the Bastille spread through France and intensified activity among the peasantry.
- The revolt of Paris led to the emigration of some nobles, led by the King's brother the Comte d'Artois: 20,000 *émigrés* fled abroad in two months.

Key terms

Citizens' militia
A bourgeois defence force set up to protect the interests of property owners in Paris. After the storming of the Bastille it became the National Guard.

Menu peuple
Used to describe ordinary people living in towns.

Émigrés
People, mainly aristocrats, who fled France during the Revolution. Many *émigrés* joined foreign opponents of the Revolution.

On 17 July, the King journeyed to Paris from Versailles, where the people gave him a hostile reception. Louis recognised the new revolutionary council – the Commune – and the National Guard, and wore in his hat the red, white and blue cockade of the Revolution (red and blue – the colours of Paris, were added to the white of the Bourbons). The significance of the King's humiliation was not lost on foreign diplomats. Gouverneur Morris, later the US ambassador to France, told George Washington: 'You may consider the Revolution to be over, since the authority of the King and the nobles has been utterly destroyed'. Far from the Revolution being over, as news of events in Paris spread throughout France, it influenced what occurred elsewhere in the country.

Summary diagram: The revolt in Paris of 1789

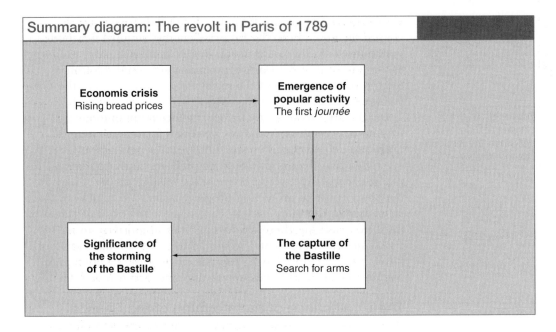

Economis crisis
Rising bread prices

Emergence of popular activity
The first *journée*

Significance of the storming of the Bastille

The capture of the Bastille
Search for arms

3 | The Revolution in the Provinces

The movement, which is known as the Municipal Revolution, covered the whole of the month of July 1789. It varied in scope and extent from one area to another. The provinces followed events in Paris with great interest, and received regular news of events in the letters sent back by their deputies in Versailles. There was activity in some towns before the revolt in Paris, but the Paris revolt had far-reaching implications. News of the storming of the Bastille was known in the provinces between 16 and 19 July, depending on the distance from Paris. As a consequence of the revolt of Paris, the authority of the King collapsed in most French towns. His orders would now be obeyed only if they had been approved by the newly formed National Constituent Assembly.

Most provincial towns waited to hear what had happened in Paris before they acted. 'The Parisian spirit of commotion', wrote the English traveller and writer Arthur Young, from Strasbourg on 21 July, 'spreads quickly'. Nearly everywhere there was a municipal revolution in which the bourgeoisie played a leading part. This took various forms.

In some towns the old council merely broadened its membership and carried on as before. In Bordeaux, the electors of the Third Estate seized control, closely following the example of Paris. In most towns, including Lille, Rouen and Lyon, the old municipal corporations which operated during the *ancien régime*, and which excluded ordinary people, were overthrown by force; in others, like Dijon and Pamiers, the former councils were allowed to stay in office, but were integrated into a committee on

Key question
What was the significance of the municipal revolution in those areas beyond Paris?

Key term

Counter-revolutionaries
Those groups and individuals who were hostile to the Revolution and the changes it imposed, and wished to reverse them at the earliest opportunity.

Key question
Why did events in Paris contribute to revolt in the countryside?

which they were a minority. Citizens' militias were set up in several towns, such as Marseille, before the National Guard was formed in Paris. In Rouan revolutionaries seized power at the beginning of July, before the revolt in the capital, following food riots.

In nearly every town a National Guard was formed, as in Paris, it was designed both to control popular violence and prevent **counter-revolution**. Nearly all *intendants* abandoned their posts. The King had lost control of Paris and of the provincial towns. He was to lose control of the countryside through the peasant revolution.

The Rural Revolt

The peasants played no part in the events that led up to the revolution until the spring of 1789. It was the bad harvest of 1788 that gave them a role, because of the great misery and hardship in the countryside. Most peasants had to buy their bread and were, therefore, badly affected by the rise in its price in the spring and summer of 1789. They also suffered from the depression in the textile industry, as many owned hand-looms and were small-scale producers of cloth. From January 1789 grain convoys and the premises of suspected hoarders were attacked. Since this violence tended to occur when food was scarce it would probably have died out when the new crop was harvested in the summer.

What made these food riots more important than usual were the political events that were taking place. The calling of the Estates-General aroused general excitement amongst the peasants. They believed that the King would not have asked them to state their grievances in the *cahiers* if he did not intend to do something about them.

Events in Paris, particularly the fall of the Bastille, also had a tremendous effect on the countryside. Risings immediately followed in Normandy and Franche Comté. Demonstrations and riots against taxes, the tithe and feudal dues spread throughout the country; it appeared that law and order had collapsed everywhere.

On the great estates of the Church and other landowners, there were storehouses of grain that had been collected as rents, feudal dues and tithes. In the spring and summer of 1789 they were the only places where grain was held in bulk. Landlords were regarded as hoarders. The President of the Grenoble *parlement* wrote on the 28 June: 'There is daily talk of attacking the nobility, of setting fire to their châteaux in order to burn all their title-deeds'.

The main features of rural protest were:

- grain stores were looted
- chateaux were attacked and frequently burnt
- documents known as 'terriers' which listed peasant obligations were seized and destroyed.

The Great Fear

Although hundreds of châteaux were ransacked and many were set on fire, there was remarkably little bloodshed – landowners or their agents were killed only when they resisted. On 20 July 1789, the attacks on the châteaux which started on the 20 July 1789 were part of what became known as the Great Fear (*Grande Peur*). These disturbances lasted until 6 August 1789. They began with local rumours that bands of brigands, in the pay of the aristocracy, were going to destroy the harvest. The peasants took up arms to await the brigands and when they did not appear, turned their anger against the landlords. The Great Fear spread the peasant rising throughout most of France. However, some areas that were further away from Paris, such as Brittany, Alsace and the Basque region, were unaffected.

Key dates

The start in the countryside of widespread attacks on the property of large landowners, during what is known as the 'Great Fear': 20 July 1789

The start of the process of dismantling the feudal system: 4 August 1789

4 | Dismantling the *Ancien Régime*

The Assembly was in a dilemma. It could not ask the King's troops to crush the peasants, because afterwards they might be turned against the Assembly itself. Yet the Assembly could not allow the anarchy in the countryside to continue. This could be ended, and the support of the peasants gained for the Assembly and for the Revolution, by giving them at least part of what they wanted.

Key question
How did the actions of the peasantry contribute to the collapse of the *ancien régime*?

The August Decrees

On 3 August, leaders of the **patriot party** drew up a plan for the liberal nobles to propose the dismantling of the feudal system. On the night of 4 August 1789, the Vicomte de Noailles, followed by the Duc d'Auguillon, one of the richest landowners in France, proposed that obligations relating to personal service should be abolished without compensation: these included serfdom and the *corvée*. Other rights such as *champart* and *lods et ventes* (see page 10) were regarded as a form of property and, although proposed to be abolished, were to be redeemed (paid for by the peasant). But these were the dues that affected the peasant most severely, so there was little satisfaction in the countryside with the limited nature of the reforms.

The proposed changes were given legal form in the decrees of 5–11 August, which stated that:

> The National Assembly abolishes the feudal system entirely. It decrees that, as regards feudal rights and dues … those relating … to personal serfdom … are abolished without compensation; all the others are declared to be redeemable …
>
> All seigneurial courts are abolished without any compensation.

Amid great excitement, the example of Noailles and Auguillon was followed by other noble deputies, who queued up to renounce their privileges in a spirit of patriotic fervour. The changes proposed went far beyond those demanded by the *cahiers*.

Key term

Patriot party
A loose group of progressive reformers, mainly nobles and bourgeoisie who wanted changes to the political structure – a reduction in royal power in order to enhance their own positions.

The main ones were:

- tithes payable to the Church were abolished
- abolition of venality
- all financial and tax privileges relating to land or persons abolished
- all citizens to be taxed equally
- special privileges (including tax exemption) for provinces, principalities, pays, cantons, towns and villages were abolished
- all citizens without distinction of birth were eligible for all offices – whether ecclesiastical, civil or military.

When the Assembly adjourned at 2 am on 5 August the deputies were weeping for joy. One of the deputies Duquesnoy exclaimed 'What a nation! What glory. What honour to the French!'

Key question
How important were the August decrees?

Significance of the Decrees

The August Decrees were very important in starting the process of dismantling the *ancien régime*. Although there was still a great deal to be done, they marked the end of noble power and the privilege of birth by establishing a society based on civil equality. All Frenchmen had the same rights and duties, could enter any profession according to their ability and would pay the same taxes. Of course, equality in theory was different from equality in practice. The career open to talent benefited the bourgeoisie rather than the peasant or worker, who lacked the education to take advantage of it. Nevertheless, French society would never be the same again – the old society (the *ancien régime*) of orders and privilege had gone.

The peasants – the vast mass of the population – were committed to the new regime, at least in so far as it removed their feudal obligations. They did not like having to compensate landowners for the loss of their feudal dues. Many stopped paying them, until they were finally abolished without compensation in 1793. Some peasants, in areas such as Brittany and the Vendée, were to become active opponents of the Revolution (see Chapter 4). For most peasants, the Revolution marked the end of the feudal system and they feared that if they did not support the changes, then aristocratic privilege and the tithe would return and they would lose all they had gained.

The August Decrees had swept away institutions like the provincial estates and cleared the way for a national, uniform system of administration. As most institutions had been based on privilege, the Assembly now began the laborious task, which would take two years to complete, of replacing institutions and often personnel relating to local government, law, finance, the Church (whose income was halved by the loss of the tithe, so that it could no longer carry the burden of funding education, hospitals and poor relief) and the armed forces. Yet many thought that those who had lost power would try to recover it. There was a widespread fear of an aristocratic plot and a feeling that, without constant vigilance, the victories of July and August could be quickly reversed.

The Declaration of the Rights of Man and the Citizen

The August Decrees prepared the ground for the creation of a constitution. Before this, the deputies drew up the principles on which this should be based – the Declaration of the Rights of Man and the Citizen. It condemned the practices of the *ancien régime* and outlined the rights of citizens, as demanded in the *cahiers* of all three orders. The following are some of the key points from the Declaration:

- all men are born free and equal, in their rights
- the main rights of man are liberty, property, security and resistance to oppression
- power (sovereignty) rests with the people
- freedom of worship
- freedom of expression – speech and publication
- taxation to be borne by all in proportion to their means
- freedom to own property.

The Declaration would outlast the constitution to which it was later attached and was to be an important inspiration to liberals throughout Europe in the nineteenth century. For all its well-meaning sentiments, the Declaration mainly represented the interests of the property-owning bourgeoisie. Its significance, according to the historian George Rudé, is that '… it sounded the death-knell of the *ancien régime*, while preparing the public for the constructive legislation that was to follow'.

The nationalisation of Church land

By September the government was facing a serious financial crisis. Tax revenue was not flowing in and the government was unable to raise a loan to meet its costs. Many in the Assembly were contemplating radical action against the Church – one of the largest landowners in the country – in order to raise funds. After prolonged debates during late October and early November 1789, the Assembly agreed on 2 November 1789 that all the property owned by the Church should be placed at the disposal of the nation. This meant that Church land was nationalised. The State, for its part, would assume responsibility for looking after the clergy and carry out their work of helping the poor.

Bonds called **assignat** were issued and sold, backed up by the sale of Church land. These were used to settle debts and for purchasing goods and were accepted as currency. Royal land was also sold. It was anticipated that the sale of Church and royal land would raise around 400 million *livres*. This would go a long way towards meeting the financial needs of the government.

Key question
What was the Declaration of the Rights of Man and the Citizen and why was it important?

Key dates
The issuing of the Declaration of the Rights of Man and Citizen: 26 August 1789

The National Constituent Assembly agrees to nationalise Church property, and in return the State will pay the salaries of priests and fund poor relief: 2 November 1789

Key question
Why did the State take over the property of the Church?

Key term

Assignat
Bonds backed up by the sale of Church land that circulated as a form of paper currency.

Summary diagram: Dismantling the *ancien régime*

```
                    ┌─────────────────────┐
                    │   The 'Great Fear'   │
                    └─────────────────────┘
                               │
                               ▼
                    ┌─────────────────────┐        • Tithes abolished
                    │                     │        • Venality abolished
                    │  The August Decrees │ ◄────  • Financial and tax privileges abolished
                    │                     │        • All citizens to be taxed equally
                    └─────────────────────┘        • Special privileges abolished
                               │                   • All citizens eligible for all offices
                               ▼
              ┌──────────────────────────┐    ┌──────────────────────────────┐
              │  Declaration of the Rights│◄── │ All men are born free and equal│
              │  of Man and the Citizen   │    │        in their rights         │
              └──────────────────────────┘    └──────────────────────────────┘
                               │
                               ▼
                    ┌─────────────────────┐
                    │   Nationalisation of │
                    │      Church land     │
                    └─────────────────────┘
```

5 | The Reaction of the Monarchy

Key question
What effect did the changes have on the power of the monarchy?

The King did not share the general enthusiasm for the changes that were taking place and on 5 August he wrote to the Archbishop of Arles: 'I will never consent to the spoliation of my clergy and of my nobility. I will not sanction decrees by which they are despoiled'. He could not use force against the Assembly as the loyalty of the army was in doubt, with many officers and men sympathetic to the Revolution. Louis adopted instead a policy of non-cooperation and refused to officially support the August Decrees and the Declaration of Rights.

This forced the Assembly to consider the important question of what rights the King should have. Should he be able to veto or delay legislation passed by the Assembly? The deputies decided that the King should have a 'suspensive veto' – the power to suspend or delay all laws other than financial ones passed by the Assembly for a period up to four years.

No-one, at this stage, considered abolishing the monarchy and setting up a republic. It was agreed by the deputies that **legislative power** should reside with the National Assembly and that no taxes or loans could be raised without its consent, while '… supreme **executive power** resides exclusively in the King's hands'.

Key terms

Legislative power
The power to make laws. In an absolute system this power belongs solely to the Crown. In a democracy legislative power rests with an elected parliament.

Executive power
The power to make decisions relating to the government of a country.

The October Days

The King's refusal to approve the Assembly's decrees caused considerable tension. That he was forced to do so was the consequence of another revolutionary *journée*. Louis decided to reinforce his guard by summoning to Versailles the loyal Flanders regiment. On the evening of 1 October, they were given a

A print showing the women of Paris going to Versailles to bring Louis back to the city. What does this print suggest about the mood of ordinary Parisians in the autumn of 1789?

banquet by the King's bodyguard in the opera house of the palace to celebrate their arrival. Both the King and Queen were present at the banquet, during the course of which there were anti-revolutionary demonstrations. Officers trampled on the tricolour cockade and replaced it with the white cockade of the Bourbons. When news of this reached Paris, feelings ran high and there were demands that the King should be brought back to the capital.

This demand coincided with a food shortage in Paris. On 5 October a crowd of women stormed the Hôtel de Ville, the headquarters of the Commune, demanding bread. They were persuaded to march to Versailles to put their complaints to the King and the Assembly. Six or seven thousand of them set off on the five-hour march. Later in the day 20,000 National Guards, under Lafayette, followed them.

When the women reached Versailles they invaded the Assembly and sent a deputation to the King, who agreed to provide Paris with grain. He also agreed to approve the August Decrees and the Declaration of Rights. On 6 October, at the request of the crowd, the King and Queen appeared on a balcony and were greeted with cries of 'To Paris'. That afternoon the royal family left Versailles. The National Assembly also moved to Paris. These dramatic events are known as the October Days.

Louis XVI and the royal family are brought to Paris: 5–6 October 1789

Key date

The significance of the October Days

The 'October Days' were a very significant event in the early phase of the Revolution. The crowd that marched to Versailles aimed to bring the royal family back to Paris where their freedom of action and political influence would, it was hoped, be significantly reduced. Once in Paris the King regarded himself as a prisoner of the Paris mob and therefore not bound by anything he was forced to accept. When Parisians had revolted in July, they had seen the Assembly as their ally. In October, the Assembly had been ignored and humiliated by the decisive action of ordinary Parisians. When the deputies followed the King to Paris, some of them felt as much imprisoned as the King did. Most deputies wanted to work out a compromise with Louis, but this was much more difficult for them in Paris, surrounded by a population which could impose its will on the Assembly by another *journée*.

Following the 'October Days' the Assembly issued a decree that changed the title and status of the monarch, from 'King of France and Navarre' to 'Louis, by the grace of God and the constitutional law of the State, King of the French'. Louis was now subordinate to the law, and his subjects now became citizens. There had been a shift in the balance of power towards Paris and its increasingly politicised population. Many moderate deputies distrusted the population of Paris almost as much as they did the King, although it was the popular movement and their *journées* that had enabled them to defeat Louis in the first place.

6 | The Key Debate

The storming of the Bastille on 14 July 1789 has become for large numbers of people the symbol of the start of the French Revolution. The anniversary of its fall is commemorated annually in France amidst great pomp and ceremony. Many historians have studied the event and a central question that they address is:

Was the storming of the Bastille of any significance?

E.D. Bradby
E.D. Bradby, writing in the early part of the twentieth century, concluded that the fall of the Bastille had momentous consequences, particularly for the old order. When the population saw that when a government could be successfully defied, the power of that government was broken. The princes and nobles of the Court party saw it, and many of them fled during the first wave of emigration. He argues that whenever an old form of government is suddenly overturned, disorder and anarchy will follow.

H.A.L. Fisher
H.A.L. Fisher was a prominent historian turned Liberal politician. He suggested that the storming of the Bastille was part of a conspiracy financed by capitalists to get Necker back into office, as the only man who could ensure financial recovery. While the event was soiled by the brutal slaughter of the garrison he considered its capture to be a political masterpiece. Fisher stresses the international repercussions and argued that its fall was hailed throughout Europe as the end of secretive tyranny and arbitrary imprisonment, and heralded the dawn of a new age.

Jacques Godechot
Jacques Godechot seeks to set the storming of the Bastille firmly within the domestic French context. He dismisses the notion that the event was a plot or conspiracy instigated by the duc d'Orleans or anyone else, and argues that it needs to be viewed as part of a much wider revolutionary movement within France. Godechot considers that the Parisian rising of 14 July represents not only the peak of the national rising but also a stage in it. After this

date most of the towns and many of the villages of France were to imitate Paris with extraordinary swiftness. During the weeks that followed the fall of the Bastille, there arose everywhere revolutionary town councils, and citizens' militias, which soon assumed the name of National Guards. The Fourteenth of July, he believes is indeed one of the great days that made France.

William Doyle

William Doyle focuses on the events preceding 14 July when the domestic crisis facing the Crown deepened. Louis was compelled to accept that his authority was diminishing rapidly, and that the newly declared National Assembly was in the ascendant. For four tense weeks in the summer of 1789, the Queen, Artois and their circle plotted and schemed to reverse these achievements. Ultimately they were foiled by a wave of popular support for the stand taken by the Third Estate. The storming of the Bastille marked the climax of the movement. Challenged by it Louis XVI drew back, leaving the people of Paris convinced that they alone had saved the National Assembly from destruction. From that moment on events in Paris would largely dictate the course and shape of the Revolution.

Some key books in the debate

E.D. Bradby, *A Short History of the French Revolution 1789–1795* (Oxford University Press, 1926).
William Doyle, *The Oxford History of the French Revolution* (Oxford University Press, 1989).
H.A.L. Fisher, *A History of Europe*, Vol II (Fontana, 1960).
Jacques Godechot, *The Taking of the Bastille July 14th 1789* (Faber, 1970).
George Rudé, *The French Revolution* (Weidenfeld, 1988).

Study Guide: AS Questions

In the style of AQA

(a) Explain why issues of voting procedure created problems for the Estates-General in May to June 1789. (12 marks)

(b) How important was the rural revolt of the spring and summer 1789 in the dismantling of the *ancien régime* by the National Assembly in August 1789? (24 marks)

Exam tips
The cross-references are intended to take you straight to the material that will help you to answer the questions.

(a) This question asks you to produce a range of reasons as to why methods of voting were the cause of dissension at the Estates-General. You will need to refer to the lack of precedent and the government's failure to establish a voting procedure before the Assembly met. You will also need to outline the problems likely to be caused if voting by estate was adopted (see page 28). More particularly you will need to refer to the government's continuing failure to address voting issues when the Estates-General opened and the attitude displayed by the Third Estate to separate estate meetings. You might want to explain that for the Third Estate the voting issue may well have been the final 'tipping point', given the range of grievances they brought to the Estates-General and their seeming determination to challenge the King's power.

(b) To answer this question you will need to evaluate the contribution of the rural revolt and balance it against other factors leading to the August Decrees and the Declaration of the Rights of Man in August 1789. You will find details of the former on page 40. You will need to examine the impact of the Great Fear and consider the Assembly's dilemma (it could hardly use royal troops to crush the revolt). The August Decrees might be considered a mere recognition of what was being established by the peasants, but there are also other factors to take into account – the impact of enlightened thinking, the determination of the National Assembly to bring about change, the long-standing grievances of men (especially those of middling status) to whom equality had been denied. It is probably worth pointing to the compensation clauses to show that the decrees were more than a display of the peasants' power. The declaration of rights was also an abstract document, little affected by rural revolt, save perhaps in its timing. Try to provide a summative and judgemental conclusion that flows easily from what you have written.

In the style of OCR B

Answer **both** parts of the question.

(a) Why were the Estates-General convened in 1789?
[Explaining actions and events.]   (25 marks)

(b) How significant were economic problems as a factor explaining the course of the revolutionary events of 1789?
[Explaining events and circumstances.]   (25 marks)

Exam tips

Read again the General introduction at the start of the study guide to Chapter 1, page 24.

(a) The prompt in the square brackets is there to set you off in the right direction: recognising and explaining the interaction of a variety of factors, both causal and intentional, to explain a specific event. Note that this question, like **(a)** in Chapter 1 (page 24), gives you two distinct things to explain: why the estates were called and why they were called in 1789. To explain the first, consider longer term developments such as the impact of the Enlightenment and the increasingly desperate state of royal finances. To explain the second, you will have to assess the short-term and immediate causes, e.g. Louis XVI's failure to secure reform and being forced to recall Necker, demonstrating to the opposition the weakness of royal power. When linked to bad harvests in 1787–8 and rising bread prices in 1788–9, you will have established a clear chain of causal factors. Your job is then to assess their relative importance so you can explain why its calling had become the only viable alternative.

(b) The prompt reminds you to start by mixing causal and intentional explanations. Give serious space to weighing up the significance of economic problems, even if you want to argue that other reasons were more significant. That is the factor singled out in the question so it must not be dismissed without good justification. Also, note that the whole year is identified so don't just look at the causes of the Storming of the Bastille and the Great Fear, but the October Days too.

Strong answers must relate economic problems to key moments in the course of the Revolution in 1789. Royal financial problems might be a good place to start since, for example, they led directly to calling of the Estates-General. Remember, however, that 'economic problems' covers the wider French economy, not just the Crown's finances.

The question 'How significant ...?' means you must go beyond economic problems and consider other influences too. They have all got to be weighed against each other before you can come to a definitive judgement on how to explain the course of revolutionary events in 1789. So in your relative evaluation of the significance of the various influences you are going to need to consider the influence of other issues such as: the attitude and policy of the King and Court (weak leadership, incompetence, indecision, reluctance to accept change), new ideas and political groups (e.g. ideas for constitutional government), friction over the Estates-General, the problem of the veto, the attitudes of members of the Third Estate, religious divisions. Doing that, you can also assess the inter-relationships between longer term developments and short-term causes. Cause and effect are always central to historical explanation.

Study Guide: Advanced Level Question

In the style of Edexcel

To what extent was the course of the revolution in the months May to October 1789 influenced by popular protest in Paris?

(30 marks)

Exam tips

The cross-references are intended to take you straight to the material that will help you to answer the question.

In planning your answer you will need to consider:

- Changes directly brought about by revolutionary *journées* in Paris (the Fall of the Bastille and the October Days).
- Changes where the events in Paris had an influence in combination with protests elsewhere.
- Additional influences and other factors.

The direct influence of popular protest can be seen in the power shifts that were brought about by the Fall of the Bastille (page 37) and the October Days (pages 43–5).

The widespread influence of the July revolt in Paris can be seen in its effects in intensifying or radicalising protest in the towns and rural areas of France (pages 38 and 39–40), which were in turn influential in bringing about the August Decrees (pages 40–1). But be careful also to note the evidence of action in some municipalities that predated 14 July. And you will need to consider the role of the economic crisis and the state of the harvest in creating the conditions which made revolt in the provinces likely.

The question requires a focus on the course of the revolution, so it is important to address what brought about the changes of the period May to October.

The key constitutional changes and attacks on privilege were the work of the National Assembly (pages 40–2) clearly part of the chain of events set in train by reactions to popular protest in July, but they were the work of forces within the Assembly as well as outside it.

The role of the King in radicalising, rather than defusing, the tension in Paris also needs to be considered (pages 43–4).

You are asked to come to an overall conclusion. You may see the events in Paris as a catalyst, and, in dealing with the course of the revolution, it will be important not to overlook the forces at work in the countryside and the significance of the August Decrees. But also ask yourself how far the July and October Days in Paris fundamentally and sharply altered the position of the King in relation to his people.

3

The Constitutional Monarchy: Reforming France 1789–92

POINTS TO CONSIDER

Following the overthrow of the *ancien régime* (Chapter 2) the main aim of the assembly was to reform France. This would involve changing the country's institutions and restructuring the way in which it was governed. The Declaration of the Rights of Man and the Citizen provided some of the guiding principles which underpinned these reforms. This chapter will consider three important themes:

- The reform programmes undertaken by the National Assembly to consolidate the Revolution, and the extent to which they changed France
- The rise of the Jacobins and the Cordeliers and their impact on political life
- The emergence of the republican movement

Key dates

1789	November 2	Nationalisation of Church property
1790	May 21	Creation of the Paris Sections
	July 12	Civil Constitution of the Clergy
	August 16	Reorganisation of the judiciary
1791	March 2	Dissolution of Guilds
	June 14	The Le Chapelier Law
	June 20	Flight to Varennes
	July 17	Champ de Mars massacre
	September 14	Louis XVI accepts the new constitution
	November 9	Decree against *émigrés* (vetoed by Louis on 12 November)
1792	March	Guillotine to be used for all public executions
	May 27	New decree against Refractory Priests
1793	July 17	Final abolition of Feudalism in France

Key question
What principles underlay the new political system?

1 | The Reform Programmes of the National Assembly

A significant start had been made to reforming France by the end of 1789. The feudal system had been abolished by the August Decrees (see page 40) and the ground had been prepared for the creation of a constitution. Following this, the deputies drew up the principles on which this should be based – the Declaration of the Rights of Man and the Citizen (see page 42). It condemned the practices of the *ancien régime* and outlined the rights of citizens, as demanded in the *cahiers* of all three orders.

After October 1789, most French people believed that the Revolution was over. For the next year there was broad agreement amongst the different groups in the Assembly, as they set about reorganising how France was governed, its legal system and the finances, taxes and economy of the country.

In doing this they tried to apply the principles of the Declaration of Rights to give France a uniform, **decentralised**, representative and humanitarian system which treated people equally and with dignity. Many of the deputies regarded themselves as products of the Enlightenment, and as such sought to end cruelty, superstition and poverty. Most people by the end of 1789 wanted a **constitutional monarchy**, and there were few regrets about the passing of the *ancien régime*. France was fundamentally changed in many ways. New structures, such as the **departments**, were created that have survived until the present day.

The deputies in the National Assembly set about their task of reforming France with considerable dedication. While most people waited in anticipation for reforms which they hoped would improve their lives, many in the privileged classes prepared themselves for the worse. The main areas where changes would be made were:

- local government
- taxation and finance
- the economy
- the legal system
- the Church
- the constitution.

Key terms

Decentralised
Where decision making is devolved from the centre to the regions of a country.

Constitutional monarchy
Where the powers of the Crown are limited by a constitution. Also known as a limited monarchy.

Departments
On 26 February 1790, 83 new divisions for local administration in France were created to replace the old divisions of the *ancien régime*.

Local government

The reforms to local government involved significantly restructuring it. In restructuring local government the deputies wanted to make sure that power was decentralised, passing from the central government in Paris to the local authorities. This would make it much more difficult for the King to recover the power he had held before the Revolution. It was hoped that the administrative chaos of the *ancien régime* would be replaced by a coherent structure. The Assembly also wanted to ensure that the principle of democracy was introduced to all levels – whereby

Key question
How far did the reforms to local government reflect the principles of the Assembly?

officials would be elected and would be responsible to those who elected them.

By decrees of December 1789 and February 1790 France was divided into 83 departments, which were subdivided into 547 districts and 43,360 **communes** (or municipalities). Communes were grouped into **cantons**, where **primary assemblies** for elections were held and justices of the peace had their courts. All these administrative divisions, except the cantons, were run by elected councils. There were also changes in Paris. On 21 May 1790 the Constituent Assembly passed a decree which reorganised the local government of the city into 48 Sections.

The right to vote

The reforms which revealed the real intention of the Assembly related to voting qualifications. It became clear that deputies did not intend that those who had taken part in the popular protests should have a direct role in government. A law in December 1789 introduced the concept of '**active citizens**', of which there were three tiers:

1. Men over 25 who paid the equivalent of three days' labour in local taxes. It was estimated in 1790 that almost 4.3 million Frenchmen fell into this category. Citizens who did not pay this amount in taxes had no vote and were known as '**passive citizens**'. In reality the only thing active citizens could do was to choose electors – the second tier.
2. Electors – active citizens who paid the equivalent of 10 days' labour in local taxes. About 50,000 men met this qualification and they elected members of the canton and department assemblies and could become officials there. They also elected the deputies to the National Assembly – the third tier
3. To be eligible to become a deputy in the National Assembly an 'active citizen' had to pay at least a *marc d'argent* (a silver mark), the equivalent to 54 days' manual labour, in direct taxation. This was way beyond the reach of most Frenchmen.

The electoral system was, therefore, heavily weighted in favour of the wealthy, although 61 per cent of Frenchmen had the right to take part in some elections (in England only four per cent of adult males had the vote). At local level, most peasants had the right to vote and were qualified to stand for office. This amounted to an administrative revolution. Before 1789 government officials ran the provincial administration, where there was not one elected council. In 1790 there were no government officials at the local level: elected councils had totally replaced them.

Control of the new councils

In the south, bourgeois landowners controlled the new councils. In the north, the bourgeoisie was largely urban and took office in the towns, which left the rural communes in the hands of

Key date

The administrative structure of Paris was reorganised into 48 Sections. These Sections became the power base of the *sans-culottes* until they were swept away in October 1795: 21 May 1790

Key terms

Commune
The smallest administrative unit in France.

Canton
An administrative subdivision of a department.

Primary assemblies
Meeting places for voters.

Active citizens
Citizens who, depending on the amount of taxes paid, could vote and stand as deputies

Passive citizens
Approximately 2.7 million citizens who enjoyed the civic rights provided by the Declaration of the Rights of Man, but paid insufficient taxes to qualify for a vote.

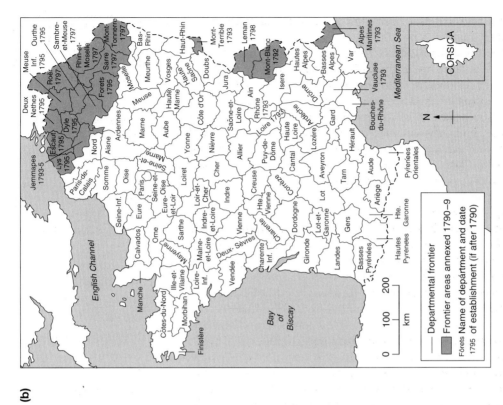

(b)

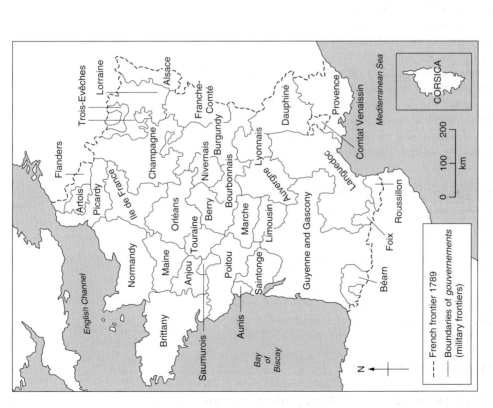

(a)

Figure 3.1: Local government: (a) Old France – the provinces of *ancien régime* France. (b) New France – the departmental framework 1790–9. Look closely at both maps. How do you think that people would have benefited from the reorganisation that took place?

laboureurs, small merchants and artisans. People belonging to social groups which had never held any public office now had the opportunity of doing so. It is estimated that in the decade 1789–99 about a million people were elected to councils and gained experience in local administration.

These councils had an enormous burden of work thrust upon them in December 1789 – much more than the *cahiers* had asked for. They had to assess and collect direct taxes, maintain law and order, carry out public works, see to the upkeep of churches and control the National Guard. Later legislation added to their responsibilities: they had to administer the clerical oath of loyalty, register births, marriages and deaths, requisition grain, and keep a watch on people suspected of opposing the Revolution.

In the towns there was usually an adequate supply of literate, talented people who provided a competent administration. It was often impossible, however, in the villages, to fill the councils with men who could read and write. Rural communes, therefore, often carried out their duties badly. In strongly Catholic areas officials disliked persecuting priests who had refused to take the oath of loyalty (see page 60). Consequently, many resigned and areas were left without any effective local government.

Taxation and finance

After the royal administration collapsed in 1789 very few taxes were collected. The Assembly needed money quickly, particularly when it decided that venal office-holders should be compensated for the loss of their offices. Yet a new tax system could not be set up immediately as considerable planning would be required before any new systems could be created.

It was decided that the existing system of direct and indirect taxation should continue until 1791. This was very unpopular. People wanted the demands made in the *cahiers* to be met at once. When there were outbreaks of violence in Picardy, one of the most heavily taxed areas under the *ancien régime*, the government gave way. The *gabelle* was abolished in March 1790 and within a year nearly all the unpopular indirect taxes, except for external customs duties, were also abolished.

The sale of Church land

As a first step to dealing with the financial crisis, Church land was nationalised on 2 November 1789 and *assignats* were introduced. The National Assembly had three main reasons for selling Church land:

1. To provide money for the State in the period before the new and fairer taxation system was introduced.
2. To guarantee the success of the Revolution since those who bought Church lands would have a vested interest in maintaining the revolutionary changes, and would be more likely to oppose a restoration of the *ancien régime*, which might lead to the Church recovering its land.

Key terms

Biens nationaux
The nationalised
property of the
Church as ordered
by the decree of
2 November 1789.

State monopoly
A system whereby
the State exercises
total control over an
industry and can set
whatever price it
wishes.

Tax rolls
Lists of citizens who
had to pay taxes to
the State.

3. It was also hoped that the clergy would support the new regime, as they would be dependent on it for their salaries.

The government would issue bonds, known as *assignats*, which the public could buy and use for the purchase of Church lands. In April 1790 the Assembly converted the bonds into paper money, which could be used like bank notes in all financial transactions.

Buying Church land

Sales of land in 1791–2 were brisk. In Haute-Marne, for example, nearly 39,000 hectares of Church land, representing a tenth of the arable land in the department, were sold. The main beneficiaries were the bourgeoisie, as they had the ready cash. This was necessary because the *biens nationaux* were sold off in large plots. Members of the bourgeoisie bought most of the available land near the towns. Peasants fared better away from the towns.

A leading historian of the French Revolution, George Lefebvre, in a special study of the Nord department, found that 25 per cent of the Church land there had been sold by 1799: of this peasants had bought 52 per cent and the bourgeoisie 48 per cent. About a third of the peasants were first-time owners, so land did not only go to the wealthier *laboureurs*. Even where the bourgeoisie bought most of the land, they often resold it in smaller quantities to the peasants. It is estimated that the number of peasant smallholders increased by a million between 1789 and 1810.

Key question
Was the new taxation
system better than
the old?

Reforming the taxation system

Before the reforms were introduced the assembly abolished:

- indirect taxes – *aides, traites, octrois, gabelle* (see page 5)
- the **state monopoly** on growing, distributing and selling tobacco
- the old direct taxes – *taille*, capitation, *vingtièmes*
- tax farming.

The new financial system, which came into effect in January 1791, established three new direct taxes:

1. The *contribution foncière* – a land tax from which there were no exemptions or special privileges.
2. The *contribution mobilière* – a tax on movable goods such as grain payable by active citizens.
3. The *patente* – a tax on commercial profits.

In line with the principle of equality, citizens would pay according to their ability to do so. It was planned that the new taxes would be collected by the municipal councils.

This system might have worked well if there had been a systematic valuation of the land, but for this a large number of officials were needed. The Assembly would not provide them, as they would cost too much. Consequently, a survey of land values was not begun until 1807 and was not completed until the 1830s. Meanwhile, the new **tax rolls** were based on those of the *ancien régime*, so that great regional variations remained. People in the

Seine-et-Marne department, for example, paid five times as much in taxes as those in the Ariège. It was also easier to avoid paying direct taxes than indirect ones, since it was easier to conceal incomes than goods.

However, the new system did benefit the poor, as the burden of taxation fell on producers rather than consumers, with the abolition of indirect taxes. It was a fairer system, as all property and income was to be taxed on the same basis. There would no longer be any special privileges or exemptions. Citizens would pay according to their means. The new financial structure would in the main last throughout the nineteenth century.

Economic reforms

During the *ancien régime* many commentators noted how limited French economic progress was when compared with the rapid developments taking place across the Channel in Britain. They viewed the restrictive social structures and internal barriers as inhibiting economic development. The Revolution presented opportunities for reform. All the deputies in the Constituent Assembly believed in **laissez-faire**. Therefore, they introduced **free trade** in grain in August 1789 and removed price controls. These measures were extended to other products in 1790–1, though this is not what the people as a whole desired. They wanted the price and distribution of all essential goods to be controlled, in order to avoid scarcity, high prices and possible starvation.

In October 1790 internal tariffs were abolished, so a national market was created for the first time. For the first time goods could move freely from one part of France to another without having to pay internal customs duties. This was helped by the creation of a single system of weights and measures – the decimal system – which applied to the whole of France.

Employer/worker relations

The deputies were determined to get rid of any organisations which had special privileges and restrictions regarding employment. The aim was to open up a range of crafts and occupations to more people. Guilds were, therefore, abolished in 1791, as they had restricted the entry of people into certain trades in order to ensure that wage levels and prices charged for goods and services had remained high.

In June 1791 a coalition of 80,000 Parisian workers was threatening a general strike to obtain higher wages, so the Assembly passed the Le Chapelier law, named after the deputy who proposed it, which forbade trade unions and employers' organisations. **Collective bargaining**, **picketing** and strikes were declared illegal. No-one in the Assembly objected to the measure. Strikes remained illegal until 1864. The ban on trade unions was not lifted until 1884.

Key question
What was the underlying aim of the economic reforms?

Laissez-faire
Non-interference in economic matters, so that trade and industry should be free from state interference.

Free trade
Trade without the imposition of taxes and duties on the goods.

Collective bargaining
Where a trade union negotiates with employers on behalf of workers who are members.

Picketing
The practice of strikers trying to get others to join in.

The assembly passes the Le Chapelier Law which outlawed trade unions and strikes: 14 June 1791

The poor and needy

The Assembly regarded relief for the poor as a duty of the State. The Church had provided what little assistance the poor had received but it could do so no longer when its land was sold and it lost its main sources of income. Therefore, there was an urgent need for a national organisation, financed by taxation, to take over this role. The Assembly set up a committee which, in 1791, showed for the first time just how serious the problem was. It concluded that nearly two million people could support themselves only by begging. When it came to taking practical measures to help the poor, the committee found itself impotent. There was simply not enough money available to deal with such an appalling problem, so nothing was done.

The legal system

Key question
Why were changes made to the French legal system?

The Constituent Assembly applied the same principle of uniformity to the legal system as it had done to local government. It abolished many features on 16 August 1790 and imposed a new structure. Among those areas removed were the following:

Key dates
Reorganisation of the judiciary: 16 August 1790

The guillotine was approved as the only method for public execution: March 1792

- The different systems of law in the north and south of the country.
- The different types of law court, the *parlements*, seigneurial and ecclesiastical courts.
- The *lettres de cachet* (see page 33): in place of the old structure a new, uniform system, based on the administrative divisions of the reformed local government, was introduced.

The main features of the new system were:

- In each canton there was to be a justice of the peace, dealing with cases previously handled by seigneurial courts.
- The justice's main task was to persuade the different parties to come to an agreement; he could also judge minor civil cases, such as trespass, without appeal.
- Serious civil cases such as property disputes were dealt with in a district court.
- A criminal court would be located in each department, where trials would be held in public before a jury. The idea of having a jury, like that of having justices of the peace, was taken from English law.
- At the head of the judicial system was a Court of Appeal, whose judges were elected by the department assemblies.
- All judges were elected by active citizens but only those who had been lawyers for five years were eligible. This ensured that all judges were well qualified and accountable.

Key term
Penal code
A list of the laws of France and the punishments for breaking those laws.

There were other improvements in the quality of French justice. The **penal code** was made more humane: torture and mutilation were abolished. Anyone arrested had to be brought before a court within 24 hours. The number of capital crimes was vastly reduced. In March 1792 a new and more efficient method of

execution – the **guillotine** – was approved by the Legislative
Assembly. It replaced all other forms used on those condemned
to death. This mechanical device with its angular blade would
become one of the most feared and lasting images of the
Revolution following its first use in April 1792.

The new judicial system was to prove one of the most lasting
reforms of the Constituent Assembly. For the first time, justice was
made free and equal to all, and was therefore popular. The
French system of justice had been one of the most backward,
barbarous and corrupt in Europe. In two years it became one of
the most enlightened.

The Church
The Constituent Assembly wanted to create a Church that was:

- free from abuses such as absenteeism and plurality
- free from foreign (papal) control – independent of Rome
- democratic
- linked to the new system of local government – primarily the
  department
- linked more closely to the State in order to strengthen the
  Revolution.

Key question
How far did the
government want
to go in reforming
the Church?

Guillotine
A machine
introduced in 1792
for decapitating
victims in a
relatively painless
way. It became
synonymous with
the Terror.

Annates
Payments made by
the French Church
to the Pope.

The deputies were not in the main anti-religious or anti-Catholic
and simply wanted to extend to religion the principles they
applied elsewhere. They certainly had no intention of interfering
with the doctrines of the Church or with its spiritual functions.

In August 1789 the Assembly abolished the tithe, **annates** and
pluralism. It also ended the privileges of the Church, such as its
right to decide for itself how much tax it would pay. Most parish
clergy supported these measures. They also accepted the sale of
Church lands, because they would be paid more than they had
been under the *ancien régime*.

In February 1790, a decree distinguished between monastic
orders which did not work in the community and those which
provided education and charity. The former were suppressed, as
they made no direct contribution to the common good. The latter
were allowed to remain 'for the present', although the taking of
religious vows was forbidden.

These changes took place without creating much of a stir
among the clergy as a whole. Less popular was the decree in
December 1789 giving civil rights to Protestants. These rights
were extended to Jews in September 1791.

The Civil Constitution of the Clergy
There was no serious conflict with the Church until the Civil
Constitution of the Clergy was approved on 12 July 1790. This
measure reformed the Catholic Church in France, and adapted
the organisation of the Church to the administrative framework
of local government. Dioceses were to coincide with departments.
This meant that the number of bishoprics would be reduced from
135 to 83. There would not only be fewer bishops but fewer clergy
generally, as all other clerical posts except for parish priests and

Key question
How significant was
the civil constitution
of the clergy on the
Revolution and
counter-revolution?

Key date

The Civil Constitution of the Clergy became law: 12 July 1790

bishops ceased to exist. The attempt to extend democracy to all aspects of government was also applied to the Church. But there was no intention of ending the Catholic Church's position as the State Church in France.

Some of the key terms of the Civil Constitution of the Clergy were:

- each department would form a single diocese
- there would be no recognition of any bishop appointed by the Pope but not approved by the French State
- all titles and offices, other than those mentioned in the Civil Constitution, were abolished
- all priests and bishops were to be elected to their posts
- all elections were to be by ballot and by absolute majority of those who voted
- priests were to be paid by the State
- there was to be no absenteeism by priests or bishops – no bishop was to be absent from his diocese for more than 15 days consecutively in any year.

Most clergy opposed the principle of election which was unknown in the Church, but even so, the majority (including many bishops) were in favour of finding a way of accepting the Civil Constitution and avoiding a split in the Church. They demanded that the reforms be submitted to a **national synod** of the French Church. This would have made a compromise possible but the Constituent Assembly would not agree to this, as it believed that it would give the Church a privileged position in the State once again, something which had just been abolished.

Key term

National synod
An assembly of representatives of the entire Church.

A constitutional priest taking the civic oath. Study the print carefully. What do you think is the significance of the large storm cloud gathering behind the priest?

The oath of loyalty

As a Church assembly was not allowed to discuss the matter, the clergy waited for the Pope to give his verdict. He delayed coming to a decision, as he was involved in delicate negotiations with the French over the status of **Avignon**. The Assembly grew tired of waiting and in 27 November 1790 decreed that clergy must take an oath to the Constitution. This split the clergy. In the Assembly only two of the 44 bishops and a third of the other clergy took the oath. In France as a whole seven bishops and 55 per cent of the clergy took the oath. When the Pope finally condemned the Civil Constitution in March and April 1791, many clergy who had taken the oath retracted it.

Two Churches

The Civil Constitution of the Clergy had momentous results. It was one of the defining moments of revolution. It effectively destroyed the revolutionary consensus that had existed since 1789. Deputies in the Assembly were shocked when it was rejected by so many clergy and by the Pope.

There were now, in effect, two Catholic Churches in France. One was the constitutional Church, which accepted the Revolution but was rejected by Rome. The other was a **non-juring** Church of '**refractory**' priests, approved by the Pope but regarded by patriots as rejecting the Revolution. Nigel Aston, a modern historian, concludes: 'Faced with what was crudely reduced to a stark choice between religion and revolution, half the adult population (and the great majority of women) rejected revolution'.

A major effect of this split was that the counter-revolution, the movement which sought to overturn the Revolution, received mass support for the first time. Before this, it had been supported only by a few royalists and *émigrés*. In the most strongly Catholic areas – the west, north-east and south of the Massif Central – few clergy took the oath. On 27 May 1792 the Legislative Assembly attempted to take a firmer line with those priests who refused to take the oath by passing a measure which enabled their deportation, if 20 citizens were prepared to denounce them.

Many villagers complained that the Assembly was trying to change their religion, especially when refractory priests were expelled. They felt a sense of betrayal which, combined with their hostility to other measures of the Assembly, such as conscription, was to lead to open revolt in 1793 in areas such as the Vendée.

Disaffection with the Revolution, which eventually turned into civil war, was, therefore, one result of the Civil Constitution of the Clergy. Another was the King's attempt to flee from France in June 1791, precipitating a series of events which was to bring about the downfall of the monarchy (see pages 65–8).

The Constitution of 1791

One of the main aims of the Constituent Assembly had been to draw up a constitution that would replace an absolute monarchy with a constitutional one. Under the new proposals power would pass from the constituent assembly (which would be dissolved)

Avignon
Territory controlled by the Pope in southern France.

Non-juror
Those members of the clergy who refused to take the new oath of allegiance to the Civil Constitution.

Refractory priests
Those who refused to take the oath.

Decree passed compelling the clergy to take an oath of loyalty to the Civil Constitution of the Clergy: 27 November 1790

Any non-juring priests who were denounced by 20 citizens could be deported: 27 May 1792

Louis vetoed the measure on 19 June

Key question
How did the new constitution propose to limit the powers of the Crown?

Key terms

Legislative assembly
Came into existence in October 1791 and was the second elected Assembly to rule during the Revolution. It differed from the National/Constituent Assembly in that members were directly elected.

Suspensive veto
The right to reject a measure proposed by the assembly.

Key date

Louis accepts the Constitution:
14 September 1791

to a **legislative assembly** of 745 members. These members would be elected every two years and would have significant power. Much of the Constitution – that the King should have a **suspensive veto** and that there should be one elected assembly – had been worked out in 1789, but the rest was not finally agreed until 14 September 1791. Under the terms of the constitution, the King:

- had the right to appoint his ministers (although they could not be members of the Assembly) and military commanders
- was given a suspensive veto, although this could not be applied to financial or constitutional matters such as new taxes
- was dependent on the Assembly for his foreign policy, as he needed its consent before he could declare war
- agreed that his office, although hereditary, was subordinate to the Assembly, as it passed the laws which the King had to obey. 'In France there is no authority superior to the law … it is only by means of the law that the King reigns.'

Louis XVI facing both ways. In this contemporary cartoon Louis is shown promising both to support and to destroy the constitution.

In September Louis XVI reluctantly accepted the Constitution. Marie Antoinette's attitude was that it was 'so monstrous that it cannot survive for long'. She was determined to overthrow it at the first opportunity.

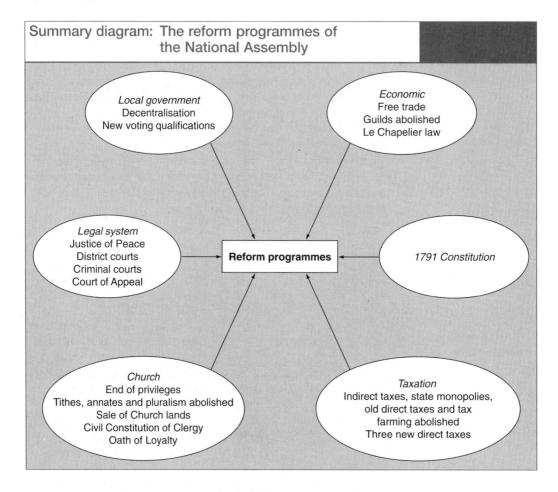

Summary diagram: The reform programmes of the National Assembly

2 | The Rise of the Jacobin and the Cordeliers

In the absence of political parties, clubs were established to support the popular movement. They were set up soon after the Estates-General met in May 1789. For many ordinary people they provided a stage from which speakers could debate the great issues of the day. The majority of Frenchmen who had never been involved in political life discovered that they provided a crash course in political education. This section will examine two of the most important of these clubs and the growth of popular activity which they helped ferment.

The revolutionary clubs

As there were no political parties, the clubs played an important part in the Revolution. They kept the public informed on the major issues of the day, supported election candidates and acted as pressure groups to influence deputies in the Assembly and to

Key question
What impact did the political clubs have on the course of the Revolution?

promote actions which the deputies seemed reluctant to undertake. In essence, they provided education in political participation.

The Jacobin Club

The Jacobin Club originated in meetings of radical Breton deputies with others of similar views. When the Assembly moved to Paris after the October Days these deputies and their supporters rented a room from the monks of a Jacobin convent in the Rue Saint-Honoré, hence the name by which they are now universally known. Their official title remained the 'Society of the Friends of the Constitution'. At the club, members debated measures that were to come before the Assembly.

The Jacobin Club set a high entrance fee for its members. There were 1200 by July 1790 and they came mainly from the wealthiest sections of society. To begin with they associated themselves with the ideas of the **physiocrats**. They raised no serious objections to the introduction of free trade in grain, or the abolition of guilds in 1791. That they started to move towards accepting a more controlled economy can be explained by the problems posed by war and counter-revolution. Even then these measures were forced on them by their more extreme supporters – the *sans-culottes*.

Jacobin ideology was based upon a combination of Enlightenment thought and revolutionary practice. They came to reject the notion of monarchy. What distinguished the Jacobin from other contemporary clubs was that they were highly political men of action. As the Jacobin moved further to the left in the summer of 1792 they favoured increased **centralisation** of government in order to defend the Republic. The key figure to emerge during this period was Maximilian Robespierre, leader of a minority group of radical Jacobin deputies (see page 112).

A national network of Jacobin clubs soon grew up, all linked to the central club in Paris with which they regularly corresponded. By the end of 1793 there were over 2000 Jacobin clubs across France. It has been estimated that between 1790 and 1799 the movement involved two per cent of the population (about 500,000 people). The significance of the clubs is that they enabled for the first time large numbers of people to become directly involved in the political life of their country.

The Cordeliers Club

The Cordeliers Club, founded in April 1790, was more radical than the Jacobin Club and had no membership fee. It objected to the distinction between 'active' and 'passive' citizens and supported measures which the *sans-culottes* favoured:

- direct democracy where voters choose deputies
- the recall of deputies to account for their actions, if these went against the wishes of the people
- the right of insurrection – rebellion, if a government acted against popular wishes.

Key terms

Physiocrats
A group of French intellectuals who believed that land was the only source of wealth and that landowners should therefore pay the bulk of taxes.

Centralisation
Direct central control of the various parts of government, with less power to the regions.

Key question
In what way did the policies of the Cordeliers Club differ from those of the Jacobin?

It had much support among the working class, although its leaders were bourgeois. Georges Danton and Camille Desmoulins were lawyers. Jacques-René Hébert was an unsuccessful writer who had become a journalist when freedom of the press was allowed. Brissot was also a journalist. But the most notorious writer of all was Marat, a failed doctor turned radical journalist. He hated all those who had enjoyed privileges under the old regime and attacked them violently in his newspaper, *L'Ami du Peuple*. He became the chief spokesman of the popular movement.

During the winter of 1790–1, the example of the Cordeliers Club led to the formation of many 'popular' or 'fraternal' societies, which were soon to be found in every district in Paris and in several provincial towns. In 1791 the Cordeliers Club and the popular societies formed a federation and elected a central committee. The members of the popular societies were drawn mainly from the liberal professions such as teachers and officials, and skilled artisans and shopkeepers. Labourers rarely joined, as they did not have the spare time for politics.

Popular discontent in rural and urban areas

By the start of 1790 many peasants became disillusioned with the Revolution. The sense of anticipation which followed the 'Night of 4 August' quickly diminished once they realised in the spring of 1790 that their feudal dues were not abolished outright but would have to be bought out (see page 40).

A rural revolution began in 1790 in Brittany, in central France and in the south-east. This lasted until 1792 and placed pressure on the Jacobin. Peasants fixed the price of grain, called for the sale of Church land in small lots and attacked châteaux. The rising in the Midi (Languedoc, Provence and the Rhône valley) in 1792 was as important as any in 1789 in size and the extent of the destruction. These risings, and the deteriorating military situation contributed to the most serious crisis of the Revolution. On 10 August 1792 Louis was deposed. Shortly afterwards all feudal and seigneurial dues which could not be justified were abolished. Feudalism was finally abolished without compensation by the Jacobin on 17 July 1793.

The *sans-culottes*

The *sans-culottes* were the workers in the towns. They were not a class, as they included artisans and master craftsmen, who owned their own workshops, as well as wage-earners. They had been responsible for the successful attack on the Bastille and for bringing the royal family back to Paris in the October Days, yet they had received few rewards.

Many of them were 'passive' citizens, who did not have the vote. They suffered greatly from **inflation**. To meet its expenses the government printed more and more *assignats* (paper money), whose value therefore declined. There was a wave of strikes by workers against the falling value of their wages early in 1791. Grain prices rose by up to 50 per cent after a poor harvest in

Key question
Was peasant pressure on the Jacobin in any way successful?

Key date
Final abolition of feudalism in France: 17 July 1793

Key question
How did popular societies seek to take advantage of concerns among workers?

Key term
Inflation
A decline in the value of money, which leads to an increase in the price of goods.

1791. This led to riots, which resulted in shopkeepers' being forced to reduce prices.

The discontent of the urban workers could be used by the popular societies, which linked economic protests to the political demand for a republic whose representatives were directly elected by the people, and by groups in the Assembly who were seeking power. This made the Revolution more radical in ways which the bourgeois leaders of 1789 had neither intended nor desired.

Summary diagram: The rise of the Jacobin and the Cordeliers		
	Jacobin	Cordeliers
Key members	Maximilian Robespierre	Georges Danton Camille Desmoulins Jaques-René Hébert Brissot Marat
Supporters	Wealthy radical deputies	Bourgeois and working-class radicals
Key ideas	Centralisation	Direct democracy Right of insurrection

Key question
How did the actions of the King contribute to the emergence of a republican movement?

3 | The Emergence of a Republican Movement

The outstanding politician and orator in the Constituent Assembly was Mirabeau, a nobleman who was elected for the Third Estate in 1789. His willingness to deal directly with the King cost him a great deal of popular support by the time of his death in April 1791. He was fairly typical of a group of moderate politicians who were becoming increasingly influential in the Assembly.

Three of the leading figures were Barnave, Du Port and Lameth, who were known as the triumvirate. Their broad aim was to try and heal the divisions between the aristocracy and bourgeoisie that had emerged during 1789. They feared the extremism of the new clubs and the emergence of an organised working-class movement and wished to bring the Revolution to an end. In order for this to happen there had to be a compromise with the King. This was difficult, as anyone suspected of negotiating with the King was likely to be accused of selling out to the Court. There was also no means of knowing if the King was sincerely prepared to co-operate with the moderates. Louis dashed all their hopes by attempting to flee from Paris.

The flight to Varennes

Louis XVI was a devout man. He deeply regretted his acceptance of the Civil Constitution of the Clergy, which offended his conscience. He decided to flee from Paris, where he felt restricted by the Constituent Assembly, to Montmédy in Lorraine, on the border of Luxembourg, and put himself under the protection of the military commander of the area. He hoped that from there, in a position of strength, he would be able to renegotiate with the Constituent Assembly the parts of the Constitution he disliked. Military action would, he hoped, be unnecessary, although the King was aware that there was a danger that his flight might open up divisions and bring about civil war.

Louis left Paris with his family on 20 June 1791. When he reached Varennes, during the night of 21–2 June, he was recognised by the local postmaster, Drouet, and stopped. He was brought back to Paris in an atmosphere of deathly silence. Louis' younger brother, the Comte de Provence, was luckier than the King. He also fled from Paris on 20 June with his wife but he arrived safely in Brussels the next day.

Key date
Louis and his family flee Paris and are stopped at Varennes: 20–2 June 1791

How significant was the flight to Varennes?

The flight to Varennes was one of the key moments of the early phase of the French Revolution. Before leaving, Louis had drawn up a proclamation to the French people which set out in great detail his true feelings regarding the developments that had taken place. Writing in the third person he concluded that: 'The king does not think it would be possible to govern so large and important a kingdom as France by the means established by the National Assembly such as they exist at present'. The significance of the event was:

Key question
Was the flight to Varennes a turning point in the Revolution?

- in the declaration it is obvious that Louis had failed to understand the popularity of the changes which had taken place since 1789
- it became clear that once again (see Civil Constitution of the Clergy, pages 58–60) that the French people would have to make choices that many of them would have preferred to avoid
- Louis in his declaration had emphatically renounced the Revolution. Could he continue to remain as head of state?

'The family of pigs brought back to the sty'. What is the significance of the way the artist has chosen to portray the royal family in this contemporary cartoon?

Key terms

Republic
A political system which does not have a hereditary head of state and where the supremacy of the people is recognised through mass democracy.

Feuillants
Constitutional monarchists, among them Lafayette, who split from the Jacobin Club following the flight to Varennes.

- the credibility of the new constitution was undermined before it had even been implemented
- support for a **republic** started to grow, while the popularity of the King declined.

On the 24 June, 30,000 people marched to the National Assembly in support of a petition from the Cordeliers Club calling for the King's dismissal from office.

Results of the flight

One immediate result of the flight was that the King lost what remained of his popularity, which had depended on his being seen to support the Revolution. Royal inn signs and street names disappeared all over Paris. His flight persuaded many who had hitherto supported him that he could no longer be trusted. People started to talk openly of replacing the monarchy with a republic.

The deputies in the Assembly acted calmly in this situation. They did not want a republic. They feared that the declaration of a republic would lead to civil war in France and war with European monarchs. Nor did they want to concede victory to the radicals, who wanted more democratic policies. 'Are we going to end the Revolution or are we going to start it again?' one deputy asked the Assembly.

On 16 July the Assembly voted to suspend the King until the constitution was completed. Governing without the head of state would encourage those who favoured republicanism. He would be restored only after he had sworn to observe it. This was going too far for some deputies – 290 abstained from voting as a protest. For others, suspension did not go far enough.

Division among the Jacobins

After the flight to Varennes, radicals were appalled when the King was not dethroned or put on trial. Their anger was directed against the Constituent Assembly, which they claimed no longer represented the people. The Cordeliers took the lead with the popular societies and persuaded the Jacobins to join them in supporting a petition for the King's deposition. This split the Jacobin Club. Those who did not want the King deposed – and this included nearly all the members who were deputies – left the Club.

They set up a new club, the **Feuillants**, which for the moment had control of the Assembly. Robespierre remained as leader of a small group of radical members. It seemed as though the Jacobins had destroyed themselves. However, only 72 of the provincial Jacobin clubs in France defected from the control of the Parisian club, and most of these drifted back in the next few months.

Key question
Why were the events on the Champ de Mars important?

The Champs de Mars massacre

On 17 July 1791, 50,000 people flocked to the Champ de Mars, a huge field in Paris where the Feast of the Federation, celebrating the fall of the Bastille, had been held three days previously. They

The shooting of demonstrators at the Champ de Mars. What would circulation of images such as this hope to achieve?

were there to sign a republican petition on the **'altar of the fatherland'**. This was a political demonstration by the poorer sections of the Paris population. The Commune, under pressure from the Assembly, declared **martial law**. They sent Lafayette with the National Guard to the Champ de Mars, where the Guards fired on the peaceful and unarmed crowd. About 50 people were killed.

This was the first bloody clash between different groups in the Third Estate, and it was greeted with pleasure in the Assembly. Messages of support for the Assembly poured in from the provinces. Martial law remained in force for a month, during which time some popular leaders were arrested. Others, such as Hébert, Marat and Danton, fled or went into hiding. The moderates had won – it took nearly a year for the popular movement to recover – and could now work out a compromise with the King without facing mob violence. As far as the extremists were concerned only the overthrow of the monarchy would satisfy their demands.

The Feuillants were more determined than ever to make an agreement with the King. Although they did not trust him and had lost popular support, for the moment they controlled Paris and the Assembly. Their long-term success however depended on the co-operation of Louis, and this was far from certain.

The Legislative Assembly

The acceptance of the Constitution by the King on 13 September 1791 marked the end of the Constituent Assembly. Its final meeting was on 30 September. On 1 October the first meeting of the new Legislative Assembly was held. But by now suspicion and hatred amongst the deputies had replaced the optimism of 1789. The mood among the deputies in the new Legislative Assembly was far from co-operative. There were a number of reasons why this change had came about:

Key date

The National Guard opens fire on a crowd killing about 50 people: 17 July 1791

Key terms

'Altar of the fatherland' A large memorial to commemorate the Revolution.

Martial law When there is severe rioting or public disorder, the authorities can declare martial law which would impose restrictions on movement and may suspend civil liberties.

Key question What effect did the lack of trust between politicians and the King have on the Legislative Assembly?

Key terms

Self-denying ordinance
Approved by the Constituent Assembly to ensure that none of its members could belong to the new assembly.

Left
Those seated on the left of the speaker favouring extreme policies such as removing the King and having a republic.

Right
Those seated on the right of the speaker and supporting a limited monarchy.

Centre
Those who sat facing the speaker favouring neither left nor right.

Girondins
A small group of deputies from the Gironde and their associates – notably Brissot.

Parlementaire
Judges who held hereditary positions on one of the 13 *parlements*.

- The King's reluctance to accept measures he disliked.
- Suspicions regarding the King's commitment to the Revolution as revealed by the flight to Varennes.
- The fear of counter-revolutionary plots.

To prevent his political opponents in the Constituent Assembly from dominating the next Assembly, Robespierre proposed a **self-denying ordinance**. This was passed and stated that no member of the Constituent Assembly, including Robespierre, could sit in the next Legislative Assembly.

In the elections for the new Legislative Assembly (29 August to 5 September), under a quarter of the 'active' citizens voted. The Assembly of 745 members which was elected was almost wholly bourgeois. In the semicircular meeting chamber the seating arrangement in front of the speaker gave rise to new political labels – **left**, **right** and **centre**. There were few nobles, most of whom had retired to their estates and kept themselves to themselves, hoping for better times. Only 23 clergy were elected. There were no peasants or artisans, and few businessmen. At the opening of the Legislative Assembly, it was possible to identify three broad groups of deputies:

1. The Left – 136 deputies most of whom were members of the Jacobin Club. The most prominent were a small group of deputies from the Gironde department, known as the **Girondins**.
2. The Right – 264 deputies who were members of the Feuillant Club and considered the Revolution to be over.
3. The Centre – 345 deputies making up the largest group who were unattached.

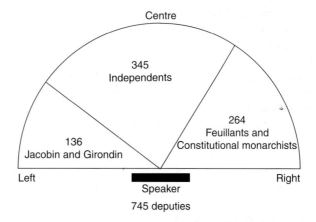

Figure 3.2: Main political groups in the Legislative Assembly, 1 October 1791 to 20 September 1792

Key question
What impact did the flight to Varennes have on the *émigrés*?

The growth of the counter-revolution

From the very start the deputies were worried by the non-juring clergy and by the *émigrés*, whose numbers had increased greatly since the flight to Varennes. Nearly all the *ancien régime* bishops and many of the great court and ***parlementaire*** families had emigrated to Austria and the small German states along the river Rhine. What alarmed the Assembly most was the desertion of army officers. By early 1791, 1200 noble officers had joined the *émigrés*, though a large majority of pre-Revolution officers remained at their posts. All this changed after Varennes.

By the end of 1791, about 6000 had emigrated, 60 per cent of all officers. The Assembly passed two laws in November. One declared that all non-jurors were suspects. The other said that all *émigrés* who did not return to France by 1 January 1792 would forfeit their property and be regarded as traitors. When the King vetoed these laws his unpopularity increased. He appeared to be undermining the Revolution.

Conclusion

This chapter has largely focused on the significant reforms passed by the Assembly which altered so many of France's institutions. It has also dealt with the increasing politicisation of many sections of society as the Revolution took hold in the country. The changes were certainly not to everyone's liking as the growth of the counter-revolution suggests. At the centre of all these changes was the King. His distaste for what was happening within France and to his authority became evident during his attempt to flee the country. Whatever assurances he might give to the contrary, he was clearly ill at ease in the role of a constitutional monarch. His opponents for their part were uncomfortable with him, as the growth of republicanism would indicate. The next chapter will examine why and how Louis was overthrown.

4 | The Key Debate

As the First Estate the Catholic Church during the *ancien régime* was the most important of the Estates of the Realm. The decision to reform it in incremental stages was certainly one of the boldest of the policies taken by the Constituent and National Assemblies. A central theme which scholars address is:

> Why was the Catholic Church reformed and did this decision have any significance on the course of the Revolution?

Jacques Solé

Jacques Solé believes that the Catholic Church on the eve of the Revolution was in a relatively healthy state and that its priests and bishops were good administrators and effective clerics. According to Sole the reform of the Church, undertaken by the Constituent Assembly, was the result of a misunderstanding. This misunderstanding arose because the Constituent Assembly, impressed by the revolutionary enthusiasm of the lower clergy who sat in it, failed to understand that the Church was deeply unified in 1789. These clerical deputies had many grievances against the Church and drove the reform process for their own ends.

John McManners

John McManners points out that on the eve of the Revolution the Catholic Church was providing an enormous amount of charity, poor relief and education along with its spiritual role. However the unity of the Church was more apparent than real. Like Solé he noted that within the Church many of its priests were vocal in asking for an improvement in their situation. Their complaints influenced clerical deputies, who in turn promoted and supported reform of the Church, culminating in the Civil Constitution of the Clergy. McManners considers however that this was the point when the Revolution 'went wrong'.

D.M.G. Sutherland

D.M.G. Sutherland identified the Civil Constitution of the Clergy as one of the great crises of the Revolution. The decision to reform the Catholic Church was notable for the boost it gave to the counter-revolution, because it provided it with a popular base. The large numbers of ordinary peasants in various parts of rural France were mobilised by refractory priests to oppose the Revolution. Showing loyalty to the refractories was one way of demonstrating hostility to the Revolution, while making the religious settlement unworkable in many areas of the country.

Nigel Aston

Nigel Aston broadly supports McManners' view that the Church on the eve of the Revolution was facing severe internal stresses, resulting from a top-heavy organisation which was crushing the ordinary parish clergy. This led large numbers of ordinary clergy to align themselves with the progressive forces directing the Revolution in 1789. Their support however was largely undermined by the Civil Constitution of the Clergy. This, according to Aston, led to a schism within the Church which helped pave the way for a republic that actively sponsored alternative beliefs to Christianity – Robespierre's Cult of the Supreme Being.

Some key books in the debate

Nigel Aston, *Religion and Revolution in France 1789–1804* (Macmillan, 2000).
John McManners, *The French Revolution and the Church* (SPCK, 1969).
Jacques Solé, *Questions of the French Revolution* (Pantheon, 1989).
D.M.G. Sutherland, *France 1789–1815 Revolution and Counterrevolution* (Fontana, 1985).

Study Guide: AS Questions

In the style of AQA

(a) Explain why the National Assembly reformed local government in France in the years 1789 and 1790. (12 marks)

(b) How important was the Civil Constitution of the Clergy in bringing about counter-revolution in France in the years 1790–4? (24 marks)

Exam tips

The cross-references are intended to take you straight to the material that will help you to answer the questions.

(a) To answer this question you would need to give some indication of the problems of local government under the *ancien régime* – the corrupt intendants and the chaotic incoherence of different government structures. You should also be able to supply some more immediate reasons for the reform from 1789, referring to:

- the undermining of the King's powers from May 1789
- the disappearance of the old feudal hierarchy
- the deputies' concern to create a more democratic system using elections
- a desire for decentralisation (to prevent the return of strong central control by the King)
- the concern for uniformity.

Try to offer some explanation of how such factors link together and their relative importance.

(b) You will need to consider how the Civil Constitution affected the growth of counter-revolution by explaining the position of the refractory priests and the reaction of the laity: particularly the peasants (see page 60). You will then need to balance the importance of this measure against other issues that turned Frenchmen against the revolution, such as the loss of land and privileges, loyalty to the monarchy, dislike for conscription and economic anxieties. You should make it clear that non-religious factors were prominent in the Vendée and federalist revolts (see page 97) and you may wish to argue that such issues were of greater importance. What you argue is really of less importance than how you argue and support your opinions. Your answer should show clear judgement with a weighing of the evidence.

In the style of OCR A

Study the four sources on the problems facing the King in the period 1790–2, and then answer both sub-questions. It is recommended that you spend two-thirds of your time in answering part **(b)**.

(a) **Study Sources B and D.**
Compare these sources as evidence of hostility to the monarchy. (30 marks)

(b) **Study all the sources.**

Use your own knowledge to assess how far the sources support the interpretation that the main reason for the problems facing the monarchy during 1790–2 was the actions of Louis XVI. (70 marks)

Source A

From: Letter from Pope Pius VI to Louis XVI, 7 December 1790. Pope Pius VI was very concerned with the new Civil Constitution of the Clergy, fearing that it would cause deep divisions within the Church. He expressed his thoughts to Louis XVI in a letter.

Our beloved son, we have no doubt of your devotion to the Catholic Church but we fear that through false arguments your love for your people may be led astray and that Your Majesty's wish to see order and peace restored to the Kingdom may be abused. We must say to you, with firmness and paternal love, that if you give your approval to the decrees concerning the clergy, you will plunge the kingdom into schism* and perhaps into cruel war of religion.

[* Religious division.]

Source B

From: Marat, L'Ami du Peuple, a radical French newspaper, 22 June 1791. The Jacobin were very suspicious of the motives of the King and doubted his commitment to the new constitution which the flight to Varennes appeared to confirm. One of Louis most outspoken critics was the radical journalist and leading Jacobin J-P Marat.

This perjurer* of a King, without faith, without shame, without remorse, this monarch unworthy of the throne, has been restrained only by the fear of being shown up as an infamous beast. The thirst for absolute power that consumes his soul will soon turn him into a ferocious murderer. Meanwhile he is laughing at the folly of the Parisians who stupidly took him at his word. Citizens the flight of the Royal family was prepared by traitors in the National Assembly.

[* Liar.]

Source C

From: A letter from Jean-Marie Roland to the King, 10 June 1792. Roland was a leading supporter of the Girondin and in this letter to Louis he advises that the King's decision on the 19 June 1792 to veto proposals to deport non-juring priests and for the establishment near Paris of a camp of 20,000 fédérés, might have serious repercussions.

Sire the present condition of France cannot last long: it is in a state of crisis, the violence of which is reaching its height: it must be ended by a measure which should interest your Majesty as much as it concerns the whole realm. Devotion to the Constitution has increased; not only did the people owe it obvious benefits, but they thought it would bring them greater ones. The Declaration of Rights has become a political gospel, and the French constitution a religion, for which the people are ready to perish. Two important decrees have been passed the vetoing of their enactment arouses mistrust: if it is continued it will cause discontent, and I dare say that in the general stirring of passions, the malcontents will be able to carry all with them.

Source D

From: A petition from the Paris Sections for the Dethronement of Louis XVI, 3 August 1792. The Paris sections were the power base of the sans-culottes. *In this petition they are demanding the overthrow of Louis XVI.*

The chief of the executive power of the State is the main link in the counter-revolutionary chain. He seems to participate in the plots of those *émigrés* at Pillnitz, which he has so tardily made known. He has separated his interests from those of the nation. Far from having opposed by any formal act the enemies without and within, his conduct is a perpetual act of disobedience to the Constitution.

Exam tips

The cross-references are intended to take you straight to the material that will help you to answer the questions.

(a) In question (a) you will be expected to compare the way each source presents its hostility to the King. Note:

- Marat's use of language – perjurer, beast. He also blames elements in the National Assembly
- Source D emphasises Louis' links with counter-revolutionary elements and willingness to disobey the Constitution.

(b) The key word in question (b) is *main*. Ensure that you examine all four sources together thematically as a set and that you do not provide half the answer on the sources and the second half based on your own knowledge. You must then come to a conclusion about whether you agree with the view or not and why. Examine closely the sources for evidence that Louis was largely responsible for the predicament he was in. The flight to Varennes, vetoing decrees might suggest that this is the case. There is certainly evidence in the sources to support this. On the other hand the growth of political extremism meant that Louis was always reacting to events, rather than controlling them. Some of the actions taken by others – the Champ de Mars Massacre, did rebound on the King. Louis, to a degree, was the author of his own misfortunes but other groups must also shoulder some of the blame for the King's predicament. *Émigrés* and foreign sympathisers of the Crown were also behaving in a provocative manner (pages 80–1).

In the style of OCR B

Answer **both** parts of the question.

(a) What do the reforms of 1789–92 reveal about the aims of those directing the Revolution during those years?
[Explaining ideas, attitudes and beliefs.]   (25 marks)

(b) How is the rise of the Jacobins best explained?
[Explaining events and circumstances.]   (25 marks)

Exam tips

Revise the General introduction at the start of the study guide to Chapter 1, page 24.

(a) The prompt guides you to begin your explanation in the empathetic mode, considering the intentions and motives that lie behind actions. In this case, consider the aims of the Revolution's leaders during the given period. Next, look at the question carefully. It gives you several specific things to do: (i) explain the aims of reformers judged through reforms actually introduced; (ii) consider only those (groups and individuals) who directed the Revolution; (iii) look at a specific four-year period. If you don't address each, your essay will not answer the question set.

Differentiate between the different aims of the various key groups and individuals that helped to direct the Revolution and for each establish a hierarchy of importance for their various aims. Lastly, note that the question wants you to consider those aims, not as theoretical ideas but being applied through political actions. In this question, you are concerned with individuals, judging how their behaviour reveals their ideals and beliefs.

(b) Starting with a causal explanation you will also be able to expand into an empathetic consideration of the appeal of Jacobin ideas. Note that the question asks for your view on how the rise of the Jacobins is 'best explained'. That phrase tells you clearly that your explanation must be rooted in relative evaluation: the various factors that you consider must be ordered in a clear hierarchy of importance.

A firm place to start might be to consider the significance of timing: what was going on when the Jacobins began to become important? Only after the revolutionary events of 1789 did the Jacobin Club become significant as the divide between monarchy and radicals widened. Indeed, it was only after the split of 1791 (in the aftermath of the flight to Varennes) that the Jacobins' role became increasingly central. So your answer can focus in on factors such as fear of counter-revolution, the impact of war, the role of the *sans-culottes* and the people of Paris in radicalising the Revolution, and the very radicalisation of the Revolution itself, in terms of politics (ardent republicanism, direct democracy, revolutionary *journées* such as that of June 1793 which secured victory of the Jacobins over the Girondins), in terms of economics (the desire to control prices and bread supply), in terms of religion (de-Christianisation).

Study Guide: Advanced Level Question
In the style of Edexcel

Source 1

Adapted from: N. Aston, Religion and Revolution in France 1780–1804, *2004.*

The dispute over the Civil Constitution of the Clergy destroyed the revolutionary consensus of 1789. The responsibility for this lay with the politicians in the National Assembly. The *cahiers* had made clear the hopes the French public held out for religious reforms and renewal. Such prospects were seen as part of revolution not at odds with it and had the two remained in alliance beyond eighteen months, events would have taken a more moderate course and thousands of lives would have been saved.

Source 2

Adapted from: George Rudé, The French Revolution, *1988.*

The most intractable of all the problems tackled by the Constituents and the most fateful in its consequences, was their settlement of the affairs of the Catholic Church. When the Civil Constitution was declared to be in force it divided the clergy into two more or less evenly balanced opposing blocks of jurors and non-jurors.* From this followed the tragic and fateful sequence of emigration, denouncement and even massacre of priests, the civil war in the west, terror and counter-terror.

* jurors were priests who took the new oath to the civil constitution while non-jurors refused.

Source 3

Adapted from: D.G. Wright, Revolution and Terror in France 1789–1795, *1974.*

The Civil Constitution of the Clergy was a sensible settlement: parishes were reorganised according to a more logical pattern, the aristocratic monopoly of high Church office was eliminated and reasonable salaries guaranteed to priests. Bishops and priests were to be elected by active citizens: even if some clerics stood to lose, the clergy did not rush to reject the Civil Constitution.

Use Sources 1, 2 and 3 and your own knowledge.
How far do you agree with the view that the settlement of the affairs of the Church was mishandled by the National Assembly and with fateful consequences? Explain your answer, using the evidence of Sources 1, 2 and 3 and your own knowledge of issues related to this controversy. (40 marks)

Exam tips

The cross-references are intended to take you straight to the material that will help you to answer the question.

In answering this type of question you are asked to use the sources and your own knowledge. It is important to treat this type of question differently from the way you would plan an essay answer. The sources raise issues for you. See them as a support. You can use them as the core of your plan since they will always contain points that relate to the claim stated in the question. Make sure you have identified all the issues raised by the sources, and then add in your own knowledge – both to make more of the issues in the sources (add depth to the coverage) and to add new points (extend the range covered). In the advice given below, links are made to the relevant pages where information can be found.

These sources make the following points:

- The Civil Constitution of the Clergy was potentially a sensible settlement.
- The Civil Constitution divided the Church and fateful consequences followed.
- The disputes and division were the responsibility of the politicians of the National Assembly.

Identify which points can be found in which of the sources, and cross-refer between them when they make related points. For example, Sources 1 and 2 both refer to the extremism and loss of life that followed from division over the Church. Note how they do this. It is good practice to select just a few words from the source to support the point you wish to make.

Essentially there are two issues to explore: whether the blame for the ending of the 'revolutionary consensus' (Source 1) should be placed chiefly on the National Assembly, and how far the consequences of this were 'fateful', i.e. did it lead directly to 'the civil war in the West, terror and counter terror' (Source 2) and if so, were other factors also involved? Was this solely the result of division over the Church, or have the consequences of the division over the Church been over-stated here?

If you are working through a study of the French Revolution for the first time, you should concentrate mainly on the first of these issues, using the material in Chapter 3. When you revise, come back to this question and explore the second issue more thoroughly. You should then use Chapter 4 to explore other reasons for the growth of counter-revolution. Non-religious factors were prominent in the Vendée and areas of Federalist revolt (page 97 in Chapter 4).

The Assembly's decree (page 60) resulted in a Church divided into a constitutional and a non-juring Church. How far did the politicians mishandle the negotiations? In dealing with this, you should aim to integrate your own knowledge with the material in the sources.

You can develop the point that at first there was some revolutionary consensus over religious reform (pages 58–9), but see the debate (pages 70–1) to consider the extent of that agreement.

From your own knowledge (page 59) you can explore the significance of attempts by the clergy to negotiate elements of the settlement. Were their demands for a national synod particularly difficult for the deputies in the Assembly to accept?

The link between the religious divide and the growth of counter-revolution (page 60) is clear, but what other factors were involved? The King's actions were also crucial (pages 60 and 65–8). However, they were in part prompted by his regrets over his acceptance of the Civil Constitution of the Clergy.

In planning your answer you will need to keep in mind that this question is asking for a judgement about how far the statement is valid. There is no doubt that the split in the Church was associated with the growth of counter-revolutionary attitudes and activity, but does the statement overstate the blame to be attached to the politicians? Does it overstate the consequences? The issues for you to explore are how far it was the fault of the politicians that the future of the Church was not settled without dispute and division, and the extent to which that division was responsible for the stimulating forces of counter-revolution and conflict which followed. In coming to an overall conclusion you will find pages 70–1 useful.

4

War, Revolt and the Overthrow of the Monarchy 1792–3

POINTS TO CONSIDER

As you read in Chapter 3, the government undertook an ambitious reform programme to modernise France. This led to increased tensions among those opposed to these policies. Many *émigrés* left France, and from exile became active opponents of the government. A number of politicians of widely differing views urged war as a means of dealing with these opponents. The decision to go to war had momentous consequences for both France and Europe. These are examined in three themes:

* The outbreak of war
* The overthrow of the monarchy
* The Republic at war 1792–3

Key dates

1791	August 27	Declaration of Pillnitz
1792	April 20	War declared on Austria
	June 13	Prussia declared war on France
	August 10	Overthrow of the monarchy
	August 19	Prussian forces entered northern France
	August 20	Capture of Longwy
	September 2–6	September Massacres
	September 22	Proclamation of the Republic
	November 6	Battle of Jemappes
	November 19	Decree of Fraternity
1793	January 21	Execution of Louis XVI
	February 1	War declared on Great Britain and the Dutch Republic
	March 11	Revolt in the Vendée
	October 16	Battle of Wattignies

1 | The Outbreak of War

Despite mistrust of the King, it seemed likely that the
Constitution of 1791 would survive. What prevented this was the
outbreak of war with Austria in April 1792. This event had more
decisive and far-reaching results than any other in the whole of
the Revolution. Almost everything that happened in France from
that time was caused, or was affected, by this decision. The war
finally destroyed the consensus of 1789. It led directly to the fall
of the monarchy, to civil war and to the Terror.

Foreign reaction to the Revolution

The **Great Powers** had shown no inclination to intervene during
the first two years of the French Revolution. Leopold II, ruler of
the **Habsburg Empire**, approved of many of the liberal reforms
in the Revolution and did not want a return to absolutism in
France. He, like other sovereigns, was pleased at the collapse of
French power and no longer regarded France as a serious rival.
In any case, Russia, Austria and Prussia were pre-occupied
elsewhere. From 1787, Russia and Austria were at war with the
Ottoman Empire. Leopold abandoned the fight in July 1790 to
concentrate on the Austrian Netherlands (the area between
Holland and France which 40 years later became Belgium),
where there was a revolt. He crushed this in the winter of 1790
and then turned his attention to Poland, where Russia and
Prussia were seeking to gain territory. All three powers were
essentially more interested in trying to secure a partition of
Poland to their own advantage, than in what was going on in
France.

Declaration of Pillnitz

After the flight to Varennes (see page 65), the Austrians felt they
had to make some gesture in support of Louis. On 27 August
1791, they issued the Declaration of Pillnitz in association with
Prussia. This stated that:

- both countries regarded the present situation of the French
  King of common interest to all other European rulers
- they hoped to restore the powers of the French crown
- force would be used if necessary to bring about this
  restoration.

The Declaration was significant because it appeared to be a threat
to interfere in French internal affairs. Enemies of the King
considered that the declaration justified their opposition to, and
mistrust of, the monarchy. In reality however, it was no threat at
all since the Austrians knew that the other powers, such as
Britain, would not join them. This meant that the Declaration was
unlikely to lead to any action. In France the Declaration did not
create much of a stir. The Assembly did not debate it and most
newspapers ignored it. When the Constitution was passed in
September, Leopold gave it a warm welcome, so the possibility of
Austrian intervention was even more remote.

Key question
Why did France go to
war in April 1792?

Great Powers
Countries that were
more powerful than
others on the basis
of their military,
economic and
territorial strength
– the major ones
were Austria,
France, Prussia,
Russia and Great
Britain

Habsburg Empire
Territory that
roughly
corresponds to
modern-day
Austria, Hungary,
the Czech Republic
and Slovakia. The
empire also
considered itself to
be the leading
German state.

Rulers of Austria and
Prussia issue a joint
declaration of support
for Louis XVI known
as the Declaration of
Pillnitz: 27 August
1791

Key question
Why did Brissot
believe war to be in
France's best
interest?

Key terms

**'Austrian
Committee'**
A group of
influential
politicians and close
confidants who
gathered around
Marie Antoinette,
the daughter of the
Austrian Empress
Maria Theresa.
They kept in close
secret contact with
Vienna, the capital
of the Austrian/
Habsburg Empire.

Brissotins
A group of deputies
who supported
Jacques Brissot and
later merged with
the Girondins.

Support for war

In France, several people, for very different reasons, came to
believe that war was either in their own best interests or in those
of France. Marie Antoinette ('the only man in the family',
Mirabeau called her) wrote to her brother, the Emperor Leopold
II, in September 1791: 'Conciliation is out of the question now.
Armed force has destroyed everything and only armed force can
put things right'. She hoped for a war in which France would be
defeated, enabling Louis to recover his old powers. The King
shared her view that France would be defeated. 'The physical
condition and morale of France', he wrote, 'is such that it will be
unable to sustain even half a campaign.' The deputies were not
convinced. There were widespread rumours that the country's
foreign policy was being run by an **'Austrian Committee'**, headed
by Marie Antoinette, and that secret agents were being sent to
Koblenz (the headquarters of the *émigrés*) and Vienna to plot
counter-revolution. These rumours were well founded.

Army commanders such as Lafayette and Dumouriez also
wanted war. Lafayette, the first commander of the National
Guard, had brought the King from Versailles to Paris during the
October Days and was responsible for the 'massacre' of the
Champ de Mars (see page 67). He had become disillusioned by
the failure of the Revolution to produce political stability and
wanted the authority of the King to be strengthened. This could
be done by waging a short, successful war against Austria, which
he believed would increase his prestige as a general. It would also
enable him to dictate his own terms to both the King and the
Assembly.

The desire for war resulted in the co-operation of Lafayette and
his followers with the **Brissotins**, who also wanted war. The
Brissotins were not a party, but a group of deputies, led by
Jacques Brissot, who merged with the Girondins to create a much
more powerful group. Brissot was one of the first to support
demands for a republic. After the flight to Varennes he argued for
the abolition of the monarchy and the trial of Louis XVI. He saw
that the King had not really accepted the Constitution and that
the Court was plotting against the Revolution and seeking the
armed intervention of the European powers. Brissot believed that
war would force the King to reveal his true sympathies – either
being for or against the Revolution. He also argued that it would
expose any traitors who were opposed to the Revolution.

There were about 130 Girondins in the 745-member Legislative
Assembly, so to obtain a majority they needed the support both of
Lafayette and his followers and of the unorganised centre. Brissot
obtained this by playing on their hopes and fears by waging a
campaign calling for war, which he began in October 1791. The
main points in his case for war were:

- a successful conflict would rouse enthusiasm for the Revolution
  and show the permanence of the new regime
- a war would allow France to extend its revolutionary ideals
  abroad

Profile: Marquis de Lafayette 1757–1834

1757   – Born at Chavaniac on 6 September into an ancient noble family

1774   – Married the daughter of the Duc d'Ayen

1777   – Used part of his enormous fortune to fit out a ship and set sail for America
       – Distinguished service in the cause of liberty made him a hero in France and opened up his mind to the need for reform in his homeland

1787   – Member of the Assembly of Notables, called for the summoning of the Estates-General, was closely connected with the reform movement

1789   – Representative of the nobility to the Estates-General.
       – Appointed commander of the new Parisian National Guard following the storming of the Bastille. During the October Days his troops saved the royal family from a hostile crowd who attacked Versailles. He escorted them to Paris where they effectively became captives of the Revolution

1790   – Occupied a pivotal role in the *Fête de la Fédération* to celebrate the first anniversary of the Revolution. Within weeks the champion of liberty appeared to be supporting repression, when an army mutiny was suppressed

1791   – The National Guard under Lafayette's command shoot demonstrators during the Champ de Mars massacre. This appeared to confirm the popular belief that he was hostile towards ordinary people. His fall from power was rapid

1792   – At the outbreak of war he was appointed commander of the Army of the Centre
       – June – Left his post during the *journées* to try and organise the Legislative Assembly against the Jacobin
       – August 19 – After the overthrow of Louis he tried to turn his army against Paris, failed and defected to the Prussians

1797   – Imprisoned by the allies

1799   – Returned to France under Napoleon and retired to farm his estates

Marriage into the great Noailles family gave Lafayette good connections into the circle of courtiers around the young Louis XVI. During the early years of the Revolution he allied himself with the Revolutionary bourgeoisie and became one of the most powerful men in France. Over-ambition proved to be his undoing and his attempts to seize power failed.

- French armies would have the active support of their enemy's own repressed subjects
- the international situation was favourable as the European powers were unlikely to unite against France – Russia was preoccupied with Poland, and Britain would not join in unless its home security or empire was directly threatened.

Opposition to war

Key issue
Why did Robespierre oppose the call for war?

Most deputies were won over by these arguments but some politicians outside the Assembly were not. Robespierre expressed his attitude to the war in these terms:

> You propose to give supreme power to those who most want your ruin. The only way to save the State and to safeguard freedom is to wage war in the right way, on our enemies at home, instead of marching under their orders against their allies across the frontiers.

He believed that the real threat came from soldiers like Lafayette, who were still popular enough to mislead the public. Robespierre believed that the aim of the European powers was to intimidate France, not to invade her. War would be more difficult than Brissot expected, because foreigners would not rise up in support of French invaders. Robespierre memorably observed: 'No one loves armed missionaries.' As a result of his opposition to the war, Robespierre became an isolated and unpopular figure, who was convinced that his opponents were plotting to betray the Revolution. His relations with Brissot were poisoned by bitter personal quarrels and mutual suspicion.

The declaration of war

Key issue
Why were the foreign powers confident of victory in any war against France?

Key term

United Provinces
Present-day Holland ruled at the time by the House of Orange.

The Girondins were pressing hard for war but it is doubtful whether they would have gained the support of the majority of deputies without the bungling of Austria and Prussia. On 7 February 1792 Austria and Prussia became allies and thought they could intimidate the French by threatening war. They had great confidence in their own armies: in 1789 a small Prussian army had conquered the **United Provinces** in under a month and in 1790 a small Austrian army occupied Belgium in under two weeks. They believed France to be weak from internal division, while mutinies in the army and the loss of so many officers who had fled the country would undermine her ability to defend herself effectively. Added to this was the bankrupt nature of French finances, which would limit the purchase of munitions. It was anticipated that France would have neither the will nor the ability to resist Austrian pressure.

Austrian threats and Girondin attacks on the 'Austrian Committee' at Court forced the King to dismiss his Feuillant ministers in March 1792 and to appoint a more radical government, including some Girondins. This was a decisive change. The old ministers had carried out the wishes of the King: the new ones obeyed the Assembly. Both the Assembly and the government now wanted war, especially the new Foreign Minister,

General Dumouriez. He hated Austria but had aims similar to those of Lafayette: a short successful war would increase his own personal power and prestige along with that of the Crown.

In Austria, the cautious Leopold had died on 1 March and had been replaced by the young and impetuous Francis II. When rumours reached Austria that Marie Antoinette was to be put on trial, it decided reluctantly on war. But it was the French who actually declared war, on 20 April 1792. Only seven deputies voted against it. The French hoped to fight solely against Austria but Prussia declared war on France a month later and took the lead in the campaign under its Commander-in-Chief the Duke of Brunswick. For very different reasons, influential groups in the Assembly and supporters of Louis XVI decided that war would serve their interests best. They hoped for a short decisive war – this did not happen. The resulting conflict – known as the **Revolutionary War** – would:

- last 10 years until the Treaty of Amiens 1802
- result in the loss of 1.4 million French people
- dramatically alter the whole direction of the Revolution.

France declares war on Austria: 20 April 1792

Key date

Revolutionary War Fought by France against other European powers between 1792 and 1802.

Key term

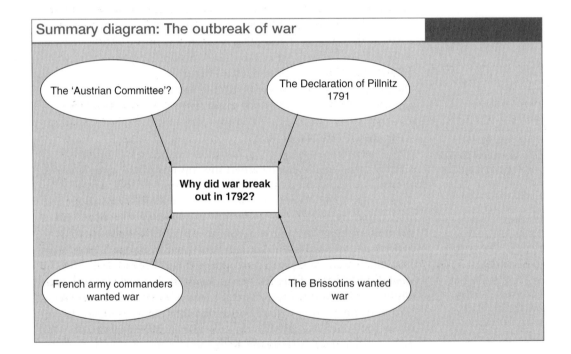

Summary diagram: The outbreak of war

The 'Austrian Committee'?

The Declaration of Pillnitz 1791

Why did war break out in 1792?

French army commanders wanted war

The Brissotins wanted war

2 | The Overthrow of the Monarchy

This section will consider the events that immediately preceded the overthrow of Louis XVI. Having taken France into war the early military engagements showed how badly prepared the French army was. Military defeat and the desertion of many commanders to the enemy created great tension and fear in Paris

Key question
How well prepared was France for the war in 1792?

Fédérés
Mainly national guardsmen sent from the provinces to display national unity during the *Fête de la Fédération* that commemorated the fall of the Bastille.

Paris Sections
Paris was divided into 48 sections to replace the 60 electoral districts of 1789 – the section became the power base of the *sans-culottes*.

Key question
Why did Louis' actions lead to demands for greater democracy?

that the capital would be captured. The royal family and Louis were suspected of being less than fully committed to gaining a French victory, and some of Louis' actions were seen as hostile to the Revolution. In this climate the King's political opponents became increasingly determined to overthrow the monarchy.

The military crisis

When war was declared, the French army was far from ready. It was badly depleted. Of its 12,000 officers, half had emigrated. There were 150,000 men under arms in 1791 comprising both regular and newly recruited volunteers. However, a combination of desertion and revolutionary propaganda in the many new newspapers and magazines destroyed the discipline of the regular army, while the volunteers were poorly trained and equipped.

When French forces advanced into the Austrian Netherlands (Belgium) on 20 April 1792 they were faced with determined opposition. The army panicked and retreated headlong to Lille, where they murdered their commander. Whole units deserted. By the end of May all three field-commanders were advising that peace should be made immediately. The allies counter-attacked and invaded northern France. Treason and traitors were blamed for French defeats and with some justification: Marie Antoinette had sent details of French military plans to the Austrians.

Royal vetoes

The government also had other problems to cope with, such as opposition from refractory priests and counter-revolutionaries who wanted to restore the authority of the Catholic Church and the monarchy. The Girondins had to satisfy demands for action against 'traitors'. On 27 May, the Assembly passed a law for the deportation of refractory priests. Another law disbanded the King's Guard and a third set up a camp for 20,000 National Guards (they were known as *fédérés* because their arrival was to coincide with the *Fête de la Fédération* on 14 July) from the provinces. They were to protect Paris from invasion and the government from a *coup* by the generals, especially Lafayette.

Louis refused to approve these laws. When Roland, the Girondin Minister of the Interior, protested, Louis dismissed him and other Girondin ministers on 13 June. Dumouriez resigned soon afterwards. On 19 June Louis vetoed the laws on refractory priests and the *fédéré* camp. There was an expectation of a military *coup* in support of the King.

The rise of the *sans-culottes*

Leaders of the **Paris Sections** responded to these events by holding an armed demonstration on 20 June, the anniversary of the Tennis Court Oath and of the flight to Varennes. Their leaders came from the Cordeliers Club. The Jacobins did not get involved, as they had done at the time of the Champ de Mars petition. About 8000 demonstrators, many of them National Guards, poured into the Tuileries. One participant described seeing Louis '… wearing the **bonnet rouge** on his head and drinking from a bottle, to the health of the nation'. Louis behaved with great dignity. He was not intimidated and his calmness may have saved his life. This *journée* did not achieve its desired end: the King did not withdraw his veto or recall the Girondin ministers. However, it did show very clearly the weakness of the King and the Assembly and the growing power of the Sections.

The Assembly soon took steps which recognised the growing importance of the *sans-culottes* but which also increased the likelihood of a rising. On 11 July it declared a state of emergency by issuing a decree '*la patrie en danger*', which called on every Frenchman to fight. This tilted the balance of power in favour of those who called for greater democracy. How could you ask a man to fight and not give him a vote? The Sections, whose assemblies were allowed to meet in permanent session, and *fédérés* demanded the admission of 'passive citizens' into the sectional assemblies and National Guard. These requests were granted by the end of the month. The bourgeois middle-class control of 1789 had begun to give way to the popular democracy of the *sans-culottes*.

Tension in Paris

Tension in Paris was increased by the arrival of *fédérés* from the provinces in late July 1793, and by the publication of the Brunswick Manifesto.

The *fédérés*

The *fédérés* were militant revolutionaries and republicans, unlike the Paris National Guard, whose officers were conservative or royalist. Their patriotism was expressed in the war song of the Rhine army, composed in Strasbourg by Rouget de l'Iisle. It acquired its name '*La Marseillaise*' as it was sung by the *fédérés* of Marseille on their march to the capital. In July their total number in Paris was never above 5000 but they were a powerful pressure group in the radical sections, calling for the removal of the King.

The situation in Paris was deteriorating rapidly and extremists were becoming much more active in the political life of the capital. With a new insurrection being prepared by radicals and *fédérés* from the middle of July, the Girondins changed their attitude of opposition to the King and tried to prevent a rising. They were alarmed that events were getting out of their control. Girondin leaders warned the King that there was likely to be a more violent uprising than that of 20 June and that it was very likely that he would be deposed. They offered to do all they could to prevent such an uprising, if he would recall the ministers dismissed on 13 June. Louis rejected their offer.

The Jacobin leader, Robespierre, was co-operating with the central committee of the *fédérés* and on 29 July, in a speech to the Jacobin Club, he put forward his proposals:

- Abandonment of the Constitution of 1791.
- The overthrow of the monarchy.

Key question
How did the *fédérés* and the Brunswick manifesto lead to the removal of the King?

Key terms

Bonnet rouge
The red cap popularly known as the cap of liberty, which became an important symbol of the Revolution.

La patrie en danger
'The fatherland is in danger' became a rallying cry to ordinary people to help save the country.

La Marseillaise
The rousing song composed by Rouget de l'Isle in 1792 and adopted as the anthem of the Republic on 14 July 1795.

- The establishment of a National Convention, elected by **universal male suffrage** to replace the Legislative Assembly.
- A **purge** of the departmental authorities, many of which were royalist.

Until this date Robespierre had warned the *fédérés* and the Sections against hasty action, as this might lead to a backlash in the King's favour. Now he felt the moment had come to strike. Petitions were pouring in from the *fédérés*, the clubs and provinces for the removal of the King.

The Brunswick manifesto

To add to the worsening tension the Brunswick Manifesto, issued by the commander-in-chief of the Austro-Prussian armies, was published in Paris on 1 August. Its main terms were:

- to ensure the welfare of France, and not to conquer any French territory
- to restore the liberty of Louis XVI and his family
- that the city of Paris set Louis free without delay, and make it responsible for the safety of the royal family
- if the Tuileries palace was attacked and the royal family harmed then the joint Austrian-Prussian army would inflict 'an exemplary vengeance' on the city and its citizens.

The Manifesto was intended to help the King but it had the opposite effect. Frenchmen were infuriated by what they considered to be foreign intervention in their affairs. Many who had previously supported the monarchy now turned against it.

On 3 August, Pétion, the Mayor of Paris, went to the Legislative Assembly and demanded, on behalf of 47 out of the 48 Sections, the abolition of the monarchy. Yet the Assembly refused to depose the King and defeated a motion to put Lafayette on trial. This finally persuaded many that a rising was necessary.

The attack on the Tuileries

On the night of 9 August *sans-culottes* took over the Hôtel de Ville, expelled the city council and set up a revolutionary Commune. Among its leaders was Hébert, who had taken part in the Cordeliers agitation the previous year and had strong links with the Sections and the *fédérés*.

The next morning – 10 August 1792, several thousand of the National Guard, which was now open to 'passive citizens', and 2000 *fédérés*, led by those from Marseille, marched on the Tuileries. The palace was defended by 3000 troops, 2000 of whom were National Guards. The others were Swiss mercenaries who were certain to resist. During the morning the King sought refuge in the Assembly to protect his family. The National Guard defending the Tuileries joined the crowd, who entered the courtyards. They believed the attack was over until the Swiss began to fire. The men from Marseille replied with grapeshot and it seemed that a violent battle was about to take place. At this point the King ordered his Swiss guards to cease fire. This left

Storming of the Tuileries Palace, 1792. What does the painting suggest about the attack on the Tuileries?

them at the mercy of the attackers: 600 Swiss were massacred. Among the attackers, 90 *fédérés* and 300 Parisians (tradesmen, craftsmen, wage-earners) had been killed or wounded. It was the bloodiest *journée* of the Revolution.

The rising was as much a rejection of the Assembly as it was of the King. The rebels invaded the Assembly and forced it to recognise the new revolutionary Commune, which had given the orders for the attack on the palace. The deputies had to hand over the King to the Commune, who imprisoned him in the Temple (see the map on page 35) – an old fortress in the north-eastern suburbs of Paris. They also had to agree to the election, by universal male suffrage, of a National Convention that was to draw up a new, democratic constitution. The Commune was now in control in Paris, though in the rest of France it was the authority of the Assembly alone that was recognised.

The proclamation of the Republic

Following the overthrow of Louis, the **constitutional monarchists** who made up about two-thirds of the deputies, did not feel safe, so they stayed away from the Assembly and went into hiding. This left the Girondins in charge, the beneficiaries of a revolution they had tried to avoid. The 300 or so deputies remaining in the Assembly appointed new ministers, including the three who had been dismissed earlier. A surprise appointment was that of Danton (see profile on page 125). He had made his career in the Cordeliers Club and the Paris Sections and was appointed Minister of Justice to please the *sans-culottes*. In its final six weeks before the National Convention replaced it, the Assembly did all that the Commune wanted. It passed several radical measures:

- Refractory priests who did not leave France were to be deported to the French colony of Guiana.

Key question
What measures did the National Assembly pass in its last six weeks?

Constitutional monarchists
Supporters of Louis who welcomed the granting of limited democratic rights to the French people.

Key term

Key date
Abolition of the
monarchy and
proclamation of a
republic:
21–2 September 1792

- Abolition without compensation of all feudal dues unless the *seigneur* was able to produce title-deeds detailing specific rights. This was an attempt to win over the peasantry, many of whom resented the attack on the monarchy. It effectively ended the feudal system, which peasants had unsuccessfully been trying to do since the August Decrees of 1789.
- House-to-house searches ordered for arms and suspects – many were arrested.
- Divorce legalised. Registration of births, deaths and marriages became a state responsibility rather than a Church one.

After the 10 August *journée*, Louis XVI was suspended from exercising his powers. It was left for the National Convention to decide whether or not to dethrone him. The Convention met for the first time on 20 September 1792. By then there was little doubt that Louis would be deposed. Royal documents found in the Tuileries after the 10 August confirmed what was widely suspected – that the King had behaved treacherously in that he had maintained links with France's enemies. On 21–2 September 1792 the monarchy in France was abolished and a republic was proclaimed. Abolishing the monarchy was one thing, how to deal with Louis was an entirely different issue.

Girondins versus Jacobins: the power struggle in the Convention

Key question
What were the main
divisions in the newly
elected Convention?

In the elections to the Convention, which were held at the end of August and the beginning of September 1792, all men over 21 could vote. The results for the new 749-seat Convention were distorted by fear and intimidation. In Paris, all who had shown royalist sympathies were **disenfranchised**. Thus, all 24 members for Paris were Jacobins, republicans and supporters of the Commune. Robespierre came head of the poll in the capital. For those deputies in the Convention where it is possible to identify their political allegiance, there were about 180 Girondins and 300 Jacobins. A total of 250 deputies were uncommitted to either group and were known as **the Plain**. Forty-seven per cent of the deputies were lawyers. The proportion representing business and trade had declined to nine per cent (compared with 13 per cent in the Constituent Assembly). Only six deputies were artisans.

Until 2 June 1793, the history of the Convention was that of a struggle between the Girondins and Jacobins. The latter came to be known as the **Montagnards** or 'the Mountain' or simply the Left, because they sat on the upper benches of the Assembly to the left of the President's chair. This is a better name for them than Jacobins, as the Girondins too were members of the Jacobin Club, where both groups argued fiercely with one another. Neither group was a party in the modern sense, with an agreed programme and common discipline. People disapproved of parties, which were regarded as pursuing the selfish interests of the members rather than the common good, very much like the corporations and guilds of the *ancien régime* had done. It is,

Key terms

Disenfranchised
Stripped of the
right to vote.

The Plain
The majority of
deputies in the
Convention who sat
on the lower seats
of the tiered
assembly hall.

Montagnards
The Mountain – the
name given to
Jacobin deputies
who occupied the
upper seats in the
tiered chamber of
the National
Assembly.

therefore, very difficult to say how many deputies belonged to any one group at any time.

As neither side had a majority in the Assembly, each needed to gain the support of the Plain who were also bourgeois, believed in economic liberalism and were deeply afraid of the popular movement. At first they supported the Girondins, who provided most of the ministers and dominated the majority of the Assembly's committees.

Table 4.1: The main differences between the Girondins and the Montagnards

	The Girondins	The Montagnards (the Left)
Deputies	Bourgeois	Bourgeois
Leaders	Brissot, Roland	Robespierre, Danton, Marat Couthon, Saint-Just
Policies	• Believed in the Revolution and the Republic • Hated privilege • **Anti-clerical** • Wanted a more enlightened and humane France • Liberal economic policy, market determines wages and prices. Free market economics • Favoured federalism – more power given to the provinces • Committed to winning the war	• Believed in the Revolution and the Republic • Hated privilege • Anti-clerical • Wanted a more enlightened and humane France • Tight control over wages and prices by central government. Policies of the 'maximum' • Favoured strong central government control from Paris • Committed to winning the war but willing to make greater concessions to ordinary people
Areas of support	Most of the Paris press, considerable provincial support from outside Paris. Lost some popular support because they did not fully back 10 August journée	Strong support among the Paris Sections, political clubs in Paris and the Paris deputies. Very popular with the sans-culottes and the popular movement
Beliefs and attitudes	Suspected Robespierre of wanting to create a bloody dictatorship. Were accused by the Montagnards of supporting the counter-revolution	Believed that the Girondins were seeking to attract support from the Right – former nobles and royalists – in order to remain in power. Strong government and firm policies needed to ensure survival of the Republic

Key term

Anti-clericalism Opposition to the Catholic Church.

The trial of Louis XVI

The Jacobins insisted on the trial of the King, in order to establish the Republic more firmly. While Louis remained alive it might be easier for the royalists to plot a restoration. The *sans-culottes*, upon whom the Jacobins came to rely more and more, wanted the King tried and executed, as they held him responsible

Key question
What did the trial and execution of Louis XVI reveal about divisions in the Convention?

The discovery of the *armoire de fer*. Why do you think the artist has chosen to portray a skeleton in the chest?

for the bloodshed at the Tuileries on 10 August 1792. The Girondins tried to prevent a trial and, when they were unable to do this, made two attempts to save Louis' life. They firstly suggested that the King's fate should be decided by a referendum. When this was rejected and the King was found guilty and sentenced to death, they then proposed a reprieve.

Two factors sealed Louis XVI's fate. The first was the incriminating royal correspondence between Louis and the Austrian royal family revealed in the *armoire de fer* documents, which were carefully examined by a special Commission set up by the Convention. The second was Marat's proposal that a decision should be reached by **appel nominal**, 'so that traitors in this Assembly may be known'. In an Assembly of 749 deputies, no-one voted that Louis was innocent, while 693 voted that he was guilty.

When it came to the sentence 387 voted unconditionally for the death penalty, and 288 for imprisonment. The Convention then voted against a reprieve by 380 votes to 310. What the voting patterns reveal is that there was a solid bloc of moderates in the Convention who were reluctant to support the execution of the King.

Key term

Appel nominal
Each deputy was required to declare publicly his decision on the guilt or innocence of Louis XVI.

The execution of Louis XVI

Louis XVI was executed on the morning of 21 January 1793. As Saint-Just, a leading Jacobin, said

> ... he was executed not for what he had done but for what he was: a menace to the Republic.

An alternative view is that Louis was executed because his actions in the period after 1789 showed that he was not to be trusted. This was to all intents and purposes confirmed by the discovery of the *armoire de fer*.

Securing the execution of Louis was the first Jacobin victory in the Convention and it left the factions more hostile to one another than ever. Although over half the Girondin leaders, including Brissot, had voted for the death penalty, they were branded as royalists and counter-revolutionaries by the Montagnards. By securing Louis' execution the Montagnards gained an ascendancy in the Convention which they rarely lost afterwards. Brissot hardly spoke there after the trial.

Key date

Louis XVI was executed in the *place de la revolution* in Paris: 21 January 1793

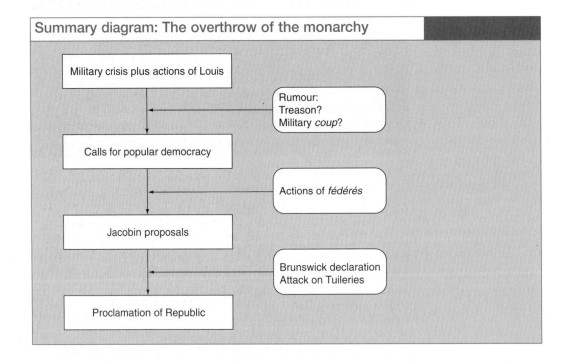

Summary diagram: The overthrow of the monarchy

- Military crisis plus actions of Louis
  - Rumour: Treason? Military *coup*?
- Calls for popular democracy
  - Actions of *fédérés*
- Jacobin proposals
  - Brunswick declaration Attack on Tuileries
- Proclamation of Republic

3 | The Republic at War 1792–3

In the summer of 1792 the situation of the French armies on the frontier was desperate. Lafayette had defected to the Austrians on 17 August. With a leading general deserting, who could still be trusted? Panic and fear of treachery swept the country. This was increased when the Prussians crossed the French frontier and captured Longwy. By the beginning of September, Verdun, the last major fortress on the road to Paris, was about to surrender.

Key question
How serious was the military crisis in August–September 1792?

The execution of
Louis XVI in the
*Place de la
Revolution*,
21 January 1793

The French capital was under immediate threat from enemy
forces, and the Revolution itself was in danger of being
overthrown by foreign powers.

The September Massacres

In the worsening situation with panic and desperation setting in,
the authorities appealed to the forces of nationalism and
patriotism. The Commune called on all patriots to take up arms.
Thousands volunteered to defend the capital and the Revolution.
But, once they had left for the front, there was growing concern
about the overcrowded prisons, which contained many priests and
nobles as counter-revolutionary suspects. A rumour arose that
these were plotting to escape, kill the helpless population and
hand the city over to the Prussians. Marat, a powerful figure in
the Commune, called for the conspirators to be killed. The
massacre of prisoners was the first appearance of **the Terror**.
It began on 2 September and continued for five days. Between
1100 and 1400 of the 2600 prisoners in Paris jails were murdered.
Only a quarter were priests and nobles: the rest were common
criminals. The killers were the *sans-culottes* of the Sections. The
Commune made no attempt to stop them, neither did Danton,
the Minister of Justice. This would have meant **mobilising** the
National Guard and risking another Champ de Mars.

The massacre cast a shadow over the first meeting of the
Convention. Most deputies from the provinces were shocked by
the killings and rallied to the Girondins. The hatred of the
Girondins for the Jacobins and their *sans-culotte* supporters was
intensified. From now on, moderates and foreign opinion
regarded Montagnards and *sans-culottes* as bloodthirsty savages –
buveurs de sang (drinkers of blood).

Key terms

The Terror
The period roughly
covering March
1793–August 1794
when the Jacobin
government used
execution and
brutal repression to
maintain the
survival of the
Republic against
both its internal and
external enemies.

Mobilising
Calling up part-
time soldiers or
national guardsmen
for military service.

Contemporary print showing the September Massacres 1793. What does this print suggest about the actions carried out in early September 1792 in the prisons of Paris?

The Battle of Valmy

Just as the fortunes of war had brought about the September Massacres, they also brought an end to this first phase of the Terror. On 20 September 1792 at Valmy 52,000 French troops defeated 34,000 Prussians. This was a very significant victory. If the Prussians had won, there is little doubt that Paris would have fallen. This would probably have meant the end of the Revolution.

The new forces summoned by the decree of 12 July 1792 were very effective, particularly as they were supplemented by many volunteers, and National Guardsmen. In the main, these men were workers and traders who belonged to the *sans-culottes* rather than being the sons of the bourgeoisie. Their commitment to the revolutionary cause was likely to be considerable. Following the Prussian defeat and responding to what he had seen, the German writer Goethe noted in response to the French victory 'This day and this place open a new era in the history of the world'.

The French Republic would not be easily defeated. Brunswick, the Prussian commander-in-chief, retreated to the frontier. French armies once again took the offensive. Within a month they had occupied much of the left bank of the Rhine. In November, Dumouriez defeated the Austrians at Jemappes and occupied most of Belgium. This was the first major battle won by Republican forces.

From defence to offence

With the Republic apparently secure from external threat, the government now began to talk about expanding to reach France's **natural frontiers** – the Rhine, the Alps and the Pyrenees – and in January 1793 it passed a decree claiming them for France. This

Key question
How did the course of the war change during the winter of 1792?

The Battle of Valmy: 20 September 1792

Key date

Natural frontiers
A barrier, such as a river, mountain range, the sea, etc., that separates countries.

Key term

Key terms

Annex
To incorporate foreign territory into a state – usually forcibly and against the will of the local people.

Decree of Fraternity
Set out the intention of the Convention to support those of any state who wished to overthrow their rulers and establish a democratic political system.

would mean **annexing** territory, which was contrary to the policy laid down by the Constituent Assembly in May 1790: 'the French nation renounces involvement in any war undertaken with the aim of making conquest'.

The change in policy was accompanied by propaganda. On 19 November 1792 the Convention issued the **Decree of Fraternity**, which promised '… to extend fraternal feelings and aid to all peoples who may wish to regain their liberty'. Some politicians were attracted to the prospect of extending the Revolution to other states. Brissot wrote 'We can only be at peace once Europe … is blazing from end to end'. He argued that as long as France was under threat from hostile monarchs there would be little prospect of security. But, if these monarchs could be defeated, the Republic would be secure.

Avignon, which had been papal territory in France since 1273, had been annexed in 1791. Savoy (November 1792) and Nice (January 1793) were the first foreign territories to be added to the Republic. A revolutionary administration was set up in the conquered lands. French armies had to be paid for and fed at the expense of the local population. Church lands and those belonging to enemies of the new regime were confiscated. Tithes and feudal dues were abolished. These measures alienated much of the population, and confirmed Robespierre's prediction that French armies would not be welcomed abroad (see page 83).

The War of the First Coalition

Key question
What factors led to war between France and the First Coalition?

Key date

The French Republic declares war on Britain and Holland: 1 February 1793

The Republican Convention posed a threat to the European monarchs with its Decree of Fraternity. The Great Powers were alarmed at the annexation of Nice and Savoy and Britain was particularly concerned at France's extension to the Rhine as this would lead to the annexation of a large part of the United Provinces as well as the whole of Austrian Netherlands (modern Belgium). William Pitt, the British Prime Minister, was determined that both of these should be kept out of French hands since they possessed good ports from which to launch any potential invasion of Britain. They were seen as central to Britain's security, not only in the English Channel but also on the routes to India (as the Dutch possessed the Cape of Good Hope on the southern tip of Africa and Ceylon). The British also disliked the French re-opening the River Scheldt to navigation (its closure since 1648 had led to the decline of the port of Antwerp as a rival to London).

The Convention unanimously declared war on Britain and Holland on 1 February 1793. The Spanish royal family, who were related to the French Bourbons, were shocked at the execution of Louis and expelled the French envoy. When it appeared that Spain was preparing to join an anti-French alliance, in March the Convention declared war on their southern neighbour. With the exception of Switzerland, Sweden and Denmark, France was at war with most of Europe. The French misunderstood the situation in Britain. They mistakenly thought that there would be a revolution there. They also thought that in war Britain would crumble as Prussia and Austria had done at Valmy and Jemappes. The British, for their part, thought that France was bankrupt and on the verge of civil war. Each side believed that the war would be short and easy and entered into it confidently. **The first coalition** emerged slowly between March and September 1793. Britain was the driving force binding the other powers together as there was no formal treaty. Her diplomacy persuaded a number of other countries to join the anti-French crusade.

The 1793 campaign

The campaign in 1793 began very badly for the French. An attack against Holland failed and the French commander, Dumouriez, was defeated by the Austrians at Neerwinden in March. Following his defeat he reached an agreement with the Austrian commander and planned to march on Paris, dissolve the Convention and restore the Constitution of 1791 and the monarchy. His action prompted some politicians to suspect the loyalty of the army commanders. When his army refused to follow him, Dumouriez deserted to the Austrians along with the Duc de Chartres. Chartres was the son of the Duc d'Orléans (Philippe Égalité), who later became King Louis Philippe of France (ruled 1830–48). Since the Girondins had enthusiastically backed Dumouriez, his defection was very important as it further weakened their position in the Convention and within the Paris clubs.

Meanwhile, the French lost Belgium and the left bank of the Rhine bordering their country. Once again there was fighting on French soil. Leading figures such as Danton were urging conciliation with the coalition. With the military situation deteriorating rapidly, a large rebellion broke out in the Vendée.

The role of Lazare Carnot – organiser of victory

Carnot (1753–1823) trained as a military engineer and served as a captain in the Royal army. During the Revolution he was elected firstly to the Legislative Assembly and following the overthrow of the monarchy, to the national Convention. As the military situation deteriorated, Carnot's military skills were called into use. He was sent to Bayonne, in the south, to organise the defences of the area against a possible attack from Spain. During the trial of Louis XVI, Carnot voted for the King's execution. Although his political inclination was towards the centre ground, he did lean towards the Jacobin in 1793. In the summer of 1793 he joined the Committee of Public Safety (CPS), and his military expertise was put to good use. He studied the military problems facing the Republic and presented a number of reports to the CPS. Following one such report 82 representatives were sent into the departments to speed up the conscription of 300,000 men into the army. The military front causing greatest concern to the Republic was in the north. He was sent by the CPS to lend his support to this demoralised and dispirited army. The essence of his contribution was:

Key term

The first coalition
A loose anti-French alliance created by Britain and consisting of Holland, Spain, Piedmont, Naples, Prussia, Russia, Austria and Portugal. Russia refused to commit soldiers to the coalition when Britain did not send money to support her armies.

Key question
What contribution did Carnot make to military successes in northern France?

Key dates

Austrian forces defeated at the battle of Wattignies: 16 October 1793

Start of a large-scale revolt in the Vendée: 11 March 1793

- reorganising the army
- re-establishing discipline
- leading by example in military engagements.

Before joining the Army of the North, Austrian forces were besieging Maubeugne. Following the measures suggested by Carnot, the siege was raised and enemy forces were defeated at the battle of Wattignies on 16 October 1793. During the campaign, Carnot fought alongside the generals and was in the heart of the action. He made a vital contribution to the eventual success of the campaign, and was honoured with the description **'organiser of victory'**.

The Vendée Rebellion

Key question
Why did the Vendée rebel against the republican government?

By the winter of 1792–3 the counter-revolution in France had virtually collapsed. It is appropriate to describe the Vendée as an 'anti-revolution' rather than a 'counter-revolution' in that it was directed more against the Revolution and its demands rather than for the restoration of the *ancien régime*. The basic causes of the uprising were the expansion of the war and the introduction of **conscription**. The government ordered a **levy** of 300,000 troops in February 1793. This triggered a massive uprising on the 11 March 1793 in four departments south of the Loire in what became known as the 'Vendée militaire' or simply the Vendée.

Key terms

'Organiser of victory'
Description given to Carnot for his help in securing victory in Belgium and reversing the tide of defeat.

Conscription
Compulsory military service.

Levy
An assessment to raise an agreed number of conscripts.

Monarchist
Active supporters of the Bourbon monarchy.

Guerrilla warfare
Military action by irregular bands avoiding direct confrontation with the larger opposing forces. They did not wear uniforms in order to blend in with civilians.

In reality, discontent in the Vendée had been present long before 1793 and the proposed conscription. Since 1789 peasants in the area had found themselves paying more in the new land tax than they had paid under the taxes of *ancien régime*. They came to dislike the revolutionary government, and with the introduction of the Civil Constitution of the Clergy (see pages 58–60) this dislike turned into hatred and open hostility. The religious changes were strongly resisted in the Vendée, which was deeply attached to the Catholic Church, and there were many non-juring priests in the area.

The sale of Church lands was also unpopular, because most were bought by the bourgeoisie of the towns, who then often raised rents. Those who bought *biens* became supporters of the Revolution, which was a guarantee they could keep the land (see page 55). Those who were not successful became hostile to the government.

The peasants looked to the nobles as their natural leaders. Many of these were **monarchist**, so the rising became caught up in counter-revolution. New local officials, constitutional priests and National Guards were massacred. The situation was so serious that in May the government had to withdraw 30,000 troops from the front to deal with the rising. Yet the rebels were never a serious threat to the government in Paris. They were ill-disciplined – better at **guerrilla warfare** than set-piece battles – and unwilling to move far from their homes.

Economic issues

The economic problems that the war had created added to the difficulties of the government. To pay for the war more and more *assignats* were printed, which reduced the value of those already in circulation. By February 1793, the purchasing power of the *assignat* had fallen by 50 per cent. This pushed up prices as more *assignats* were needed to buy goods. The harvest in 1792 was good but bread was scarce. Saint-Just pointed out why in a speech in November 1792: 'The farmer does not want to save paper money and for this reason he is most reluctant to sell his grain'. The results of high prices and scarcity were, as usual, widespread riots against grain stores and demands from the *sans-culottes* for price controls and **requisitioning**.

Requisitioning Compulsory purchase by the government of supplies of food and horses paid for in *assignats* – the new paper currency.

Key term

The Republic saved

Of greater concern to the government was that the war against the allies continued to go badly in the summer of 1793. The Austrians pushed into France. The Spaniards invaded Roussillon in the south. The allies had 160,000 men on the Netherlands' border with France, with a smaller French force opposing them. If York and Coburg, the allied commanders, had joined forces and moved on Paris the French would have faced disaster. Fortunately for them, the allies did not co-ordinate their plans. Pitt ordered the Duke of York to capture Dunkirk as a naval base, so he turned west. The Austrians turned east, and the allied army broke in two. This enormous blunder saved France.

Key question
Why was France not defeated?

Summary diagram: The Republic at War 1792–3		
	War	*At home*
1792	Military crisis Battle of Valmy	September Massacres
1793	Decree of Fraternity Annexations Declaration of war on Britain and Holland War goes badly for France	Popular discontent: Vendée Rebellion

4 | The Key Debate

Few issues rouse greater passions among historians of the Right and the Left than the role played by the *sans-culottes* in the Revolution during the period 1789–94. A central issue concerning scholars is:

> Who were *sans-culottes* and to what extent did they influence the Revolution?

Albert Soboul

Soboul, a leading Marxist historian (see page 19), researched very carefully the *sans-culottes*. He suggested that they played a major role in the political struggle leading to the consolidation of the revolutionary government and the organisation of the CPS (see page 108). He argued that in social terms they can clearly be identified in a number of ways, for instance by their dress, their egalitarian social relationships and hostile attitude towards trade. According to Soboul, extreme *sans-culottes* such as Babeuf saw the Revolution in terms of a 'war between the rich and the poor'. This obvious class-based attitude was one of the features that drew Marxist historians in both France and Russia to study this group.

Alfred Cobban

Cobban, in contrast to Soboul, dismissed the notion that the *sans-culottes* were a social class. He considered that they should be defined essentially in political and not in social terms. In Cobban's view there has been an enormous concentration of attention on what was after all only a transient episode in the Revolution and which left little permanent mark on the evolution of French society. According to Cobban the *sans-culottes* were almost literally a red-herring to divert attention away from the basic rural and urban social problems of French Revolutionary history.

Gwyn A. Williams

Gwyn Williams places a different perspective on *sans-culottisme* by describing it as a type of morality. This morality had a firm social base. The heart and core of *sans-culotterie* were the artisans, tradesmen and journeymen, the further one moves from this base the more honorary *sans-culottes* become. Its embodiment was Hébert's *Le Père Duchesne* (see page 123). By 1793–4 the movement, however primitive and precarious, was recognisably a political movement, organised through popular societies and Section assemblies. Their point of entry into politics was the first war crisis of 1792 and the proclamation of *La Patrie en Danger*. Both the *sans-culottes* and Jacobins were self-conscious minorities compelling the people to be free. In this sense, according to Williams, there is a direct line from Robespierre's Despotism of Liberty to Marx's Dictatorship of the Proletariat.

Some key books in the debate
Richard Cobb, *The Peoples' Armies* (Yale, 1987).
Richard Cobb, *The Police and the People* (Oxford University Press, 1970).
Alfred Cobban, *The Social Interpretations of the French Revolution* (Cambridge University Press, 1964).
Albert Soboul, *The Parisian Sans-Culottes and the French Revolution 1793–4* (Oxford University Press, 1964).
Gwyn A. Williams, *Artisans and Sans-Culottes* (Arnold, 1968).

Study Guide: AS Questions

In the style of AQA

(a) Explain why counter-revolution broke out in La Vendée.

(12 marks)

(b) How important was the rebellion in La Vendée in weakening the Republic between March and December 1793? (24 marks)

Exam tips

The cross-references are intended to take you straight to the material that will help you to answer the questions.

(a) You will need to demonstrate explicit understanding of a range of factors and draw conclusions about their relative significance, for example:

- Pro-Catholic reaction to the Civil Constitution of the Clergy. Note how in the Vendée there was deep commitment to the Catholic Church and all its traditional values (page 97).
- Popular reaction to the implementation of the *levée en masse* (page 97).
- Particularism, which led to a deep-rooted suspicion of Paris and its seemingly advanced metropolitan ideas.
- The essential conservatism of the peasantry.

(b) You will need to evaluate the importance of the rebellion, showing an understanding of the threat it posed and its extent (page 97). You may wish to argue that it was not of major importance – it was only one area and it was brought under control by the army of the Republic and the rebels were crushed (see pages 119–20 in Chapter 5). However, you will also need to emphasise that it did cause considerable anxiety for the Republic, at a time of external war and it contributed to the establishment of government by terror (see Chapter 5 for details on this). You will also want to consider other factors weakening the Republic here, most important of which must be the war against external enemies, but also the threat posed by the *sans-culottes* and the radicalisation of the revolution. Try to decide which way you will argue before you begin to produce an organised and sustained analysis with an appropriate conclusion.

In the style of OCR B

Answer **both** parts of the question.

(a) Why was the monarchy finally overthrown in August 1792?
[Explain actions and circumstances.] (25 marks)

(b) How did war affect the course of the Revolution from 1792 to 1795?
[Explain events and circumstances.] (25 marks)

Exam tips

Look again at the General introduction at the start of the study guide to Chapter 1, page 24.

(a) Prompted by the bracketed guide, you can start your explanation in either the causal or the intentional mode and in due course switch to the other. Given that political ideas of monarchy versus republicanism were also involved, you will need to devote part of your essay to consideration of ideas, attitudes and beliefs (the empathetic mode). Note what the question is about: not the creation of the constitutional monarchy, but the abolition of the monarchy, so keep the focus of your essay tight. Note also that word 'finally' – ignore serious consideration of the immediate reasons for abolition (as opposed to the underlying longer term developments) and you won't have answered the question fully.

Good answers will weigh up the relative importance of reasons and the ways in which some were interconnected. One place to start might be with reasons that resulted from the culpability of Louis himself (e.g. his commitment to the new constitutional monarchy, the flight to Varennes, his correspondence). Against the King's own responsibility could then be ranged the contributions made by other reasons, such as the renewal of economic problems, growing extremism, the role of political clubs and the actions of the people of Paris (especially the *sans-culottes*), the impact of the onset of war. Would this be a good answer? No. Why not? Because you will not have answered the question: it is not about why the monarchy was overthrown.

The key word in the question is 'finally'. That one word shifts the thrust of the question away from underlying reasons to the more immediate factors that explain why the monarchy was overthrown when it was. So, your essay must weigh up the events of that summer: the invasion of France; the royal vetoes; the declaration of the state of emergency; the shift of power from a bourgeois-led revolution to the popular democracy of the *sans-culottes*; the Brunswick Manifesto; the attack on the Tuileries. Along the way, don't forget to organise the various ideas/actions/events into a hierarchy of significance.

(b) This question is not about the war or about the Revolution but about the impact of the war on the Revolution. The prompt guides you to begin your explanation in either the causal or the intentional mode and then switch to the other. A solid answer might take different areas of French life and consider how the war affected the Revolution: (i) politics (the growing extremism of

1791–2, the introduction of direct democracy, the role of revolutionary *journées*, the Reign of Terror); (ii) economics (desire to control prices and bread supply); and (iii) religion (de-Christianisation).

A better answer would not treat 'war' as a single phenomenon. Fear/anticipation of war had a significant role in radicalising the Revolution. Military defeat encouraged the abolition of the monarchy and the development of the Reign of Terror in 1793–4. Victory in war then provided a justification for ending the Terror in the summer of 1794. In other words, the changing fortunes of war explain, in whole or in part, the changing course of the Revolution from 1792 to 1795.

Study Guide: Advanced Level Question
In the style of Edexcel

Source 1

From: D. Sutherland, France 1789–1815 Revolution and Counterrevolution, *published in 1985.*

It is rare that an episode such as the flight to Varennes has such momentous and extensive consequences both short and long term. The very success of the repression of the popular protests following Varennes, and the compromises other politicians were willing to make with a tarnished monarchy, tempted others to the extremist solution of demanding a war to smoke out what Brissot called the 'great treasons'. The most immediate consequence was a precipitate decline in the popularity of the King. The flight and the fatal memorandum showed that he could no longer be trusted.

Source 2

From: Dylan Rees and Duncan Townson, France in Revolution, *published in 2008.*

Yet, in spite of the mistrust of the King, it seemed likely that the Constitution of 1791 would survive. What prevented this was the war with Austria, which began in April 1792. This event had more decisive and far-reaching results than any other in the whole of the Revolution. Almost everything that happened in France from that time was caused, or affected, by it. The war finally destroyed the consensus of 1789.

   It led directly to the fall of the monarchy, to civil war, and to the Terror.

Source 3

From: A. Goodwin, The French Revolution, *published in 1966. Here he is writing about the immediate aftermath of the flight to Varennes.*

By not acceding to the demands of the radical political clubs for the King's immediate deposition, or for the establishment of a provisional executive council, the Assembly clearly indicated that it intended to restore Louis as soon as it was safe to do so. To have deposed the King at that stage would have exposed the country to the dangers of foreign intervention. This danger was emphasised on 6 July when the Emperor issued from Padua a circular note to the European powers in which he urged concerted action. It seemed as if the failure of the King's flight had at last roused the Emperor to a sense of his responsibilities.

Use Sources 1, 2 and 3 and your own knowledge.
How far do you agree with the view that the flight to Varennes fatally damaged the prospects of successfully implementing a constitutional monarchy in France in 1791–2? Explain your answer, using the evidence of Sources 1, 2 and 3 and your own knowledge of this controversy.   (40 marks)

Exam tips

The cross-references are intended to take you straight to the material that will help you to answer the question.

All three sources make it clear that there were attempts to retain the King as a constitutional monarch. (What evidence can you find for this in the sources?) This would suggest that the prospects for constitutional monarchy were damaged, but possibly not fatally. Indeed, Source 2 suggests this directly, attributing fatal damage not to Varennes but to the war. However, you should note that Sources 1 and 2 both suggest a link between Varennes and the coming of the war, by increasing support for it from both inside and outside France. You should develop these issues from your own knowledge.

From your own knowledge you can also develop the significance of:

• Varennes in increasing Republican sentiment (pages 66–8)
• the threat of foreign invasion in increasing the challenge to the constitution of 1791 and in bringing about a republic (pages 86–7).

You can also introduce another factor that weakened the likelihood of Louis continuing in the role of a constitutional monarch: his own attitudes and actions (page 85).

In coming to an overall conclusion you should take into account the crucial role played by the war in radicalising the position in France and undermining the Constitution of 1791, but it is up to you to decide whether the position was indeed 'fatally damaged' already after Varennes.

5 Government by Terror 1793–4

POINTS TO CONSIDER
The Terror was the most dramatic phase of the Revolution.
For opponents of the Revolution it symbolised the chaos
and anarchy that France had sunk into. Supporters of the
Republic, on the other hand, believed that only the most
ruthless policies could ensure its survival. These events are
considered in a number of themes:

- Why government by Terror came about
- The dominance of the *sans-culottes*
- The impact of the Terror
- The Dictatorship of the Committee of Public Safety (CPS)
- The overthrow of Robespierre

Key dates

1793	March 10	Revolutionary Tribunal established
	April 6	Committee of Public Safety created
	June 2	Girondin deputies purged
	June 24	A new constitution approved
	July 27	Robespierre joined the CPS
	August 23	Decree of *levée en masse* issued
	September 17	Law of Suspects
	September 22	Year II began
	September 29	General Maximum introduced
	October 5	New revolutionary calendar
	December 4	Law of 14 Frimaire establishes Revolutionary Government
1794	March 24	Execution of Hébert and his leading supporters
	April 5	Danton and Desmoulins executed
	June 8	Festival of the Supreme Being
	July 27–28	*Coup* of Thermidor
	July 28	Execution of Robespierre

1 | Emergence of Government by Terror

Key question
What was the reason
for introducing
government
by Terror?

The symbol of the Terror is the guillotine and it is this image that most people have in mind when they think of the French Revolution (see page 58). Bloodthirsty purges, terrified citizens, dictatorship and the suppression of the liberties which had been so triumphantly announced in the Declaration of Rights of 1789: all are associated with the Terror.

While the Terror is the most dramatic phase of the Revolution, it had less influence on the formation of modern France than the great reforms of the Constituent Assembly. The French historians Furet and Richet saw the period from August 1792 to July 1794 as a time when extremist *sans-culottes* knocked the Revolution off course. They forced the country's leaders to adopt policies that were contrary to the liberal reforms of the Constituent Assembly. Their support was necessary to preserve the Revolution but they did not make any permanent gains for themselves or any lasting changes. After the fall of Robespierre, the Revolution, they maintain, returned to its earlier course.

Government by Terror came into being because of the need to organise the Republic against internal and external threats to its survival. There were two periods of terror and both were associated with the war abroad.

- The first began with the attack on the Tuileries on 10 August 1792, included the September Massacres, and came to an end with the Battle of Valmy, when the allied invasion was held up and then pushed back (see pages 92–4).
- The second period began with the *journée* of 31 May–2 June 1793, when some Girondin deputies were arrested, and ended with the execution of Robespierre and his supporters in July 1794. During the start of this second Terror, French armies were doing badly and the country was once again faced with invasion. Its end came shortly after the victory of Fleurus in June 1794, which secured France's frontiers.

The political crisis

It was clear to some politicians that in order to fight a war against both internal and external enemies the support of the people was necessary. To achieve this some popular demands would have to be granted. This was realised first of all by the Montagnards. And just as the Montagnards were drawing closer to the *sans-culottes*, the Plain was drawing closer to the Montagnards. Its members shared the Girondin hatred of Robespierre and Marat, but they held the Girondins responsible for the failures in the war (Dumouriez had been closely associated with them), the rising in the Vendée and the economic crisis, After all, several ministers were Girondins. The Plain, therefore, joined the Montagnards in favouring repressive measures.

Key terms

Anti-republican opposition
Forces opposed to the Republic. Comprising former members of the nobility, refractory priests and monarchists.

Committee of General Security
Had overall responsibility for police security, surveillance and spying.

Revolutionary Tribunal
A court specialising in trying those accused of counter-revolutionary activities.

Representatives-on-mission
Mainly Jacobin deputies from the Convention who were sent to reassert government authority.

Comités de surveillance
Surveillance or watch committees, sometimes known simply as revolutionary committees.

Summary execution decree
From 19 March 1793, any rebels captured with arms were to be executed immediately.

Key date

Revolutionary Tribunal set up to try counter-revolutionary suspects: 10 March 1793

Barère, a leader of the Plain, told the Convention that it should recognise three things:

1. In a state of emergency no government could rule by normal methods.
2. The bourgeoisie should not isolate itself from the people, whose demands should be satisfied.
3. Since it was vital the bourgeoisie retain control of this alliance with the people, the Convention must take the initiative by introducing the necessary measures.

The machinery of the Terror

Against a background of mounting crisis – military defeat, civil war, severe economic problems and **anti-republican opposition** which threatened to overturn the Revolution – the Convention passed a range of measures between 10 March and 20 May 1793 designed to deal with these problems and ensure its survival. They had three objectives:

- to identify, place under observation and punish suspects
- to make government more effective and ensure that its orders were carried out
- to meet at least some of the economic demands of the *sans-culottes*.

Committee of General Security (CGS)

The task of rooting out all anti-republican opposition was given to the **Committee of General Security**. On 10 March 1793 a **Revolutionary Tribunal** was set up in Paris to try counter-revolutionary suspects. It was intended to prevent massacres like those of September 1792. 'Let us embody Terror', said Danton in the debate on the decree, 'so as to prevent the people from doing so'. This tribunal was to become one of the main instruments of what became known as the Terror.

Owing to the resistance to conscription and the suspicion of generals after Dumouriez's defection, **representatives-on-mission** were sent to the provinces. They had almost unlimited powers over the department administrations and the armies and were intended as the first stage in reasserting central control over the provinces. Plots by royalists were blamed for the rising in the Vendée, so *comités de surveillance* were set up in each commune and each section of major towns. They provided many victims for the Revolutionary Tribunal.

Severe measures were to be taken against rebels. The **summary execution decree** provided for the trial and execution of armed rebels within 24 hours of capture. These trials were held without a jury and there was no appeal. They condemned many more victims than the Revolutionary Tribunal itself did. Very harsh laws were also passed against *émigrés*: their property was confiscated by government officials and they were to be executed if they returned to France.

Committee of Public Safety (CPS)

On 6 April 1793 one of the most important decisions taken by the Convention was to set up the Committee of Public Safety (CPS). Its purpose was to supervise and speed up the activities of ministers, whose authority it superseded. The CPS was not a dictatorship: it depended on the support of the Convention, which approved its powers each month.

The Committee of Public Safety was established: 6 April 1793

Key date

As to the composition of the new Committee, Danton, supported by the Plain, wanted a committee without extremists. Thus of the nine members selected in April, seven, including Barère, were from the Plain. There were only two members from the Mountain, of whom Danton was one, and no Girondins at all. Danton and Robespierre spoke of the need for winning the support of the people for the Republic. This, they felt, could be done by economic concessions. On 4 May a maximum price, which the Girondins opposed in principle, was fixed for grain and later in the month a compulsory loan was imposed on the wealthy.

All these measures – Revolutionary Tribunals, representatives-on-mission, watch committees, the CPS and the summary execution decree – were vital parts of the machinery of the Terror. At first they were applied only partially, if at all, outside the Vendée.

The overthrow of the Girondins

Danton and other Montagnards had asked the Girondins to stop attacking Parisian *sans-culottes* as *buveurs de sang* (see page 93) but to no avail.

Key question
What was the significance of the overthrow of the Girondins?

- On 26 May Robespierre came down on the side of the *sans-culottes* when he invited 'the people to place themselves in **insurrection** against the corrupt [Girondin] deputies'.
- On 31 May a rising began which spread rapidly when news of the overthrow of the Jacobins in Lyon reached Paris on 1 June.
- On 2 June 80,000 National Guardsmen surrounded the Convention and directed their cannon at it. They demanded the expulsion of the Girondins from the Assembly and a maximum price imposed on all essential goods. When the deputies tried to leave they were forced back. For the first time armed force was being used against an elected assembly.

Insurrection
An uprising of ordinary people, predominantly *sans-culottes*.

Key term

To avoid a massacre or a seizure of power by a revolutionary commune, the Convention was compelled to agree to the arrest of 29 Girondin deputies and two ministers. Following the purge of the Girondins a young royalist, Charlotte Corday, assassinated Marat in the vain belief that it would end the Revolution.

Marat Assassinated, by J.L. David, 1793. Marat was one of the most extreme of the Jacobin and was very popular with the *sans-culottes*. David has chosen to present the body of Marat in a classic pose used by many artists over the centuries to portray Christ after his removal from the cross. Why do you think he has chosen to paint Marat in this pose?

The federal revolt

Key question
How serious a threat to the government was the Federalist revolt?

Key term

Federalism
A rejection of the central authority of the State in favour of regional authority.

As the military crisis worsened Montagnard Jacobin deputies turned on the Girondins. During the political crisis of June 1793, the Girondin deputies were expelled from the Convention (see page 108) for supporting revolts backed by royalists, aimed at destroying the unity of the Republic. In fact, both sides believed in the unity of the Republic and the revolts had, initially, nothing to do with royalism or counter-revolution. The Montagnards called these revolts '**federalism**', and were concerned that not only was the unity of the Republic under threat, but that with fighting a war as well, the government's resources would be placed under very severe strain.

In many departments the rebels resented the influence of Paris and its Commune over the Convention and the power of the Jacobins. The first significant city to rebel was Marseille. Its inhabitants turned against the local Jacobin club. Encouraged by these events, anti-Jacobin supporters took control of many other towns and cities in the south. The most serious revolt occurred in Lyon (30 May) – the Republic's second city. Bordeaux reacted to the purge of the Girondin deputies by declaring the city in revolt until they were restored.

Some form of disturbance occurred in 60 of the 83 departments, although there was significant resistance to the Convention in only eight. Potentially the most serious revolt was in the great naval base of Toulon. Disillusion with the war and the course of the Revolution led to an uprising which overthrew the town council and closed down the Jacobin club. The government cut off food supplies to the city. To prevent starvation the town authorities negotiated with the British, who insisted that the monarchy be restored. British troops entered the town on 28 August. As half the French fleet was lying off the coast at Toulon, this was a most serious blow to the Republic.

Once the towns of Marseille, Lyon and Toulon rejected the authority of the Convention, many smaller towns in the Rhône valley and Provence followed suit. Despite the attempts of the Jacobin press to portray them as pro-Church monarchists, many of the federalists were supporters of the Republic. According to rebels in Toulon all they wanted was 'to enjoy our goods, our property, the fruits of our toil and industry in peace, yet we see them incessantly exposed to threats from those who have nothing themselves'. However, 'Federal' forces were pitifully small. Marseille was able to raise only 3500 men, Bordeaux 400, and none of them wanted to move far from home. This failure to co-operate enabled the government to pick off the rebel areas one by one.

The New Committee of Public Safety

After 2 June most deputies feared and distrusted the Montagnards because of the way they had dealt with the Girondin. However, they did not want to see the Republic overthrown by domestic or foreign enemies and so, for the next 14 months, they were

Key question
What was the composition of the new Committee of Public Safety?

Table 5.1: Leading members of the Committee of Public Safety

Name	Role	Fate
Barère	Spokesman for the CPS	Tried, sentenced to deportation, escaped d.1841
Collot d'Herbois	Responsible for repression in Lyon	Deported to Guiana d. 1796
Billaud-Varenne	Extreme left-winger	Deported to Guiana where he later settled d.1819
Carnot	Organised movement of supplies	Returned to private life d.1823
Couthon	Involved in repression of Lyon	Executed after *Coup* of Thermidor 1794
Lindet	Implemented General Maximum	Retired to private life d.1825
Saint-Just	Drew up Constitution 1793	Executed after *Coup* of Thermidor 1794
Danton	Urged slowing down of Terror	Executed April 1794
Robespierre	Leading figure in CPS	Executed after *Coup* of Thermidor 1794
Hérault de Séchelles	Moderate, linked to plots	Executed April 1794

reluctant accomplices of the Montagnards' Jacobin minority. When a new CPS was formed between July and September 1793, the 12 members were all either Montagnards, or deputies of the Plain who had joined them. All were middle class, except for Hérault de Séchelles, who was a former noble. Eight of them were lawyers, two were engineers. Nearly all were young: the average age was just 30. There was no chairman: all the members were jointly responsible for the Committee's actions. The new Committee was to become the first strong government since the Revolution began.

Maximilian Robespierre

Key question
How did Robespierre justify the Terror?

Maximilian Robespierre joined the CPS on 27 July 1793. Owing to his influence in the Jacobin Club and the Commune, he was expected to provide a link between the middle-class Jacobins and the *sans-culottes*. He never had much support in the Convention and many could not stand his narrow self-righteousness. Yet he was known as 'the Incorruptible' because he did not seek power or wealth for himself and was consistent in putting the good of the country above all other considerations. Some have described him as 'a moral fanatic', because his love of '*vertu*' swept aside all human feelings, as when he wrote:

Key term

Vertu
'Virtue' – meaning moral excellence.

> The spirit of the Republic is virtue, in other words love of one's country, that magnanimous devotion that sinks all private interests in the general interest.

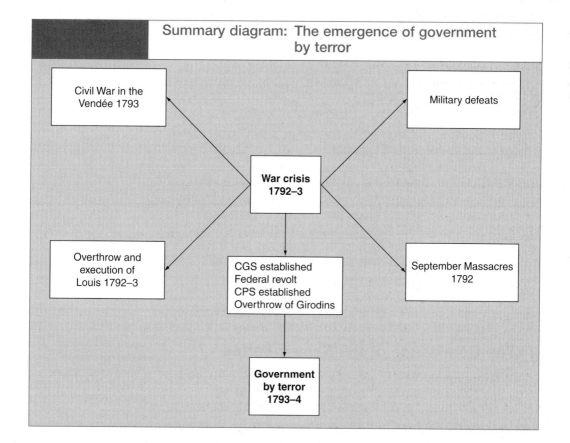

Summary diagram: The emergence of government by terror

Civil War in the Vendée 1793

Military defeats

War crisis 1792–3

Overthrow and execution of Louis 1792–3

CGS established
Federal revolt
CPS established
Overthrow of Girodins

September Massacres 1792

Government by terror 1793–4

Profile: Maximilian Robespierre 1758–94

1758	– Born into a bourgeois family in Arras
1769	– Educated at prestigious College Louis-le-Grand at Paris
1781	– Returns to Arras from Paris to practise as a barrister
1789	– Elected deputy for the Third Estate of Artois
	– Joins the Breton (later Jacobin) Club
1790	– Champions the cause of popular liberty
1791	– Elected public prosecutor of Paris criminal tribunal
	– Opposes calls for war
1792	– Demands deposing the King
	– Elected to the National Convention
1793	– Joins the CPS
1794	– Takes over police bureau
	– Speech on the Supreme Being
	– Attempted assassination
	– Elected speaker of National Convention
	– Calls for purge of those hostile to Revolution
	– Overthrown during *Coup* of Thermidor, executed

Robespierre believed that principles were everything, human beings nothing. Anyone who did not put '*vertu*' first would have to be sacrificed:

> Terror is nothing other than justice, prompt, severe and inflexible; it is therefore an essence of virtue … Break the enemies of liberty with terror, and you will be justified as founders of the Republic.

It was Robespierre's tactical skill that led him to ally with the *sans-culottes*. He saw the need for the Montagnards to be allied to the people if the Revolution was to survive. During the rising of 31 May–2 June he wrote in his diary:

> What is needed is one single will … The danger within France comes from the middle classes and to defeat them we must rally the people.

Although Robespierre shared many ideas with the *sans-culottes* and was popular with the people of Paris, he was never one of them. He dressed with the silk stockings, knee-breeches and powdered wig of the old regime. He never took part in a demonstration and was never carried shoulder-high by the people, as Marat was. Robespierre was a rather remote figure who lived comfortably, though rather modestly, in the *petit*-bourgeois household of the cabinet-maker Duplay.

2 | The Dominance of the *Sans-culottes*

The growth in power of the *sans-culottes* was largely a consequence of the war (Chapter 4, pages 85–8). They had played an important role in the Revolution in 1789 by storming the Bastille and by bringing the King to Paris during the October Days, but

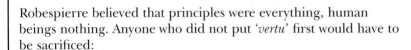

Key question
How significant was the domination of the *sans-culottes*?

Key terms

Militants
Those who differed from ordinary *sans-culottes* in that they adopted an extreme political position such as arguing for a republic, greater democracy and the destruction of privilege.

Egalitarianism
Derived from 'equality' – the aim to have all citizens equal, with no disparities in wealth status, or opportunity.

'Certificates of citizenship'
Proof of good citizenship and support for the Republic, without which no-one could be employed.

after that the bourgeois National Guard kept them under control, as at the Champ de Mars.

However, when the National Guard was opened up to 'passive citizens' in July 1792 (page 86) the *sans-culottes* **militants** grew in influence. Their power and domination was important in the overthrow of the monarchy and from the summer of 1792 to the spring of 1794 no-one could control Paris without obtaining their support. They were responsible for the *journée* of 31 May–2 June 1793, which brought the Jacobins to power.

Ideas and organisation

Who were the *sans-culottes*? Their own view of themselves in a contemporary document notes:

> A *sans-culotte*? He's a man who goes everywhere on foot, who has none of the millions you're all after, no mansions, no servants and who lives simply on the fourth or fifth floor. In the evening he's at his section to support sound resolutions. A *sans-culotte* always keeps his sword sharp. At the first roll of the drum off he goes to the Vendée or the armée du Nord.

The main characteristics of the *sans-culottes* were:

- hatred of the aristocracy and anyone of great wealth
- **egalitarianism** – they addressed everyone as citizen and *ancien régime* titles were rejected
- the wearing of red caps (*bonnet rouge*), originally associated with freed slaves, symbolising the equality of all citizens, to which they were firmly committed
- passionate anti-clericism – this was because priests had joined with aristocrats in taking the wealth created by ordinary men and women
- a belief in direct democracy.

For the *sans-culottes*, the sovereignty of the people – their right to exercise power – could not be delegated to representatives. They believed that the people had the right to control and change their elected representative at any time, and if they were betrayed they had the right of insurrection. Political life must take place in the open: the patriot had no reason to hide his opinions. The meetings of the Assembly must therefore be open to the public and deputies must vote aloud.

The Paris Sections

The Commune and the Sections were the administrative units of Parisian local government, with their officials and elected committees. They controlled the National Guard. While there was danger from internal and foreign enemies, they were encouraged by the government, as they helped the war effort, kept a watch on suspects and assisted representatives-on-mission in purging local authorities. In 1793 they were often more important than the municipalities, as they issued **'certificates of citizenship'**.

Each Section was controlled by a small minority of militants, usually the better-off members, who had the time to devote to Section business. Of the 454 members of the Revolutionary Committees in Paris in 1793–4, 65 per cent were shopkeepers, small workshop masters and independent craftsmen while only eight per cent were wage-earners. They exercised power through their own institutions, which were not responsible to the central government.

The Parisian *sans-culottes* had the force with which to seize power but they chose to persuade or intimidate the Convention, never to replace it. They wholeheartedly supported the government on basic issues, such as their hatred of the aristocracy and in their determination to win the war.

Concessions to the *sans-culottes*

As the *sans-culottes* had put the Jacobins in power a series of concessions were made to them:

- A new Constitution was presented to the people on 24 June 1793, which recognised many of their aspirations, preceded by a Declaration of Rights, which went much further than that of 1789. It stated the rights of people to work, to have assistance in time of need and to be educated. The right of insurrection was proclaimed. All adult males were to have the vote and there were to be direct elections.
- To fight the war effectively, the Sections demanded conscription. This was part of the *levée en masse*.
- Economic concessions – the maximum legislation to fix prices, making the hoarding of goods a capital offence, anti-hoarding laws (page 116).

The *levée en masse*

The *levée en masse*, which was decreed on 23 August 1793, marked the appearance of **total war**. It stated that 'Until the enemies of France have been expelled from the territory of the Republic, all Frenchmen are in a state of permanent requisition for the army'.

Nearly half a million conscripts, unmarried men between 18 and 25, were called up to the army. They had to be fed, armed and trained, so all the human and material resources of the nation were put at the government's disposal. State factories were set up to make arms and ammunition. Church bells were melted down for cannon and religious vessels, such as chalices, for coinage. The government also took control of foreign trade and shipping. Government control of the economy harnessed the energies of the nation on an unprecedented scale. It was remarkably successful in the short term: without it victory would have been impossible.

Key date

Following a series of meetings among leading Montagnards, a Constitution was drawn up on which the primary assemblies were invited to vote. The results, which were announced in August 1793, approved the new Constitution: 24 June 1793

Key terms

Levée en masse
Compelled citizens to perform duties to defend the Republic – military service for single men, married men to move supplies, women to manufacture uniforms. Buildings and horses were taken over for military use.

Total war
All aspects of the State – population, economy, buildings – were used by the government to try and ensure victory.

Summary diagram: The dominance of the *sans-culottes*

Under control of National Guard

Dominant position – in control of Paris

1794

1789
Important role in Revolution

1792
Growing influence as National Guard opened up

1793
Responsible for *journée* which brought Jacobins to power

Results of influence:
• New constitution
• *Levée en masse*
• Economic concessions

3 | The Impact of the Terror

The firm line imposed by the Jacobin government over most of France did ensure the survival of the Republic in the medium term. Yet many champions of the poor were alarmed that their economic position was getting worse, not better. This section illustrates a much more radical approach to dealing with this issue.

The *Enragés*

Key question
Why was Jacques Roux considered to be a threat?

The economic situation continued to deteriorate in the summer of 1793. In mid-August the *assignat* was below a third of its face value and drought reduced the grain supplies into Paris by three-quarters.

One group, the *Enragés*, and their spokesman Jacques Roux demanded action from the government. As a priest in one of the poorest quarters of Paris, Roux was shocked by what he saw: people starving in crowded attics. These were people for whom the Revolution had brought very little material improvement to their standard of living. His followers were wage-earners, casual labourers, the poor and unemployed. He wanted the Convention to deal immediately with starvation and poverty and when it did nothing, he denounced it. His programme was Economic Terror; he demanded the execution of **hoarders** who pushed up the price of grain and a purge of ex-nobles from the army. Robespierre wanted to destroy him, because he was threatening the Commune and the Convention with direct action in the streets. Roux was an influential figure in the *journée* of 5 September 1793, which adopted a new more extreme approach to ensure the movement of food into Paris. Roux was arrested during the course of the *journée* and after several months in prison he took his own life in February 1794.

Key term

Hoarders
Those who bought up supplies of food, keeping them until prices rose and then selling them at a large profit.

The *armée révolutionnaire*

Key question
What was the purpose behind setting up the '*armée révolutionnaire*'?

On 4 September a crowd gathered before the Hôtel de Ville to demand bread and higher wages. The following day, urged on by Roux, it marched on the Convention, forcing it to accept a series of radical measures. The Sections imposed on the Convention the proclamation of 'Terror as the order of the day'.

The Convention immediately authorised the formation of a Parisian *'armée révolutionnaire'* consisting mainly of *sans-culottes*. The purpose was to confront counter-revolutionary activity and organise the defence of the Republic. In total, 56 other unauthorised armies were set up in the provinces between September and December 1793, and were used in about two-thirds of the departments. The purpose of these civilian *armée révolutionnaires* was to:

- ensure the food supplies of Paris and the large provincial cities
- round up deserters, hoarders, refractory priests, religious 'fanatics', political suspects and royalist rebels
- mobilise the nation's resources for the war effort by confiscating church silver and bells
- establish revolutionary 'justice' in the areas of the south and west, which had shown little enthusiasm for the Revolution.

The operation of the Parisian army extended over 25 departments. Its main task was to ensure the capital's food supplies by requisitions in the major grain-producing areas of the north. A third of its men took part in the savage repression of the federal revolt at Lyon. Both the Parisian and provincial armies were engaged in **dechristianisation** (see page 121).

The Parisian army was remarkably successful in supplying Paris with bread until the spring of 1794, and so helped to preserve the Revolution. The provincial armies also did a good job in supplying major towns and the regular army on the eastern frontier. Their success, however, was unlikely to last, because their numbers were small and they met enormous hostility from the rural population. There was great joy in the countryside when they were disbanded. The CPS did not like the revolutionary armies because they were anarchic and outside the control of the authorities. They also disliked them because they created opposition to the Revolution by their heavy-handed methods in dealing with the peasants.

Economic Terror

The Convention had bowed to popular pressure from Roux and the *sans-culottes* in July by passing a law that imposed the death penalty for hoarding food and other supplies. On 29 September 1793 the law of the **General Maximum** was passed to control prices. It fixed the price of bread and many essential goods and services at one-third above the prices of June 1790. Wages, which largely determined prices, were also fixed at 50 per cent above the level of 1790. When peasants refused to sell grain at the maximum price that was set, the government was compelled to requisition supplies.

The Maximum divided the common people against each other. Peasants hated it because the rate was often below the cost of production, while the *sans-culottes* wanted it so that they could afford to buy bread. When *sans-culottes* went into the countryside with the *armée révolutionnaire* to enforce the Maximum they clashed with the peasants and the conflict between town and

'Armée révolutionnaire' *Sans-culottes* sent to the provinces to confront counter-revolutionary forces and ensure the movement of food supplies.

Dechristianisation Ruthless anti-religious policies conducted by some Jacobin supporters against the Church – aimed at destroying its influence.

General Maximum Tables that fix the prices of a wide range of foods and commodities.

What was the impact of the Maximum laws?

Introduction of the General Maximum to control prices and wages: 29 September 1793

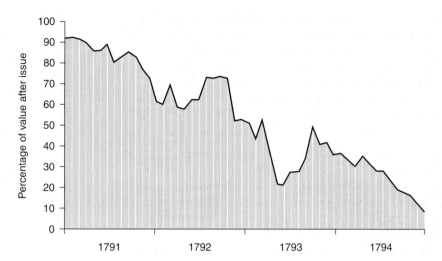

Figure 5.1: The declining value of the *assignat*. How do you think ordinary people would react to the declining value of the *assignat*?

country was deepened. The government was in a difficult position, as farmers would simply stop sowing if they could not make a profit. The co-operation of the wealthy peasants, who controlled most of the harvest, was necessary for the government. After all, they were the municipal councillors and tax collectors, who were expected to oversee requisitioning. Thus, where there was no local revolutionary army in the countryside, the Maximum had to be imposed by the rich.

To meet the concerns of farmers and other producers, the government revised prices upwards in February 1794, much to the disgust of the *sans-culottes*. In the short term, the government's measures were successful. The towns and armies were fed and the *assignat*, worth 22 per cent of its face value in August, rose to 48 per cent in December 1793 (see Figure 5.1 above).

The Political Terror

Key question
What were the main aspects of the Political Terror?

In October 1793, on the recommendation of the CPS, the recently approved Constitution was suspended and it was decreed that 'The government of France will be Revolutionary until the peace'. This paved the way for the adoption of extreme policies. The Political Terror took three forms:

1. The official Terror, controlled by the CPS and CGS, centred in Paris and whose victims came before the Revolutionary Tribunal.
2. The Terror in the areas of federal revolt such as the Vendée and Lyon, where the worst atrocities took place.
3. The Terror in other parts of France, under the control of watch committees, representatives-on-mission and the revolutionary armies.

The CGS was largely responsible for bringing cases before the Revolutionary Tribunal in Paris. Up to September 1793 the

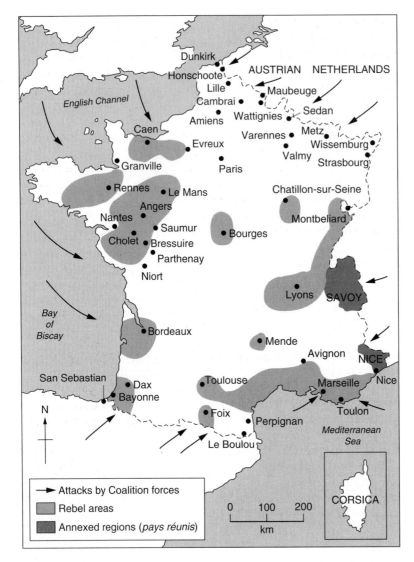

Figure 5.2: The Republic under siege July–August 1793. Note the extent of the external threat from coalition forces and the rebel areas, which are, in most instances, on the margins of the country where there was the possibility that they could be reinforced by the external enemies of the Republic.

Tribunal had heard 260 cases and pronounced 66 death sentences (25 per cent of the total). A series of celebrity trials were held which were popular with the masses and removed those regarded as enemies of the Republic. The trial of important figures almost always resulted in their execution. Acquittal would have been regarded as a vote of no confidence in the government. The Revolutionary Tribunal became the scene of many famous trials and death sentences: Marie Antoinette on 16 October, 20 leading Girondin deputies on 31 October, Philippe Égalité (formerly known as the Duke of Orleans) on 6 November and Mme Roland, wife of the Girondin ex-minister, three days later.

Key question
What measures were
used in the provinces
to restore the
authority of the
government?

Provincial repression

By the end of 1793, the federal revolt had been suppressed by the
regular army. Marseille, Lyon and Toulon were taken and the
Vendéan rebels crushed. Repression followed. From January to
May 1794, troops moved through the area, shooting almost every
peasant they met, burning their farms and crops and killing their
animals. Women were raped and mutilated. When the
'pacification' was over, the Vendée was a depopulated wasteland.
Thousands who surrendered crammed the prisons. They could
not be released in case they re-joined the rebels, and were shot
without trial – 2000 near Angers alone. In the 10 departments
involved in the Vendée rebellion, revolutionary courts condemned
some 8700 people, just over half the 16,600 executions in France
during the Terror. Most were ordinary peasants, few were
bourgeois.

Representatives-on-mission and the revolutionary armies were
often responsible for the worst atrocities. Their actions were fully
supported and, indeed, encouraged by the government. At
Nantes, the representative Carrier carried out the dreadful
noyades (drownings) by placing 1800 people, nearly half of them
women, into barges, which were taken to the mouth of the Loire
and sunk. In Toulon 800 were shot without trial and a further 282
were sent to the guillotine by a Revolutionary Commission. Lyon,
the second city in France, was to pay dearly for its rebellion. On
12 October 1793, the Committee of Public Safety ordered the
destruction of Lyon. Collot-d'Herbois, a member of the CPS and

Print of the drowning of priests in the River Loire at Nantes, November 1793. Which side in the
civil war do you think published this print?

a representative-on-mission, restored order in Lyon with great brutality: 1900 victims were either mown down by cannon fire in front of large pits during the *mitraillade* or guillotined. A total of 72 per cent of the executions during the Terror (12,000 victims) took place in these rebel areas of the west and south-east, which covered 16 departments.

Law of Suspects

In September 1793 the **Law of Suspects** was passed. Under this law the government delegated some of its powers to local revolutionary committees. These committees were packed with fanatical Montagnards and their supporters. They worked closely with representatives-on-mission and the revolutionary armies to deal with counter-revolutionary activity. Mass arrest of suspects took place (about half a million according to one estimate, of whom 10,000 died in prison). The committees could also send offenders before one of the Revolutionary Tribunals, and purge the local administration, removing moderates and replacing them by *sans-culottes* militants. These committees symbolised the Terror at the local level. By the end of 1793 most rural communes had one. They were the one permanent institution of the Terror in the countryside.

The extent of the Terror

Estimating the human cost of the Terror is difficult because of the absence of reliable figures, which vary from several hundred thousand to tens of thousands. The number of official executions that took place is believed to be 16,600. This figure however does not include the large number of deaths resulting from, imprisonment, starvation, military action, repression, etc. Of the official executions most took place in the departments involved in the Vendée Rebellion (53 per cent) and the departments in the south-east (20 per cent). In social terms the official victims were mainly peasants (28 per cent) and urban workers (31 per cent), with the nobility accounting for just 8 per cent of the total. What is clear is that the majority of the victims of the Terror perished in the Vendée. The historian Douglas Johnson suggests a figure of 80,000 deaths for the Vendée, and for the whole of the west a round figure of 200,000 would seem to be realistic.

Table 5.2: Official executions by region during the Terror

Region	No. of deaths	%
Paris	2,639	15.9
Area of the Vendée rebellion	8,713	52.5
Area of armed federalism round Lyon	1,967	11.9
Area of armed federalism in the Midi	1,296	7.8
Other areas	1,979	11.9
Total	16,594	100.0

Key question
What was the impact of dechristianisation campaign?

Religious Terror: dechristianisation

Dechristianisation was not the official policy of the central government. The main impulse for the campaign came from the *sans-culottes* in the Paris Commune, the revolutionary armies and the representatives-on-mission. They hated Catholicism, which they felt had betrayed the Revolution and fermented the cause of the counter-revolution. The Convention was drawn along with it.

Dechristianisation was a deliberate attempt by the First Republic between 1792 and 1794 to use the resources of the State to destroy Christianity as the dominant cultural form of French society. Like the abolition of the monarchy, the destruction of churches was a symbol of the revolutionaries' determination to destroy everything connected with the *ancien régime*.

The attack on the Church took various forms. Churches were closed, church bells and silver were removed, roadside shrines and crosses were destroyed. The Paris Commune stopped paying clerical salaries in May 1793 and in November ordered that all churches in Paris should be closed. Notre Dame became a Temple of Reason. Other areas of France rapidly followed the lead of Paris so that by the spring of 1794 most of the country's churches had been closed.

Priests were forced to renounce their priesthood and many were compelled to marry. Estimates of the number of priests who gave up their calling vary from about 6000 (10 per cent of all constitutional priests) to 20,000. This brutal attempt to uproot centuries of Christian belief was deeply resented in the villages. For many ordinary people outside the civil war zones, dechristianisation, which left large areas of France without priests, was the aspect of the Terror that most affected them.

Revolutionary calendar

Key dates
The start of Year II, which is closely identified with the Terror: 22 September 1793

A new revolutionary calendar and form of dating was introduced which rejected the Christian calendar: 5 October 1793

On 5 October 1793 a new revolutionary calendar was introduced. It was dated from 22 September 1792, when the Republic was proclaimed. Thus the period from 22 September 1792 to 21 September 1793 became Year 1. The year was divided into 12 months of 30 days, with five supplementary days (soon called *sans-culottides*). Each month was divided into three periods of 10 days, every tenth day (decadi) being a day of rest. Another decree gave each month a name appropriate to its season: thus Vendémiaire (the month of vintage) ran from 22 September to 21 October, Floréal (the month of flowers) from 20 April to 19 May. The new calendar ignored Sundays and festivals of the Church. In the new calendar the period of the Terror roughly coincided with Year II, which started on 22 September 1793.

Summary diagram: The impact of the Terror

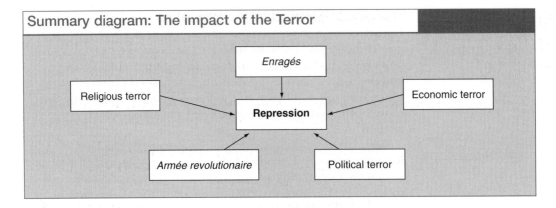

4 | The Dictatorship of the Committee of Public Safety

Key question
How did the government restore its authority?

Towards the end of 1793 the government had begun to overcome the problems that had threatened the existence of the Republic:

- the federal revolts had been crushed
- food supplies were moving into towns and cities
- the value of the *assignat* was rising
- in the west, the defeats of the rebels at Cholet and Le Mans effectively ended the civil war in the Vendée
- French armies were also doing well in the war. By the end of September they had driven the Spanish armies out of Roussillon and the Piedmontese out of Savoy. The British were defeated at Hondschoote in the same month and the Austrians at Wattignies in October.

It appeared that the CPS's policy for defending France was proving to be successful. With renewed confidence the Convention's Committees could now begin to claw back much of the power which had passed to the *sans-culottes* and their organisations.

Restoring government authority

At some stage it was likely that the government and the *sans-culottes* would come into conflict. There was administrative confusion in many departments in the autumn of 1793 as local revolutionary committees, revolutionary armies and representative-on-mission, such as Fouché and Carrier, interpreted the law, or ignored it, on a whim. The government could not tolerate anarchy indefinitely as it undermined its authority. Yet it had to act carefully in case it upset its supporters among the *sans-culottes*.

The first steps to tame the popular movement were taken in September 1793. The Convention decided that the general assemblies of the Sections should meet only twice a week. In October the Convention passed a decree that government was to be 'revolutionary until the peace'. This meant the suspension of the Constitution of 1793. Although this was planned to be a temporary measure, the Constitution was never put into operation.

Key date

The law of 14 Frimaire establishes revolutionary government: 4 December 1793

The Law of Revolutionary Government

A major step to restore central control was taken on 4 December 1793 when the law of Frimaire established revolutionary government. This law gave the two Committees full executive powers.

- The CGS was responsible for police and internal security. The Revolutionary Tribunal, as well as the surveillance committees, came under its control.
- The CPS had more extensive powers. In addition to controlling ministers and generals, it was to control foreign policy and purge and direct local government.

Key term

Agents nationaux
National agents appointed by, and responsible to, the central government. Their role was to monitor the enforcement of all revolutionary laws.

The chief officials of the communes and departments, who had been elected, were placed under *agents nationaux*. The representatives-on-mission, sent out by the Convention in April, were now put firmly under the control of the CPS. All revolutionary armies, except that in Paris, were to be disbanded. As Robespierre pointed out: 'Revolutionary Government … has no room for anarchy and disorder. It is not directed by individual feelings, but by the public interest. It is necessary to navigate between two rocks; weakness and boldness, reaction and extremism.'

The new policies resulted in:

- the end of anarchy
- breaking the power of the *sans-culottes*
- providing France with her first strong government since 1787.

However, it rejected many of the principles of 1789. The Constitutions of 1791 and 1793 had established de-centralisation, elections to all posts, the separation of legislative from executive power and impartial justice. Now all this was reversed. Robespierre justified the policy by arguing that a dictatorship was necessary until the foreign and internal enemies of the Revolution were destroyed. 'We must', he said, 'organise the despotism of liberty to crush the despotism of kings'. This was contrary to the ideas of democracy and people's rights he had advocated before he took office.

Key question
How did the government deal with opposition?

Opposition to the government – Hébert

The main challenge to the revolutionary government came from within the ranks of its former supporters. 'Left' opposition came from the publisher Jacques Hébert and his followers. His newspaper *Le Père Duchesne* demanded that more hoarders should be executed and property redistributed. This was very popular with the *sans-culottes*. The Hébertistes had few supporters in the Convention but many in the Cordeliers Club, the Commune, the Paris revolutionary army and the popular societies. Robespierre disliked their political extremism, particularly their leading part in the dechristianisation campaign, which turned Catholics against the Revolution. When Hébert called for an insurrection at the beginning of March 1794 he was arrested along with 18 supporters. They were accused of being foreign agents who wanted a military dictatorship that would then prepare the way for a restored monarchy. The populace was taken in by this government propaganda. When the Hébertistes were guillotined on 24 March 1794, Paris remained calm.

The CPS took advantage of the situation to strengthen its dictatorship. The Parisian revolutionary army was disbanded, the Cordeliers Club was closed and popular societies were forced to disband. The Commune was purged and filled with supporters of Robespierre. Representatives-on-mission, responsible for some of the worst atrocities in the provinces, were recalled to Paris.

Opposition to the government – Danton

Of greater significance, because of the higher profile of its leader, was the opposition of the Right. This centred around Danton (see Profile on page 125), a former colleague of Robespierre, and a leading Montagnard/Jacobin. In order to heal the divisions in the revolutionary movement, the **Indulgents** wanted to halt the Terror and the centralisation imposed in December. To do this, Danton argued that the war would have to come to an end, as it was largely responsible for the Terror. Since leaving office he had become very wealthy. It was not clear where his new-found wealth came from. Nearly 400,000 *livres* were unaccounted for at the Ministry of Justice while he was in charge. He was accused of bribery and corruption. Danton's friend, Camille Desmoulins, supported him in his desire to end the Terror. In his newspaper *Le Vieux Cordelier* in December 1793, Desmoulins called for the release of '200,000 citizens who are called suspects'.

Since Danton, unlike Hébert, had a large following in the Convention, he was regarded as a much more serious threat by the CPS. His call for peace and an end to the Terror would, they felt, leave the door open for a return of the monarchy. He was, therefore, brought before the Revolutionary Tribunal on charges based on his political record and on 5 April 1794 was executed with many of his followers, including Desmoulins. The Terror now seemed to have a momentum of its own. The members of the Committees had become brutalised and acted vindictively in ways that would have shamed them only two years earlier. Desmoulins' wife tried to organise a demonstration in his support. She was arrested and in April went to the scaffold, along with the wife of Hébert. They could not in any way be regarded as presenting a threat to the Committee.

The effect of the fall of Hébert and Danton was to stifle all criticism of the CPS. Everyone lived in an atmosphere of hatred and suspicion, in which deputies were afraid to say anything, because an unguarded word could lead to a death sentence.

The Great Terror

The Great Terror was centred on Paris and lasted from 10 June until 27 July. In order to control all repression, the government in May 1794 abolished the provincial Revolutionary Tribunals. All enemies of the Republic had now to be brought to Paris, to be tried by the cities Revolutionary Tribunal. This did not mean that the Terror would become less severe. Although the 'factions' of

Profile: George Jacques Danton 1759–94

1759	– Born into a bourgeois family in Arcis-sur-Aube
1785	– Called to the Bar
1789	– Appointed President of the Cordeliers Club
1791	– Administrator of the Department of Paris
	– Assistant *Procurateur* of the Commune
1792	– Appointed Minister of Justice
	– Elected deputy to the Convention
	– First Mission to Belgium
1793	– Joins the CPS
	– Retires to country because of ill health
	– Returns to Paris
	– Urges the slowing down of the Terror
1794	– Labelled by his enemies as an Indulgent, arrested and executed

Danton was one of the most controversial figures of the Revolution. He was loathed and loved in almost equal measure. Many hated him because he was suspected of being corrupt, untrustworthy and in the pay of the royal family. Others loved him for his vast energy, determination and fine oratory. As Minister of Justice he delivered a rousing speech calling for the defence of the nation, after the fall of Verdun to the Prussians (September 1792):

> The tocsin [bell] that we are going to sound is no alarm bell, it is the signal for the charge against the enemies of the fatherland. To vanquish them we must show daring, more daring, and again daring; and France will be saved.

Danton and Hébert had been crushed, some of their supporters were still alive, so the Terror would have to continue until they were eliminated. During the Great Terror, approximately 1594 men and women were executed. Robespierre had no desire to protect the innocent, if this meant dangerous enemies of the Revolution escaped.

Following assassination attempts on Robespierre and Couthon (23 May) they drafted the **Law of Prairial**, which was passed on 10 June 1794. It was directed against 'Enemies of the people' but the definitions were so broad and vague that almost anyone could be included. Under it, no witnesses were to be called and judgment was to be decided by 'the conscience of the jurors' rather than by any evidence produced. Defendants were not allowed defence counsel and the only verdicts possible were death or acquittal. This law removed any semblance of a fair trial and was designed to speed up the process of revolutionary justice. In this it succeeded. More people were sentenced to death in Paris by the Revolutionary Tribunal during June/July 1794 (1594, 59.3 per cent) than in the previous 14 months of its existence. Many of the victims were nobles and clergymen, while nearly a half were members of the wealthier bourgeoisie. No-one dared to make any criticism of the Committee. 'The Revolution is frozen', Saint-Just commented.

Key term

Law of Prairial
The most severe of the laws passed by the revolutionary government. The purpose of the law was to reform the Revolutionary Tribunal in order to secure more convictions. The law paved the way for the Great Terror.

Summary diagram: The main instruments used during the Terror		

Measure	Date of introduction	Purpose
CGS	1792 October	Deal with all matters relating to security
Representatives en mission	1793 March	Sent to Departments to enforce war effort
Revolutionary Tribunal	1793 March	Try those accused of counter-revolution
Comités de surveillance	1793 March	Monitor movements of strangers
CPS	1793 April	Effectively the government, passes decrees
First Maximum	1793 May	Fixes the prices of grain
Levée en masse	1793 August	Organise France for total war
Death penalty for hoarders	1793 July	Communes and sections to search for hoarded food
Armée revolutionnaire	1793 September	Sans-culottes sent to provinces
Law of Suspects	1793 September	Anyone suspected of counter-revolution arrested
General Maximum	1793 September	Fixes prices on all foods and goods
Law of revolutionary government	1793 December	Extends and centralises power of CPS
Laws of Ventose	1794 February	Distributes property of suspects to the poor
Law of 22 Prairial	1794 June	Reform of Revolutionary Tribunal to speed up executions

5 | The Overthrow of Robespierre

Robespierre loses support
In the spring and early summer of 1794, Robespierre started to lose support in three key areas:

- among Catholics
- the *sans-culottes*
- on the CPS and CGS.

Catholics
Robespierre believed in God and had a genuine faith in life after death, in which the virtuous would be rewarded. He loathed the dechristianisation campaign of the *sans-culottes*, partly on religious grounds and partly because it upset Catholics and created enemies of the Revolution. He wanted to unite all Frenchmen in a new religion, the **Cult of the Supreme Being**, which he persuaded the Convention to accept in a decree of 7 May 1794. It began: 'The people of France recognises the existence of the Supreme Being and of immortality of the soul'. On 8 June 1794 Robespierre organised in Paris a large 'Festival of the Supreme Being'.

This new religion pleased no-one. Catholics were distressed because it ignored Catholic doctrine, ceremonies and the Pope. Anti-clericals, including most members of the Committee of General Security, opposed it because they thought it was a first step to towards the reintroduction of Roman Catholicism. They

Key question
How did people react to Robespierre's new religion?

Cult of the Supreme Being
Robespierre's alternative civic religion to the Catholic faith.

Key term

felt that Robespierre was setting himself up as the high priest of the new religion.

Sans-culottes

Key question
Why was Robespierre losing support among the *sans-culottes*?

Robespierre's popularity among the *sans-culottes* was falling sharply for a number of reasons:

- the execution of the Hébertistes
- the dissolution of the popular societies
- the end of direct democracy in the Sections
- the raising of the Maximum on prices in March, which led to inflation and a fall in the *assignat* to only 36 per cent of its original value
- the imposing of the Maximum on wages.

While the Commune had been under the control of the Hébertistes it had not applied the Maximum on wages, which had risen considerably above the limit allowed. The government now decided it would have to act, as the profits of manufacturers were disappearing. On 23 July, therefore, the Commune, now staffed by Robespierre's supporters, decided to apply the Maximum to wages. This led to a fall in wages by as much as a half, and heightened discontent amongst the majority of *sans-culottes*, who were wage-earners.

The Great Terror sickened many ordinary people, workers as well as bourgeoisie. By the spring of 1794 the Republic's armies had driven all foreign troops from French soil, recaptured lost territory in Belgium and moved into the Rhineland. On the domestic front internal enemies had been defeated and government authority restored over all parts of the country. Many questioned whether it was still necessary to apply the ruthless policies of the Terror now that the threats to the Republic had been dealt with.

CPS and CGS

Key question
Why did tensions emerge within and between the CPS and the CGS?

The dictatorship of the two Committees remained unchallengeable, until they fell out amongst themselves. In April, the CPS set up its own police bureau, with Robespierre in charge, to prosecute dishonest officials. The CGS deeply resented this interference with its own control of internal security, so that the two Committees became rivals rather than allies. There were also conflicts within the CPS. Some members disliked Saint-Just's **Laws of Ventose** (26 February 1794) and made sure they were never put into practice. Two members of the CPS, Billaud and Collot, had been closely attached to Hébert and so felt threatened by Robespierre. Robespierre was especially critical of Collot because of the extreme measures he had used to restore order in Lyon (see pages 119–20). Many on the CPS were becoming suspicious of Robespierre particularly following the introduction of the Cult of the Supreme Being and he was losing support among former allies.

Key term

Laws of Ventose
Property of those recognised as enemies of the Revolution could be seized and distributed among the poor.

An anti-Robespierre cartoon claiming that most of the victims of the Terror were not from the privileged orders but were ordinary people. How does the cartoon seek to portray Robespierre?

The *Coup* of Thermidor

During these divisions, Robespierre took a month away from public life. He made no speeches in the Convention between 18 June and 26 July, attended the CPS only two or three times and even gave up his work at the bureau of police. It may be that he was worn out, both physically and emotionally, as all the members of the Committee had worked long hours for months without a

Key question
What was the impact of Robespierre's speech to the Convention on 8 Thermidor?

Key dates

Robespierre delivered an important speech in the Convention suggesting that some of its members were plotting to overthrow the government:
26 July 1794

Execution of Robespierre and his leading allies Couthon and Saint-Just:
28 July 1794

Key terms

Thermidor
A month in the new revolutionary calendar equivalent to 19 July–17 August.

Terrorist
An active supporter of the policies of the Terror.

Coup **of Thermidor**
The overthrow of Robespierre and his closest supporters, which marked the end of the Terror.

break. When he did reappear it was to address the Convention, not the Committee. On 26 July (8 **Thermidor**) he made a speech attacking those colleagues who, he claimed, were plotting against the government. When asked to name them, he declined. This proved to be his undoing. Any denunciation by Robespierre would have resulted in arrest and almost certainly death. Moderates like Carnot and **terrorists** like Fouché and Collot all felt threatened. Fearing that Robespierre was about to denounce them as traitors a number of his former colleagues conspired to plot against him, before he could order their arrest.

Arrest

When Robespierre attempted to speak at the Convention on 9 Thermidor (27 July) he was shouted down. The Convention then voted for the arrest of Robespierre, his brother Augustin, Couthon, Saint-Just and Hanriot, the Commander of the Paris National Guard. They were taken to prisons controlled by the Commune. Robespierre and his colleagues continued to be popular in the Commune, and its leaders ordered all gaolers in Paris to refuse to accept the prisoners and called for an insurrection in their support. Following their release, they ordered the National Guard of the Sections, still under their control, to mobilise. Hanriot was allowed to escape. However, because of the dictatorship established by the two Committees, neither the Jacobin Club nor the Commune could inspire these militants as they had done on 5 September 1792. The CGS now controlled the revolutionary committees of the Sections and the popular societies had been dissolved.

There was great confusion on the evening of 27 July, as the Convention also called on the National Guard to support it against the Commune. Most Sections took no action at first: only 17 (out of 48) sent troops to support the Commune. They included artillery units and for several hours Hanriot had the Convention at his mercy. Only a failure of nerve on his part and Robespierre's strange reluctance to act saved the Convention.

Robespierre had little faith in a popular rising for which no plans had been made and wanted to keep within the law. Barère proposed that the prisoners be declared outlaws on the basis that they had 'escaped'. This meant that they could be executed without a trial. The decree of outlawry and the enforcement of the law persuaded many Sections which were uncertain about who to support to side with the Convention. When they reached the Hôtel de Ville where Robespierre and his supporters were based, they found no one defending it.

Amid scenes of great confusion, Robespierre, who had tried to shoot himself, and his leading supporters were arrested for a second time. On the 28 July 1794 he and 21 others were executed. In the next few days over 100 members of the Commune followed Robespierre to the scaffold. The events of the *Coup* **of Thermidor** effectively meant the rejection of government by Terror. The Terror was dead although the violence would continue.

The end of Terror

The *Coup* of Thermidor brought to an end the most dramatic period of the Revolution. Through a combination of policies that were attractive to their core supporters and ruthlessness to their enemies, the Jacobin dictatorship ensured the defeat of the Republic's internal and external enemies. Many of the gains made since 1789 were preserved and even extended. In the course of defeating her enemies, the Republic created a highly motivated citizen army, which laid the foundations for future conquests in Europe. However, these successful aspects were more than balanced by a number of negative features. There was massive loss of life and devastation in the Vendée and the areas of federalist revolt. The extremist policies of the CPS and CGS alienated many Catholics and the bourgeoisie. Even the *sans-culottes* became disillusioned with the extremist policies of the revolutionary government. The ferocity of the reaction to the Terror, which will be dealt with in the next chapter, indicates the depth of hostility felt by large numbers of men and women towards the system created by Robespierre and his allies.

Key question
How successful was
the Terror?

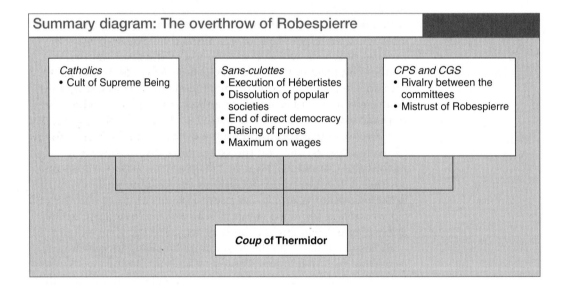

Summary diagram: The overthrow of Robespierre

Catholics
• Cult of Supreme Being

Sans-culottes
• Execution of Hébertistes
• Dissolution of popular societies
• End of direct democracy
• Raising of prices
• Maximum on wages

CPS and CGS
• Rivalry between the committees
• Mistrust of Robespierre

Coup of Thermidor

6 | The Key Debate

The political career of Robespierre is indelibly linked to the Terror. Many historians have contributed to the debate on the significance of Robespierre and his role during the Terror. The central question which historians frequently address is:

How important a figure is Maximilian Robespierre in the history of the French Revolution?

Jean Jaurès

The great French socialist politician and historian Jaurès wrote his history of the French Revolution in the early years of the twentieth century (1901–4). As a leader, he believed Robespierre to be a democrat and supporter of liberty, yet lacking in political vision. Moreover Jaurès considered his importance to be a strange mixture of optimism and pessimism – optimism as regards the moral worth of the people, pessimism as regards the equal distribution of property. While Robespierre deplored poverty he would do nothing to destroy the monopoly of wealth controlled by the *bourgeoisie*.

Richard Cobb

Richard Cobb described Robespierre as a fussy, vaguely ridiculous little man, a consistent winner of second prizes. He considered that his influence on the CPS was weak, but that he was useful to it because of the close links that he maintained with the popular movement and the Jacobins. According to Cobb, Robespierre's importance was in providing the revolutionaries with a sense of purpose, direction and vision. Had Robespierre not existed, it would have made very little difference to the course of the Revolution.

John Hardman

John Hardman argues that Robespierre would never have admitted that he enjoyed exercising power for its own sake. He suggests that his aim was to create a Republic of virtue. The positive aspect of this was the new state religion he introduced – Cult of the Supreme Being. This was balanced, however, by a negative side, which involved the elimination of those who refused to accept his policies. The importance of Robespierre, according to Hardman, was his attempting to unblock or unfreeze the Revolution by actively encouraging its most enthusiastic supporters – the *sans-culottes*.

Alfred Cobban and J.M. Thompson

Alfred Cobban emphasised the three elements of Robespierre's political creed that explain his importance:

- government should be based on ethical principles
- the people are always good
- in every community there must be a single sovereign will.

J.M. Thompson had expanded on this by arguing that no-one else at the time of the Revolution went as far as Robespierre in outlining the essential principles of the democratic state. These, which single him out as an important figure, include votes for all, equality of rights regardless of race or religion, payment for public service to enable rich and poor to hold office, and a national system of education.

Albert Soboul

A leading French historian, Albert Soboul interpreted the Revolution from a Marxist viewpoint. He supported the notion that Robespierre played an important role in attempting to provide a theoretical justification of the Terror but pointed out that he was incapable of making an accurate analysis of the social realities of his time. According to Soboul, Robespierre was very much a prisoner of his own contradictions: he was too aware of the interests of the bourgeoisie to give his total support to the *sans-culottes*, and yet was too supportive of the needs of the *sans-culottes* to win the support of the bourgeoisie. In the end this contributed to his overthrow.

François Furet

The Revisionist historian François Furet sees Robespierre as a prophet, who believed everything he said and expressed it in the language of the Revolution. There are two ways, according to Furet, of totally understanding Robespierre as a historical figure: one is to detest him while the other is to make too much of him. He is an important figure, not because he reigned supreme over the Revolution for a few months, but because he was the mouthpiece of its most tragic period.

Some key books in the debate
Alfred Cobban, *Aspects of the French Revolution* (Jonathan Cape, 1968).
François Furet, *Interpreting the French Revolution* (Cambridge University Press, 1981).
François Furet, *The French Revolution 1770–1814* (Blackwell, 1988).
Norman Hampson, *The Life and Opinions of Maximilian Robespierre* (Basil Blackwell, 1988).
John Hardman, *Robespierre* (Longman, 1999).
J.M.Thompson, *Robespierre* (Basil Blackwell, 1988).
Albert Soboul, *The French Revolution 1787–1799* (Unwin, 1989).

Study Guide: AS Questions

In the style of AQA

(a) Explain why the Committee of Public Safety was created in France in April 1793. (12 marks)
(b) How important was the Terror in helping to preserve the Republic? (24 marks)

Exam tips
The cross-references are intended to take you straight to the material that will help you to answer the questions.

(a) Try to provide some context by looking at the long-term reasons for the creation of the Committee of Public Safety (CPS). You could refer to the war against internal and external enemies, the influence of the *sans-culottes*, the power of the Jacobins and France's severe economic problems. You would need to stress that the CPS was one of a series of measures in 1793, although you should not waste time describing what else was done. The immediate reasons for its creation would include the need to supervise and speed up government by the Convention and address military defeat and civil war. Try to provide some overall comment on the factors you have given, showing an awareness of the links between them.

(b) To answer this question you will need to consider the contribution of the Terror and other factors that helped preserve the Republic. You might even wish to argue that the Terror was not important and did more harm than good. Whatever line you adopt, it is important that you are consistent and provide an analysis that leads to a supported conclusion. You will probably want to:

- Indicate the dangers to the Republic by explaining the extent of the gravity of the crisis confronting the Republic: indicating the extent of both the internal and external opposition.
- Suggest clearly how the measures adopted by the CPS during the Terror were designed to relieve the pressure on the Republic (page 18).
- Balance this against other factors such as the effectiveness of the first coalition and the military developments that were taking place, which would transform the nature of the French army (pages 177–8 in Chapter 7).

In the style of OCR B
Answer **both** parts of the question.
(a) How is the outbreak of the Terror best explained?
[Explaining ideas, attitudes and beliefs.] (25 marks)
(b) Why did the Terror come to an end in 1794?
[Explaining actions and circumstances.] (25 marks)

Exam tips
Remind yourself of the basics in the General introduction at the start of the study guide to Chapter 1, page 24.

(a) The prompt will set you going along an empathetic explanation, showing how and why the introduction of the Terror was justified and accepted. That will mean consideration of the impact on the population of the mounting crisis that resulted from the combination of military failure after Valmy, developing civil war and fear of counter-revolution. That will also enable you to consider an intentional explanation of the ideas of Robespierre and explain his rising influence.

Both of those sections could then be set in context by a causal explanation of the influence of other factors at work from later 1792 and the first half of 1793 in the struggle against internal and external enemies (real or perceived), such as the renewal of economic problems (e.g. high bread prices and the falling value of the *assignats*). Careful consideration should be given to the reasons first for the growing political alliance between the Montagnards and the *sans-culottes*, and then for the purge of the Girondins in June 1793. When to stop your essay is left to you to decide. You must explain the process up to the moment when the full apparatus of the Terror was in place so the creation of the Committee of Public Safety is a point far too soon. The Terror was still to be constructed later in 1793: the economic terror of the *enragés* in the *journée* of 5 September 1793 and the law of the General Maximum, and the political terror that followed the suspension of the constitution in October 1793. In covering the developments, your essay can examine the full impact of food supplies, the value of the currency, counter-revolution, civil war and external military threats.

(b) The bracketed prompt pushes you to begin in the intentional or causal mode of explanation and then move over to the other before considering the ways in which some component events interacted and the hierarchy of importance between them.

Circumstance will be central to your explanation because you have to account for a major change in political structures and the end of the most dramatic period of the Revolution. You need to establish what in 1794 was so significant that leading figures arranged the *Coup* of Thermidor and the overthrow of Robespierre. Careful consideration of the confusing events of 27 July will explain a lot. Why had the climate changed? Consider the longer term impact of victory in war from 1793 and the defeat of counter-revolution. Consider also the immediate situation in May to July 1794. Did the Terror become most extreme at the moment when the rationale for its existence had diminished? In which case, was the Law of Prairial the tipping point?

Why did Robespierre start to lose support among key constituent supporters, especially the *sans-culottes*. Some historians see loss of *sans-culottes* support as the key to Robespierre's downfall. Shifts in the climate mean that you must also assess ideas and attitudes. Why did the Cult of the Supreme Being appeal to so few? Why did members of the Committee of Public Safety begin to feel threatened? In this context, don't overlook the ferocity of the reaction to the Terror: it is a powerful indicator of the depth of hostility to the system created by Robespierre and his allies.

Study Guide: Advanced Level Question

In the style of Edexcel

'Robespierre fell when Terror had outlived its usefulness.' How far do you agree with this explanation of the *coup* of 9 Thermidor?

(30 marks)

Exam tips

The cross-references are intended to take you straight to the material that will help you to answer the question.

In accounting for the fall of Robespierre you will need to consider a range of factors and you will need to establish the close connection between Robespierre and the machinery of Terror (page 117), the excesses of the Great Terror (pages 124–5) and reactions to that (page 127). To address 'outlived its usefulness' you could examine the extent to which the Terror had reduced the problems faced by the Republic (page 122) and the questioning of its necessity as the military position improved (pages 127 and 130).

Other factors to examine are:

- Robespierre's loss of support from the Catholics (page 126) and the *sans-culottes* (page 127).
- The significance of divisions between the Committee of General Security and Committee of Public Safety (CPS) and within the CPS itself (pages 127–8).

How far in the end was Robespierre's increasing personal isolation (page 128), misjudgement of the political mood of the Convention and mishandling of events on 9 Thermidor responsible for his political overthrow (pages 128–9)?

In coming to an overall conclusion, you should take account of the way in which factors inside and outside the convention combined to create the circumstances in which the *Coup* of Thermidor was secured.

6

The Thermidorian Reaction and the Directory 1794–9

POINTS TO CONSIDER

Following the overthrow of Robespierre and the end of the Terror a reaction took place among those opposed to revolutionary government. A new system was created – the Directory – which, although the longest lasting of the regimes created during the Revolution, was also in the end replaced. This period is examined as three themes:

- The Thermidorian reaction
- The Directory
- The *Coup* of Brumaire and the overthrow of the Directory

Key dates

1794	August 1	Law of 22 Prairial repealed, government reorganised
	September 18	State ends financial support of the Church
	November 12	Jacobin Club closed
1795	February 21	Formal separation of Church and State
	April 1–2	Germinal Uprising
	May 20–23	Prairial Uprising
	August 22	Constitution of Year III
	October 1	Vendémiaire Uprising, Bonaparte appointed commander of the Army of the Interior
	November 2	Directory established
1796	March 11	Bonaparte appointed to command the army in Italy
1797	September 4	*Coup d'état* of Fructidor
1798	May 11	Law of 22 Floréal
1799	June 18	*Coup d'état* of Prairial
	November 9–10	*Coup d'état* of Brumaire, Bonaparte overthrows the Directory
	December 25	Constitution of Year VIII

1 | The Thermidorian Reaction

Key question
Who were the
Thermidorians?

There was a great popular outburst of delight and relief when Robespierre was executed. The journalist Charles de Lacretelle reported the reactions in Paris: 'People were hugging each other in the streets and at places of entertainment and they were so surprised to find themselves still alive that their joy almost turned to frenzy'.

Those who helped to overthrow Robespierre were known as the **Thermidorians** (after the month of Thermidor when the *coup* occurred). The Thermidorians were a mixed group – members of the two great Committees (the CPS and the CGS), ex-terrorists and deputies of the Plain. The Plain now emerged from obscurity to take control. They were the men who had gained from the Revolution by buying *biens nationaux* (land) or by obtaining government contracts. As **regicides** these men were firmly attached to the Republic and did not want to see the return of a monarchy, even a constitutional one. They also disliked the Jacobins, who had given too much power to the *sans-culottes* and had interfered with a free market through the Maximum laws. For them popular democracy, anarchy and the Terror were synonymous. These men were joined by many Montagnards who had rejected their former views and values.

Key terms
Thermidorians
Those individuals
and groups who
had helped
overthrow
Robespierre.

Regicides
Those involved in
the trial and
execution of Louis
XVI.

Ending the Terror

Key question
What measures were
taken to end the
Terror?

The Convention now set about dismantling the machinery of the Terror. With this aim, between the end of July 1794 and 31 May 1795, the Convention:

- abolished the Revolutionary Tribunal, following the execution of a further 63 people, including some who had been leading terrorists
- released all suspects from prison
- repealed the law of Prairial (see page 125) and closed the Jacobin Club.

The deputies were determined to gain control of the institutions that had made the Terror possible. This meant abandoning the centralisation established by the CPS. The Convention decreed that 25 per cent of the members of the two Committees (the CPS and the CGS) had to be changed each month. In August, 16 committees of the Convention were set up to take over most of the work of the CGS and CPS. The latter was now confined to running the war and diplomacy. In Paris the Commune was abolished. In local government power passed again to the moderates and property owners, who had been in control before June 1793.

The Thermidorians also decided to deal with religious issues by renouncing the Constitutional Church. In September 1794 the Convention decided that it would no longer pay clerical salaries. This brought about for the first time the **separation of Church and State**. On 21 February 1795 the government restored freedom of worship for all religions, and thereby formally ended

Key term
**Separation of
Church and State**
The Republic was
legally committed
to religious
neutrality. In order
to serve their
parishioners, priests
were required to
follow French law as
opposed to Church
law.

the persecution of religions waged during the Terror by the dechristianisation campaign. State recognition of the Cult of the Supreme Being was also ended. For the first time in a major European country the State was declaring itself to be entirely neutral in all matters of religious faith – in that it would not favour one belief to the exclusion of others. The consequence of this was that refractory and constitutional priests, protestants and Jews would be in free competition for popular support.

The Risings of Germinal and Prairial

The Thermidorians wanted to get rid of price controls, partly because of their support for a **free market** and partly because it was considered to be unenforceable. These were abolished in December 1794. Public arms workshops were closed or restored to private ownership. The removal of price controls led to a fall in the value of the *assignat* and massive inflation. The government now had to buy its war materials at market prices. It therefore decided to print more *assignats* to pay for them. In August 1794, before the Maximum was abolished, the *assignat* was 34 per cent of its 1790 value. It dropped to 8 per cent in April 1795 and 4 per cent in May. The situation was made worse by a poor harvest in 1794. Grain shortages led to a huge increase in the price of bread.

The winter of 1794–5 was an unprecedentedly severe one. Rivers froze and factories closed down. A combination of economic collapse and the bitter cold produced an enormous increase in misery, suicides and death from malnutrition, as scarcity turned into famine. A publisher, Ruault, described the situation: 'The flour intended for Paris is stopped on the way and stolen by citizens even hungrier no doubt than ourselves, if such there be within the whole Republic. Yet there is no lack of corn anywhere! … The farmers absolutely refused to sell it for paper money'.

Germinal

The hungry turned their fury against the Convention. **Germinal** (1 April 1795) was a demonstration rather than a rising. A large crowd of about 10,000 unarmed people marched on the Convention. Many gained access to the main hall and disrupted debates with demands for bread, the Constitution of 1793 and the release of former members of the CPS – Barère, Collot and Billaud, who had been imprisoned following the *Coup* of Thermidor. The demonstrators expected support from the Montagnards in the Assembly but received none. When loyal National Guards appeared, the insurgents withdrew without resisting.

The repression that followed Germinal was light. But to emphasise its authority the Convention sentenced Barère, Collot and Billaud to be deported to Devil's Island in the French colony of Guiana, off the coast of South America. To safeguard security, other known activists during the Terror were disarmed. During the spring of 1795, disillusionment with the Convention's inability to resolve the famine led to sporadic outbreaks of violence in the provinces, some of which were organised by royalists.

Key date
The government restored freedom of worship for all religions. Protestants had been granted religious toleration in 1787, while Jews were given citizenship in 1790: 21 February 1795

Key question
What was the impact of the economic crisis?

Key terms

Free market
A trading system with no artificial price controls. Prices are determined solely by supply and demand.

Germinal
Popular demonstration on 1 April 1795 in Paris. Named after a month in the new revolutionary calendar.

Key question
What was the
significance of the
Prairial uprising?

Key term

Prairial
A large popular
uprising in Paris on
20–1 May 1795. It
was named after a
month in the new
revolutionary
calendar.

Prairial

Prairial was a much more serious affair. It was an armed rising
like those of 10 August 1792 and 2 June 1793 (see pages 87 and
108). On 1 Prairial (20 May 1795) a large crowd of housewives,
workers and some National Guard units marched on the
Convention to demand bread. In the ensuing chaos a deputy was
killed and the mood of the crowd became increasingly hostile.
The following day forces loyal to the Convention gathered to
confront the crowd and a tense situation developed. The
Convention's gunners went over to the rebels and aimed their
cannon at the Assembly, but no-one was prepared to fire. The
crisis was resolved when the Convention agreed to accept a
petition from the insurgents and to set up a Food Commission.
In the evening loyal National Guards arrived and cleared the
Assembly.

On 3 Prairial (22 May) the Convention took the offensive. The
rebel suburbs were surrounded by 20,000 troops of the regular
army who forced them to give up their arms and cannon. This
time the repression was severe:

- 40 Montagnards were arrested and six were executed
- a military commission condemned to death a further 36,
  including the gunners who had joined the rebels
- about 6000 militants were disarmed and arrested.

Prairial marked the end of the *sans-culottes* as a political and
military force. The significance of Prairial was that the defeat of
popular movement marked the end of the radical phase of the
Revolution. No longer would the *sans-culottes* be able to threaten
and intimidate an elected assembly. In Year IV (1795–6)
conditions were just about as bad as in Year III (1794–5), yet there
was no rising. Demoralised, without arms and without leaders, the
sans-culottes were a spent force.

There were a number of reasons why the uprising of Prairial
failed:

- the workers of Paris were divided – the National Guard units in
  several Sections of the city remained loyal to the Convention
- there was no institution like the Paris Commune in 1792 to
  co-ordinate their activities
- they were politically inexperienced. When they had the
  advantage and had surrounded the Convention they allowed
  the opportunity to slip
- loss of support from the radical bourgeoisie, which they had
  enjoyed between 1789 and 1793.

The key factor, however, was the role of the army. The regular
army was used against the citizens of Paris for the first time since
the Réveillon riots in the spring of 1789 (see page 34). Its
intervention was decisive and made clear just how dependent the
new regime was on the military. This would prove to be the first
of many instances when the army would interfere in France's
internal politics.

The White Terror

The 'White Terror' was an attack on ex-terrorists and all who had done well out of the Revolution by those who had suffered under it. White was the colour of the Bourbons, so 'White Terror' implies that it was a royalist reaction. This was true in part, as returned *émigrés* and non-juring priests did take advantage of the anti-Jacobin revulsion at the persecution of the Year II. In Nîmes 'Companies of the Sun' were formed by royalists to attack former terrorists.

However, most of those who took part in the White Terror were not royalists and had no intention of restoring the Bourbons and the *seigneurs* of the *ancien régime*. Their main concern was vengeance on all those who had been members of the popular societies and watch committees. The Whites were people who had been victims of the Revolutionary Tribunals. They now turned on those who had done well out of the Revolution, such as purchasers of state land, constitutional priests and government officials.

The White Terror in Paris

The White Terror did not cover the whole of France. It was confined to a score of departments north and west of the Loire and south of Lyon. In Paris it was limited to the activities of the *jeunesse dorée*, who played an essential role in organising and co-ordinating the reactionary movement. These were middle-class youths – bankers' and lawyers' clerks, actors, musicians, army deserters and sons of suspects or of those executed. They dressed extravagantly with square collars, earrings and long hair tied back at the neck, like those about to be guillotined. They formed gangs to beat up and intimidate Jacobins and *sans-culottes*. Yet, although there was certainly some violence, it was not on the same scale as the Terror.

White Terror in the Vendée

Much more violent was the White Terror in the north-west and south-east of France. Guerrilla warfare was revived in the Vendée in 1794 after the brutal repression of Year II. In the spring, a movement known as **Chouan**, opposed to conscription, began in Brittany under the leadership of Jean Cottereau. Groups of between 50 and 100 men posed a serious threat to law and order as they roamed the countryside, attacking grain convoys and destabilising local government outside the towns by murdering officials.

From the summer of 1794 to the spring of 1796 they controlled most of Brittany and, under royalist leaders, sought English support. In June 1795, 3000 *émigré* troops based in the Channel Islands were landed at Quiberon Bay and were joined by thousands of Chouans. The total rebel force possibly numbered 22,000.

General Hoche, forewarned, sealed them off with 10,000 troops and compelled them to surrender. Six thousand prisoners were

Key question
What was the motivation behind the White Terror?

Key terms

Jeunesse dorée **(gilded youth)** Young men who dressed extravagantly as a reaction to the restrictions of the Terror. They were also known as muscadins.

Chouan Guerrilla groups operating in the Vendée between 1794 and 1796.

taken, including over 1000 *émigrés*: 640 were shot, along with 108 Chouans in the biggest disaster suffered by *émigré* forces. The government decided that the Chouan had to be eradicated, and sent Hoche with a huge army of 140,000 to wipe out the Chouan and Vendée rebels. Highly mobile flying columns of soldiers swept across the area north and south of the Loire and by the summer of 1796 they had restored government authority once again to this part of France.

White Terror in the south
In the south the murder gangs of the White Terror were not considered to be a serious threat to the Republic, so little effort was made to crush them. This allowed them to become established and to spread rapidly after the disarming of former terrorists and their supporters. Where the Terror had been at its most savage in Lyon and the Rhône valley, prison massacres reminiscent of the September Massacres in 1792 took place. Gangs of youths, like the *jeunesse dorée* in Paris, killed as many as 2000 in the south-east in 1795. The killing continued throughout 1796 and for much of the following year.

The Constitution of the Year III 1795

Key question
What did the Thermidorians hope to achieve in a new constitution?

Key date
Constitution of Year III agreed which established the Directory: 22 August 1795

The Thermidorians wanted a new constitution, which would guarantee the main features of the Revolution of 1789 – the abolition of privilege, freedom of the individual and the control of local and national affairs by an elected assembly and elected officials. They also wanted to ensure that a dictatorship, like that of the CPS, would be impossible in the future and that there would be no return to monarchy or to popular sovereignty on the *sans-culotte* model.

The main features of the new constitution were:

- All males over 21 who paid direct taxation were allowed to vote in the primary assemblies to choose electors.
- Real power, however, was exercised by the electors who actually chose the deputies. Electors had to pay taxes equivalent to 150–200 days' labour. This was so high that the number of electors had fallen from 50,000 in 1790–2 to 30,000 in 1795. Electors were, therefore, the very rich, who had suffered from the Revolution in 1793–4.
- In order to prevent a dictatorship arising, the Thermidorians rigidly separated the legislature from the executive.

The legislature
The legislature was divided into two chambers:

1. The Council of Five Hundred, all of whom had to be over the age of 30. This Council would initiate legislation and then would pass it on to a Council of Ancients
2. The Council of Ancients – 250 men over 40, who would approve or object to bills but could not introduce or change them. There was no property qualification for the councillors of either chamber.

Elections were to be held every year, when a third of the members retired.

The Executive

The Executive was to be a Directory of five, chosen by the Ancients from a list drawn up by the Five Hundred. The five Directors would hold office for five years, though one, chosen by lot, had to retire each year. Directors were not allowed to be members of either Council, and their powers were limited. They could not initiate or veto laws or declare war and they had no control over the treasury. Yet they had considerable authority, as they were in charge of diplomacy, military affairs and law enforcement. Ministers (who also could not sit in the Councils) were appointed by, and were responsible to, the Directors, as were government commissioners, who replaced the representatives-on-mission and national agents and saw that government policy was implemented in the provinces.

Weaknesses in the new Constitution

In spite of the complex system of **checks and balances** designed to prevent a dictatorship, the new Constitution had many weaknesses:

- The yearly elections promoted instability, as majorities in the Councils could be quickly overturned.
- There was no means of resolving conflicts between the legislature and the executive.
- The Councils could paralyse the Directory by refusing to pass laws that the government required.
- The Directors could neither dissolve the Councils nor veto laws passed by them.
- The legislature was not in a strong position either, if it clashed with the executive. It could alter the composition of the Directory only by replacing the one director who retired each year with its own candidate.

The new Constitution enforced quite rigidly the **separation of powers**. If a hostile majority dominated the legislature then the Constitution allowed it to paralyse the Directory. As the Directory was unable to dissolve the legislature or veto their laws, it came to rely on unconstitutional methods such as cancelling election returns and calling in the army to resolve any disputes.

Having drawn up the new constitution, the Convention, knowing that it was unpopular as an elected chamber, feared that free elections might produce a royalist majority. In order to avoid this it decreed that two-thirds of the deputies to the new Councils must be chosen from among the existing deputies of the Convention. The new constitution of Year III was agreed on 22 August 1795. This was then submitted to a **plebiscite** for approval – 1,057,390 were in favour of the Constitution, against 49,978 who opposed it. Four million voters did not vote. The Two-Thirds Decree was accepted by only 205,000 to 108,000.

Key question
How effective was the new system?

Key terms

Checks and balances
Ensuring that the power given to the executive was balanced by the power granted to the legislature.

Separation of powers
The division of executive and legislative powers in order that the government could not make laws without the support of the legislature.

Plebiscite
A popular vote on a single issue.

Key question
Why did the Verona
Declaration fail to
appeal to the French
people?

Verona Declaration

As the discussions about the proposed constitution were nearing a close, the royalists sought to promote their cause. Constitutional monarchists wanting a return to a limited monarchy similar to that in the 1791 Constitution felt they were gaining public support, as they appeared to offer a prospect of stability. They had hoped to put Louis XVI's son, a prisoner in the Temple (one of the prisons in Paris), on the throne as 'Louis XVII' but he died in June 1795. From northern Italy the Comte de Provence, Louis XVI's brother, immediately proclaimed himself Louis XVIII and on 24 June issued the **Verona Declaration**.

The Declaration, however, turned out to be a reactionary document, which made the task of restoring the monarchy more difficult. Louis promised to restore the 'ancient constitution' of France completely, which meant restoring the three orders and the *parlements*. He also promised to restore 'stolen properties', such as that taken from the Church and the *émigrés*. This antagonised all those who had bought *biens nationaux* and all who had benefited from the abolition of the tithe and seigneurial dues. Although not intended, the Verona Declaration turned out to be a great boost to those who favoured a Republic.

Key term

Verona Declaration
A reactionary
statement issued by
the new heir to the
throne promising to
reverse many of the
gains made during
the Revolution.

The Vendémiaire Uprising

The Verona Declaration failed to attract mass support for the royalist cause. Although work on the new constitution was proceeding well, news of the Two-Thirds Law came as a shock to many Parisians who had hoped that the Convention would soon be replaced. Its inability to deal with food shortages and inflation turned many ordinary people against the Convention, yet it now appeared that most of its deputies would be returned to the new assembly. Royalists in particular felt that the prospect of any restoration of the monarchy was unlikely given the known hostility of the Convention. Frustration and anger spilled over into rebellion.

On 5 October 1795 (13 Vendémiaire), a large royalist crowd of 25,000 gathered to march on the Convention and seize power. They greatly outnumbered the 7800 government troops but the latter had cannon, under the command of General Bonaparte, whereas the rebels did not. The devastating artillery fire – Bonaparte's famous 'Whiff of grapeshot' – crushed the rebellion. As over 300 were killed or wounded in the fighting, this was one of the bloodiest of the revolutionary *journées*. It also marked another watershed – the people of Paris would not again attempt to intimidate an elected assembly until 1830.

The divisions among the royalists and the unpopularity of the Verona Declaration all make the rising of Vendémiaire appear rather mysterious. It is usually presented as a royalist rising brought about by the Two-Thirds Decree, which, it is said, prevented the royalists from obtaining a majority in the elections to the Councils. Yet, the largest groups of rebels were artisans and apprentices: a third of those arrested were manual workers. The rising was not simply against the Two-Thirds Decree but had

Key question
What was unusual
about the
Vendémiaire
Uprising?

Key date

The Vendémiaire
Uprising: 5 October
1795

The defeat of the royalist uprising of Vendémiaire, 1795. The print shows the force used by the Directory to suppress the uprising. The artillery used by Bonaparte is clearly shown firing into the crowd.

economic origins too. Many people, including *rentiers* – small proprietors – and government employees, had been badly hit by inflation. These people, who were among the rebels, had supported the Thermidorians and defended the Convention in the risings of Germinal and Prairial.

The repression that followed was light. Only two people were executed, although steps were taken to prevent further risings. The Sectional Assemblies were abolished and the National Guard was put under the control of the new General of the Army of the Interior, Napoleon Bonaparte. For the second time in six months the army had saved the Thermidorian Republic.

Profile: Napoleon Bonaparte 1769–1821

1769 – Born into a minor noble family on the island of Corsica which had only been part of France since 1768
1784 – Enters the *École Militaire* in Paris
1785 – Commissioned as an artillery officer
1793 – Commands artillery at siege of Toulon
1795 – Puts down Vendémiaire Uprising
1796 – Appointed commander of the army in Italy
1797 – Negotiates the Peace of Campo Formio
1798 – Sets off on the Egyptian campaign
1799 – *Coup* of Brumaire, appointed First Consul
1804 – Proclaimed Emperor of the French
1815 – Defeated at Waterloo and exiled to St Helena
1821 – Death and burial at St Helena
1840 – Remains reburied at *Les Invalides* in Paris

The emergence of Napoleon as one of the ablest and most popular generals during the Directory is one of the key features of the Revolution. His use by the Directory to resolve political disputes made him aware of how weak the system was. When invited to join the *coup* to overthrow the Directory he agreed willingly (see Chapter 8, pages 185–210).

Summary diagram: The Thermidorian reaction

Dismantling the Terror and economic crisis → **The Thermidorian reaction**

↓

Germinal and Prairial Risings

↓

White Terror → **Constitution of Year III (1795)**

Key question
What difficulties confronted the Directory when it took up office and how was it able to survive for so long?

Key term

Conventionnels
Members of the Convention between 1792 and 1795.

2 | The Directory

The new third of members elected to the Council of Five Hundred after Vendémiaire and the dissolution of the Convention was mainly royalist, but they were unable to influence the choice of directors. As the Verona Declaration had threatened to punish all regicides, the *conventionnels* elected Directors (Carnot was the best known) all of whom were regicides, as this would be a guarantee against a royalist restoration.

The Directors wanted to provide a stable and liberal government, which would maintain the gains of the Revolution. Yet the problems they faced were daunting. The war appeared to be endless, and it had to be paid for. The treasury was empty, taxes were unpaid and the *assignat* had plummeted in value. Many Frenchmen did not expect the Directory to last more than a few months.

The Directory did, however, survive and for longer than any of the other revolutionary regimes. There were a number of factors that contributed to this:

- The Directory was committed to restoring the rule of law.
- Many of their key opponents were discredited. Few wanted a return either to the Jacobin Terror of Year II or to the absolute monarchy of the *ancien régime*.
- While many ordinary people were prepared to accept a constitutional monarchy with limited powers, the royalists themselves were deeply divided – between extremists who supported the Verona Declaration and constitutional monarchists.
- Public apathy also helped the Directory to survive – after six years of revolution and three years of war, revolutionary enthusiasm had all but disappeared.
- Significantly, the army supported the Directory, as a royalist restoration would mean an end to the war. Army officers did not wish to be deprived of any opportunity provided by war for promotion or plunder. It was the army, above all, that enabled

the Directory to overcome all challenges to its authority, but this was a double-edged weapon. The army, which kept the Directory in power, would be the most serious threat to its survival, if it became dissatisfied.

The Babeuf Plot 1796

The first real challenge to the Directory came from Gracchus Babeuf, a radical pamphleteer and editor of *Tribun du Peuple*. Babeuf disliked the Constitution of the Year III, because it gave power to the wealthy. He believed that the aim of society should be 'the common happiness', and that the Revolution should secure the equal enjoyment of life's blessings for all. He thought that as private property produced inequality, the only way to establish real equality was 'to establish the communal management of property and abolish private possession'. These ideas were much more radical than those put forward in the Year II and have led many historians to regard Babeuf as the first **Communist**, a forerunner of Karl Marx (1818–83).

From March 1796 Babeuf organised a plan to overthrow the Directory by means of a *coup*. He saw what he called his **Conspiracy of Equals** as a popular rising. Babeuf realised, however, that this would not come about spontaneously but must be prepared by a small group of dedicated revolutionaries. Through propaganda and agitation they would persuade key institutions, like the army and police, who would provide the armed force to seize power. After seizing power, the revolutionary leaders would not hand it over to an elected assembly but would establish a dictatorship, in order to make fundamental changes in the organisation of society.

Babeuf received no support from the *sans-culottes* and little from former Jacobins. He was arrested in May 1796, after being betrayed to the authorities by a fellow conspirator, and was executed the following year. Marxist historians such as Albert Soboul consider Babeuf's theories to be extremely influential. They argue that his ideas inspired not only nineteenth-century French revolutionaries, like Blanqui, but, ultimately Lenin and his followers who set up the first communist state in the Soviet Union in 1917. Babeuf's importance to the French Revolution itself however was slight.

The *Coup d'état* of Fructidor 1797

The elections of 1797 revealed a growing popular shift towards the monarchists. People were tired of war abroad and religious conflict at home and found the idea of a constitutional monarchy attractive, believing that it would offer peace and stability. Of the 216 ex-members of the Convention who sought re-election, only 11 were returned. Monarchists won 180 of the 260 seats being contested, bringing their numbers in the Councils to 330. The wealthy, populous northern departments returned the largest proportion of monarchists, which suggests that the Directory had lost the support of the richer bourgeoisie.

Key question
How important a figure was Babeuf?

Key terms

Communist
A follower of the political belief that centres on social and economic equality as outlined by Karl Marx.

Conspiracy of Equals
Babeuf's theory of how to organise a revolution – using a small group of committed revolutionaries rather than a mass movement.

Key question
What threat did the revival of monarchism pose to the Directory?

The elections, in which in some departments fewer than 10 per cent of electors voted, did not give the monarchists a majority in the Councils. However, they did mean that the Directory no longer had majority support and could rely on only about a third of the deputies. All the monarchists needed to do, it appeared, was to wait for the next elections when more *conventionnels* would have to give up their seats and, if voting followed a similar pattern to the elections of 1797, they would obtain a majority. Monarchists would then be in a position to restore the monarchy legally. The opponents of the Directory were also successful in elections to the provincial administrations.

The *coup d'état*

Key question
What was the importance of the *Coup* of Fructidor?

Key date

Republican directors purge pro-monarchist deputies and directors in the *Coup* of Fructidor: 3–4 September 1797

The royalists showed their strength when the Councils appointed three of their supporters to important positions. One was elected President of the Five Hundred and another President of the Ancients. Barthélemy, the new director, was regarded as sympathetic to the monarchists, as was Carnot, who was becoming steadily more conservative. Carnot was prepared to give up conquered territory to make a lasting peace and so was disliked by the generals.

Of the remaining Directors, two were committed republicans. They were determined to prevent a restoration of the monarchy and sought help from the army. Bonaparte had already sent General Augereau to Paris with some troops to support the republican Directors. On the night of 3–4 September 1797 (17–18 Fructidor, Year V) troops were ordered to seize all the strong points in Paris and surround the Council chambers. They then arrested two Directors, Carnot and Barthélemy, and 53 deputies.

Some of the remaining deputies who attended the Councils clearly felt intimidated, and they approved two decrees demanded by the remaining Directors. One decree cancelled the elections in 49 Departments, removing 177 deputies without providing for their replacement. Normandy, Brittany, the Paris area and the north now had no parliamentary representation at all. A second decree provided for the deportation to the penal settlements in Guiana of Carnot (who had escaped and fled abroad and was sentenced in absentia), Barthélemy, the 53 deputies arrested, and some leading royalists. The Directors also cancelled the local government elections and made appointments themselves.

It was clear to all that the *coup* was the end of parliamentary government and of the Constitution of the Year III, and that the executive had won an important victory over the legislature. The revival of monarchism had been dealt a significant blow. It also meant that the Directory could now govern without facing hostile Councils.

Terror

After Fructidor, the new Directory took action against *émigrés* and refractory priests. *Émigrés* who had returned to France were given two weeks to leave: otherwise they would be executed. During the next few months many were hunted down and were sentenced to death. Clergy were now required to take an oath rejecting any support for royalty: those refusing would be deported to Guiana. The 1400 non-juring priests were sentenced to deportation.

The terror that followed Fructidor was limited. It was carried out solely by the government and the army in an attempt to destroy the royalist movement. In the short term it succeeded but, by alienating Catholic opinion, it provided more opponents for the Directory.

Financial reform

Many of the financial problems of the Directory were the legacy of previous regimes, which had printed more and more *assignats* in order to pay for the war. As by February 1796, these were almost worthless, the Directory issued a new paper currency, known as *mandats territoriaux*. They also soon lost value, and by July were worth less than five per cent of their nominal value. In February 1797 they ceased to be legal tender.

The monetary crisis had been catastrophic for government officials, *rentiers* and workers, as they saw a rapid decline in their purchasing power. Metal coins now became the only legal currency and these were in short supply: there were only one billion *livres* in circulation in 1797, compared with two and a half billion in 1789. This resulted in **deflation**, as producers and retailers lowered prices to try and stimulate demand among consumers who were reluctant to buy goods. The inflation of 1795–7 had made the Directory unpopular with the workers. Now it became unpopular with businessmen since lower prices meant lower profits.

Decreasing the national debt

From the *Coup* of Fructidor to the spring of 1799 the Directory had little trouble with the purged Councils, and Dominique-Vincent Ramel, the Minister of Finance, had an opportunity to introduce some far-reaching reforms. In September 1797 two-thirds of the **national debt** was renounced by a one-off payment to debt holders. Their loans to the government were converted into non-interest-bearing bonds, which could be used to buy national property.

This move was of immediate benefit to the government, as it reduced the annual interest on the national debt from 240 million francs (which was about a quarter of government expenditure) to 80 million. It was not of much use to the bondholders who were denied income. Within a year the value of the bonds had fallen by 60 per cent; soon after that they became worthless, when the government refused to accept them for the purchase of *biens*. This was, in effect, a partial declaration of state bankruptcy, as two-thirds of the national debt was liquidated in this way. Although debt holders were unhappy with the measure, the **'bankruptcy of the two-thirds'**, as it was known, helped to stabilise French finances for a time.

Key question
What was the impact of the financial crisis facing the Directory?

Key terms

Mandats territoriaux
The new paper currency issued by the Directory in March 1796 and withdrawn in February 1797, when worth only one per cent of face value.

Deflation
A fall in prices as demand for goods and services falls.

National debt
Money borrowed by the government from its own people, on which it has to pay interest. This debt increased during the Revolution and the war.

'Bankruptcy of the two-thirds'
The government wrote off two-thirds of the debt it owed its creditors.

Increasing revenue

In addition to cutting expenditure Ramel wanted to increase revenue. He put in place a number of policies to achieve this:

- In 1798 four basic forms of direct taxation were established:
  - a tax on trading licences
  - a land tax
  - a tax on movable property
  - a tax on doors and windows.

  These measures were among the most lasting achievements of the Directory and survived until 1914.

- Ramel changed the method of collecting direct taxes. Whereas, previously, locally elected authorities had been responsible for collection, central control was now introduced. Commissioners appointed by the Directors were to assess and levy taxes.
- As there was a continual deficit during wartime, the government revived an unpopular practice of the *ancien régime* – indirect taxes. The *octrois* (page 5) was re-introduced and was again very unpopular, as it raised the price of goods in the towns.
- An increasingly lucrative source of income was plunder from those foreign states, especially Italy and Germany, which had been occupied by French armies.

Key term

Balance the budget
To create a situation in which the government's expenditure is equal to its income.

The impact of these policies was positive. Although very unpopular, the 'bankruptcy of the two-thirds' helped to stabilise French finances for a time. Aided by the reduced military expenditure when peace with Austria was made in October 1797, and new taxes, Ramel was able to **balance the budget** for the first time since the Revolution began.

Key question
To what extent had French forces reversed earlier defeats by the end of 1795?

War: 1794–9

The battle of Fleurus (in Belgium) in June 1794 was the first of a series of successes, which continued until all the members of the First Coalition, except Britain, had been knocked out of the war. In the summer of 1794, Belgium was occupied and, in the following winter, the United Provinces were invaded. The French conquered the Rhineland and crossed into Spain. Russia had intervened in Poland, which it was clear would be partitioned again. Prussia therefore made peace with France so that she would be free to claim Polish territory for herself. This, in reality, made very little difference as Prussia had played only a minimal part in the war against France since 1793.

At the Treaty of Basle on 6 April 1795, Prussia promised to hand over its territories on the left bank of the Rhine to France. In return she would receive land on the right bank. This treaty freed French troops to attack other enemies.

Meanwhile, the United Provinces had become the Batavian Republic in January 1795, after a revolt against William V, who fled to England. Having lost Prussian support, the Dutch hastily made peace with France, who they were forced to join as an ally. The French hoped that the powerful Dutch navy would help to tip the naval balance against Great Britain. Spain too made peace in July, giving up to France her part of the island of San Domingo. Of the Great Powers, only Great Britain and Austria remained in the fight against France.

Figure 6.1: France, 1789–95. Note how France had extended her territory particularly in the north east in order to establish a natural frontier on the Rhine.

Key question
What impact did Napoleon make on the war in Italy?

Key dates

General Napoleon Bonaparte appointed commander of the French army in Italy: 2 March 1796

Peace of Campo Formio ends the war between Austria and France: 18 October 1797

Key terms

Armistice
An agreement between two countries to end hostilities. This would precede a peace settlement that would formally mark the end of a war.

Irish Nationalists
Irish who were staunchly anti-British and wished to be free from what they considered foreign rule. During the Revolution they approached the republicans for support.

Key question
Why was France unable to take advantage of Britain's isolation?

Defeat of Austria

In 1796 the main French objective was to defeat Austria. Carnot drew up the plan of campaign and prepared a pincer movement against Austria. Armies under Jourdan and Moreau would march across Bavaria to Vienna, whilst the armies of the Alps and Italy would conquer Piedmont and Lombardy and then move across the Alps to Vienna. The main attack was to be by Jourdan and Moreau, who were given 140,000 troops.

Command of the Italian campaign was given to the 27-year-old General Napoleon Bonaparte on 2 March 1796. It was expected that he would play a secondary role as he had no field experience and only 30,000 unpaid and ill-disciplined troops under his command. Yet Napoleon was to turn Italy into the major battleground against Austria. He was able to do this by winning the loyalty of his men, to whom he promised vast wealth.

Within a month of taking command he had defeated the north Italian state of Piedmont and forced her to make peace. In the same month of May he defeated the Austrians at Lodi and entered Milan. Mantua was the key to the passes over the Alps to Vienna, and Napoleon finally captured it in February 1797. The road to Vienna seemed open but all had not been going well for the French. The Archduke Charles had driven Moreau back to the Rhine, so Napoleon signed an **armistice** with Austria at Leoben in April.

Napoleon decided the terms at Leoben, without consulting the Directory. He was already confident enough to be making his own foreign policy and, in so doing, ignoring specific instructions from the Directors. They had wanted to use Lombardy as a bargaining counter when negotiating with Austria to exchange for recognition of French control of the left bank of the Rhine. Instead, Napoleon joined Lombardy to Modena and the Papal Legations to form the Cisalpine Republic. Austria recognised Belgium, which the French had annexed in October 1795, as French territory.

As compensation for giving up Lombardy and Belgium, Napoleon gave Austria Venice and part of the Venetian Republic, which provided access to the Adriatic. The fate of the left bank of the Rhine was unclear: it was to be decided by a Congress of the Holy Roman Empire. The Directory and the generals on the Rhine were furious that they had no choice but to accept what Napoleon had done. As the royalists had won the elections in France, the Directory knew it might need him. The peace of Campo Formio 18 October 1797 confirmed what had been agreed at Leoben.

Britain isolated

With her major allies out of the war, Britain was now isolated. The French wanted to invade Britain, but for this to happen control of the seas was necessary in order to ensure safe passage for an invasion army. In particular they wanted to support **Irish Nationalists** in their attempt to overthrow British rule in Ireland. Control of the sea was also vital if the French hoped to send a military expedition to Ireland. The French hoped that with the aid of the Dutch and Spanish fleets (Spain had become an ally of France in October 1796) they would be able to obtain this. These plans were dashed by two British victories in 1797. In February the Spanish fleet was defeated off Cape St Vincent and the Dutch fleet was almost completely destroyed at Camperdown in October. The war with Britain therefore continued.

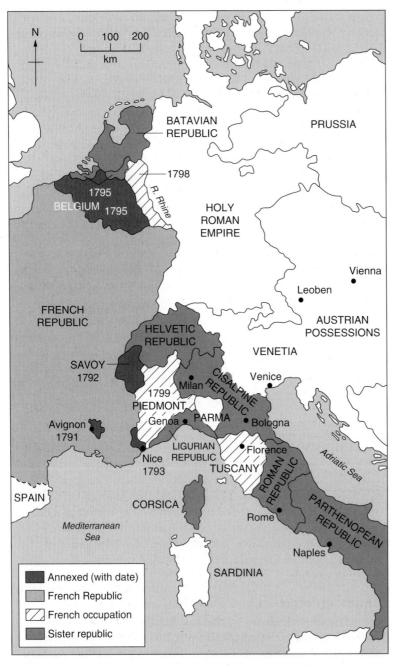

Figure 6.2: The expansion of revolutionary France. Note how the French Republic established 'sister republics' along some of her borders. Why do you think the republicans did this?

Key question
How was the creation of new states beneficial to the Republic?

Key terms

Satellite republics States that had the appearance of being independent but were in reality under French control.

Second Coalition Formed in 1799 and consisting of Britain, Russia, Austria, Turkey, Portugal and Naples.

Creating states

On the continent the prospects for a permanent peace receded. French foreign policy became increasingly aggressive as the Directors sought to keep French conquests and even extend them. France reorganised a number of foreign territories, effectively redrawing the map of Europe in some areas. These new territories were in effect **satellite republics** under French influence or control:

- The Helvetic Republic was set up in Switzerland in January 1798 with the help of Swiss Patriots sympathetic to French ideals. This was important to France, as it controlled the main Alpine passes to Italy. Geneva was annexed to France.
- In Italy three small republics were created:
  1. The Roman Republic after the French invasion and the flight of the Pope to Tuscany (1798).
  2. The Cisalpine Republic based on Milan.
  3. The Ligurian Republic, which replaced the Genoese Republic in June 1797.
- The Batavian Republic was established in the United Provinces in January 1795, after a revolt supported by the French against William V, who fled to England.
- The French were busy redrawing the map of Germany in negotiations with the Congress of the Holy Roman Empire at Rastatt. In March 1798 the Congress handed over the left bank of the Rhine to France and agreed that princes who had lost land there should be compensated by receiving Church land elsewhere in Germany.

The spring of 1798 marked the high point of the Republic's power. In western, central and southern Europe, France had attained a degree of hegemony (domination) unparalleled in modern European history (see the map opposite). Yet from this position of great external strength, the decline in the Directory's fortunes was equally dramatic. Within 18 months it would be overthrown.

Key question
What impact did the defeat of the French at Aboukir Bay have on the war?

The Second Coalition

Following his successes in Italy, Napoleon departed for Egypt in May 1798 with the aim of attacking British interests. His fleet, however, was destroyed by Nelson at the Battle of Aboukir Bay (August 1798). This defeat encouraged other countries to once again take up arms against France. A **Second Coalition** was formed, and Russia, which had not taken part in previous fighting against France, declared war in December. Tsar Paul was incensed at the French seizure of Malta, of which he had declared himself protector in 1797. France declared war on Austria in March 1799 on the grounds that Austria had allowed Russian troops to move through her territory. Immediately war resumed, France occupied the rest of Italy; Piedmont was annexed to France, and Naples was turned into another 'sister' republic – the Parthenopean.

These early successes were followed by a series of defeats. The French were pushed back to the Rhine by the Austrians, and the Russians advanced through northern Italy. French forces withdrew from the whole of Italy, except Genoa, as the Russians moved into Switzerland. It appeared that France would be invaded for the first time in six years, but, as had happened before, France was saved by quarrels among the allies. Austria, instead of supporting Russia in Switzerland, sent her best troops north to the Rhine. This allowed the French to move on to the offensive in Switzerland, where the Russians withdrew in the autumn of 1799. The immediate danger to France was over.

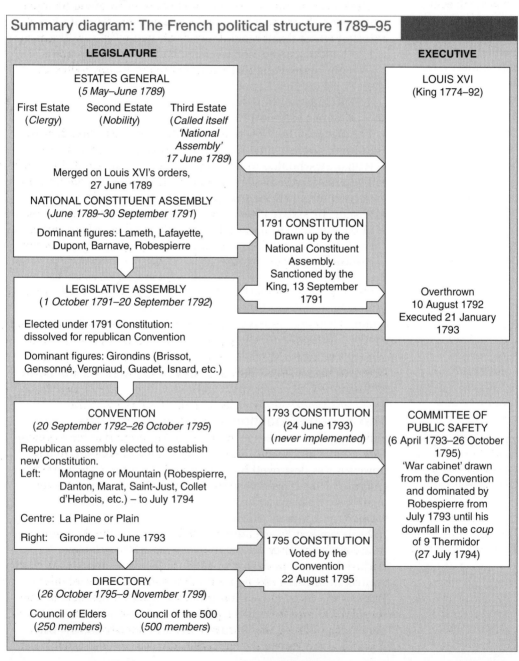

Summary diagram: The French political structure 1789–95

LEGISLATURE

EXECUTIVE

ESTATES GENERAL
(*5 May–June 1789*)

First Estate (*Clergy*)   Second Estate (*Nobility*)   Third Estate (*Called itself 'National Assembly' 17 June 1789*)

Merged on Louis XVI's orders, 27 June 1789

NATIONAL CONSTITUENT ASSEMBLY
(*June 1789–30 September 1791*)

Dominant figures: Lameth, Lafayette, Dupont, Barnave, Robespierre

LEGISLATIVE ASSEMBLY
(*1 October 1791–20 September 1792*)

Elected under 1791 Constitution: dissolved for republican Convention

Dominant figures: Girondins (Brissot, Gensonné, Vergniaud, Guadet, Isnard, etc.)

CONVENTION
(*20 September 1792–26 October 1795*)

Republican assembly elected to establish new Constitution.
Left: Montagne or Mountain (Robespierre, Danton, Marat, Saint-Just, Collet d'Herbois, etc.) – to July 1794

Centre: La Plaine or Plain

Right: Gironde – to June 1793

DIRECTORY
(*26 October 1795–9 November 1799*)

Council of Elders (*250 members*)   Council of the 500 (*500 members*)

1791 CONSTITUTION
Drawn up by the National Constituent Assembly. Sanctioned by the King, 13 September 1791

1793 CONSTITUTION
(24 June 1793)
(*never implemented*)

1795 CONSTITUTION
Voted by the Convention 22 August 1795

LOUIS XVI
(King 1774–92)

Overthrown 10 August 1792
Executed 21 January 1793

COMMITTEE OF PUBLIC SAFETY
(6 April 1793–26 October 1795)
'War cabinet' drawn from the Convention and dominated by Robespierre from July 1793 until his downfall in the *coup* of 9 Thermidor (27 July 1794)

3 | The *Coup* of Brumaire and the Overthrow of the Directory

Key question
How effective were the measures introduced in 1799 to deal with the worsening economic and military crisis?

Key date
Law of 22 Floréal – also known as the *Coup d'état of* Floréal, when the Directory excluded Jacobin deputies from the Council: 11 May 1798

The persecution of royalists after Fructidor had been severe, so they tended to keep away from the electoral assemblies in the 1798 election. Although the Jacobins did well in the elections, they captured less than a third of the seats. The Directory could be sure of a majority of support among deputies in the new legislature, yet the Directors persuaded the Councils by the Law of 22 Floréal (11 May 1798) to annul the election of 127 deputies, 86 of whom were suspected Jacobins. In another contravention of the 1795 Constitution, the Directors chose most of the deputies who replaced the expelled members. The *Coup d'état* of Floréal was less drastic than that of Fructidor but it had less justification: no-one could pretend that the Republic was in danger. Once again the Directory had shown its contempt for the wishes of the electors.

Jourdan's Law

By 1798 there were concerns about the size of the French army, which was only 270,000 strong. Desertion, low morale and a reluctance to join the military were all taking their toll. Jourdan's law proposed that conscription be re-introduced for the first time since 1793. The Councils approved this in September 1798. However, it provoked widespread resistance. Much of Belgium, where conscription was also introduced, revolted in November and it took two months to put down the rising. The prospect of conscription was viewed with great reluctance among large numbers of young men who went to great lengths to avoid military service. Of the first draft of 230,000, only 74,000 reached the armies.

The 1799 elections once again showed the unpopularity of the Directory. Only 66 of 187 government candidates were elected. Among the rest there were about 50 Jacobins, including some who had been purged during Floréal. They were still a minority but many moderate deputies were now prepared to follow their lead. The moderates had become disillusioned with the government, as news of military defeats reached Paris. The military situation was regarded as so desperate that the Councils were persuaded to pass emergency laws that were proposed by Jacobins. In June 1799 Jourdan called for a new *levée en masse*: all men between 20 and 25 were to be called up immediately.

Crisis

With her armies being forced back into France, the Republic could no longer pay for the war by seizing foreign assets. A **forced loan** on the rich was therefore decreed. This was intended to raise 100 million *livres*, a sum that meant that the wealthy might have to give up as much as three-quarters of their income. The **Law of Hostages** of 12 July was even worse for the notables. Any areas resisting the new laws could be declared 'disturbed'. Local authorities could then arrest relatives of *émigrés*, nobles or

Key terms
Forced loan
A measure compelling the wealthy to loan money to the government.

Law of Hostages
Laid down that the relatives of any French citizens challenging the authority of the Republic would be imprisoned at their own expense and their property seized to pay for damage done by anti-government rebels.

rebels. They could be imprisoned, fined and their property confiscated to pay for the damage done by those causing disturbances.

These measures appeared to be a return to the arbitrary arrests and harassment of the Terror of the Year II. Yet by November only 10 million *livres* of the forced loan had been collected. Conscription was planned to raise 402,000 troops but, as in 1798, there was widespread resistance and only 248,000 actually joined the army. Many became brigands or royalist rebels to avoid being called up. The Law of Hostages was hardly ever applied, because of opposition from local officials.

In 1799 there was a virtual collapse of government administration in the provinces. There were many reasons for this:

- the Directory could not persuade local notables to accept office and had few troops to enforce its decrees
- local authorities were often taken over by royalists, who refused to levy forced loans, persecute non-juring priests or catch deserters
- the National Guard was not large enough to keep order in the absence of regular troops, so substantial areas of the countryside were not policed at all
- government commissioners were killed as quickly as they were replaced.

The result of this administrative collapse was **brigandage**. By November 1799 there was civil war in the Ardèche region in southern France.

Brigandage
Outbreaks of lawlessness and violence by groups of bandits.

Key term

The *Coup d'état* of Brumaire

In the late summer of 1799 the military situation improved. The Russians were driven out of Switzerland in September. Sieyès (page 29), who had become a Director, saw this as an opportunity to stage a *coup*. He wanted to strengthen the executive but knew that the Five Hundred would not agree to this and that it could not be done constitutionally. Therefore a *coup* was required for which the support of the army would be necessary. But which general could be relied on?

Moreau was approached but recommended Bonaparte, who had returned from Egypt on 10 October. 'There is your man', he told Sieyès. 'He will make your *coup d'état* far better than I can.' On his way to Paris Bonaparte was greeted enthusiastically by the population, as the most successful of the republican generals and the one who had brought peace in 1797. He had made up his mind to play a leading role in French politics. He agreed to join Sieyès' *coup* but only on condition that a provisional government of three consuls, who would draft a new constitution, should be set up (page 186).

Key question
What was Sieyès hoping to achieve by a *coup*?

Saint-Cloud
A former royal palace in the suburbs of Paris away from the influence of the Parisian populace, where the plotters believed that Jacobinism was still a powerful force.

The removal to Saint-Cloud

Sieyès wanted to move the Councils to **Saint-Cloud**, as the Jacobins in the Five Hundred in Paris were numerous enough to provide opposition to his plans. The Ancients, using as an excuse the fear of a plot, persuaded the Councils to move to a safer location at Saint-Cloud. Once there it became clear on 19 Brumaire (10 November) that the only plot was one organised by Sieyès. The Council of Five Hundred was furious, so Bonaparte reluctantly agreed to address both Councils.

The appearance of Napoleon in the Five Hundred with armed grenadiers was greeted with cries of 'Outlaw' and 'Down with the tyrant'. He was physically attacked by Jacobin deputies and had to be rescued by fellow officers. It was not at all clear that the soldiers would take action against the elected representatives of the nation. Napoleon's brother Lucien, President of the Five Hundred, came to his rescue when he told the troops that some deputies were trying to assassinate their general. At this the troops cleared the hall where the Five Hundred were meeting.

Some hours later a small group of Councillors sympathetic to the plotters met and approved a decree abolishing the Directory.

Napoleon and the Council of Five Hundred at Saint-Cloud by Bouchot. The artist seeks to portray Napoleon in a heroic pose as an isolated figure surrounded by hostile opponents but determined to do what is right for France.

It was replaced with a provisional executive committee of three members, Sieyès, Roger Ducos and Napoleon. The great beneficiary of Brumaire was Napoleon but it was his brother who was the true hero of the hour.

Constitution of Year VIII

Napoleon issued a Proclamation to the French Nation on 10 November 1799 to explain why he had taken part in the *coup*: 'On my return to Paris I found all authority in chaos and agreement only on the one truth that the constitution was half destroyed and incapable of preserving liberty. Men of every party came to see me, confided their plans, disclosed their secrets and asked for my support. I refused to be a **man of party**'.

Paris remained calm, but this was a sign of apathy and reluctance to become involved in any more protest, rather than of approval. When news of the *coup* spread to the provinces there was little rejoicing at the events. Such reaction as there was varied between surprise and mild opposition. A poster that appeared in Paris expressed the disillusionment many felt towards the Directory: 'France wants something great and long-lasting. Instability has been her downfall. She has no desire for a monarchy, wants a free and independent legislature and to enjoy the benefits from ten years of sacrifices'.

Key question
What significance did Napoleon attach to the new Constitution?

Key term

Man of party
A phrase used by Napoleon to indicate he was not tied to any particular group, such as the monarchists or Jacobins, and that he was acting in the best interests of France.

A contemporary print that depicts France as a woman being dragged into an abyss by two figures representing revolutionary fanaticism. Napoleon is attempting to draw her back towards justice, unity, peace and plenty. According to this print what is Napoleon's role in the history of the Revolution?

When Napoleon presented the new Constitution of year VIII to the French people on 15 December 1799, he said that it was 'founded on the true principles of representative government, on the sacred rights of property, equality and liberty [pages 186–7]. Citizens the Revolution is established on the principles which began it. It is finished.' Many did not realise the significance of the *coup d'état* of Brumaire. The republican phase of the Revolution was drawing to a close, while another, destined to culminate in the Napoleonic Empire, was beginning (Chapter 8).

The failure of the Directory

Key question
Why did the Directory fail?

The Directors had wanted to produce a stable government, which maintained the gains of the Revolution of 1789 whilst avoiding the extremes of Jacobin dictatorship or royalism. In the final analysis they were unsuccessful, and this was due to a combination of factors:

- Their failure to create stability was partly due to the Constitution of the Year III, with its annual elections and no provision for settling disputes between the executive and the legislature or change the Constitution in a reasonable way.
- In order to try and maintain a non-Jacobin/Royalist majority in the Councils, the Directors interfered with the election results. During the *coups*, Fructidor 1797 and Floréal 1798, they purged the Councils. The effect of such action on the Constitution, as Napoleon told the Ancients, was that: 'Nobody has any respect for it now'.
- Increasing reliance on the army to settle political disputes. This started with the Thermidorians during the risings of Prairial and Vendémiaire and continued under the Directory with the *coup d'état* of Fructidor. This reliance made an army takeover a distinct possibility. Although a politician planned the *Coup* of Brumaire, and assumed the army would merely occupy a supporting role, its most important figure was General Napoleon Bonaparte, who had no intention of leaving the political stage.
- Most of the people who would normally have supported the Directory – owners of *biens*, the wealthy notables – were alienated by its policies, especially its forced loans. They showed this by refusing, in increasingly large numbers, to vote in the annual elections or to take up posts in local government. When the challenge to the Directory came, few were prepared to defend it.
- Any enthusiasm for the war had long since gone and most people wanted peace. Yet war had become a necessity for the Directory – to ensure money for the French treasury, to produce the victories and the prestige that would enable the regime to survive, and to provide an opportunity to keep ambitious generals and unruly soldiers out of France. As Napoleon observed '... to exist it [the Directory] needed a state of war as other governments need a state of peace'. One of the reasons for Napoleon's popularity was that he had brought peace at Campo Formio in 1797.

- The renewal of the war after 1797 also produced a flurry of Jacobin activity. The Jacobins pressed for and secured a forced loan and the Law of Hostages. While Jacobins by the late 1790s were never more than an urban minority, the policies they advocated revived fears of a Terror like that of Year II, and helped convince many that the Directory could not, and should not, survive.

These events discredited the Directory and produced politicians who were not as attached to the Republic as the *conventionnels* had been. Only 12 per cent of those elected to the Councils in 1799 had been members of the Convention and only five per cent were regicides. Over half the deputies chosen in 1799 were elected for the first time that year. These deputies were prepared to accept the view of Sieyès that the Constitution should be changed and that this involved getting rid of the Directory. They were not only prepared to welcome the new regime but took part in running it. Of 498 important officials of the **Consulate** 77 per cent had been deputies under the Directory. These conservative and moderates wanted stability and were prepared to accept an authoritarian regime to get it. To some extent the regime collapsed because of the contradictions within it – it claimed to favour democracy yet used the military to suppress opposition: it needed war for economic purposes, yet the war lost it considerable domestic support.

Achievements of the Directory

Despite the fact that the Directory was the longest lasting of the revolutionary regimes there has been a tendency to dismiss it as a period of little achievement. The trend in recent years has been to consider the period in a more balanced and objective way. Many of the achievements of the Consulate began under the Directory. The financial reforms and reorganisation of the tax system started during the Directory contributed to economic recovery (pages 148–9). These helped stimulate industrial and agricultural expansion that would develop much more fully in the Napoleonic era. Changes in administration within the departments preceded the roles later taken by **prefects**. Although its collapse was sudden, the Directory's achievements should not be dismissed as insignificant.

4 | The Key Debate

It is possible to dismiss the period of Thermidor and the Directory as being of little importance in the history of the French Revolution. It is considered to have lacked the idealism and spirit that drove the great reforms that re-shaped the nation. A central issue that concerns historians is:

Did the Thermidorians and the Directory make any real contribution to the Revolution?

Key terms

Consulate
The system of government that replaced the Directory. It took its name from the three Consuls of whom Napoleon was the most important as first Consul. They formed the executive in the new constitution of 1799.

Prefect
Centrally appointed government official whose task was to administer a department and ensure government policy was carried out.

Key question
Did the Directory have any achievements?

Summary diagram: Why was the Directory overthrown?

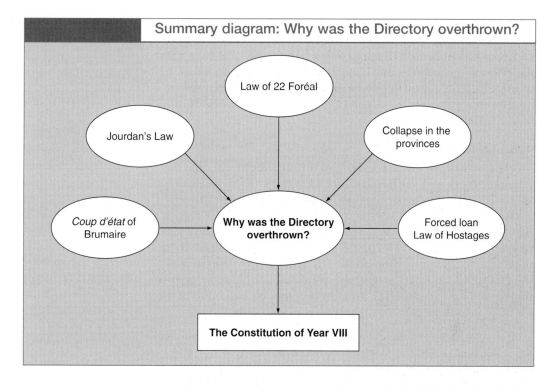

Peter Taaffe

Peter Taaffe (1989), as a Marxist writer, focuses on how the Thermidorians and the Directory sought to restore the controlling influence of the bourgeoisie over the Revolution, which had been lost during the Terror to the *sans-culottes*. It was during this period, Taaffe argues, that the bourgeoisie 'garnered [collected] the fruits of the Revolution'. The contribution of what he considers to be a corrupt regime was essentially a negative one: the suppression of the Conspiracy of Equals and the Vendémiaire uprising helped pave the way for a military dictatorship under Napoleon.

William Doyle

Doyle, Professor of History at the University of Bristol, writing in 1989, stresses the enormous economic problems that confronted the Thermidorians and the Directory. Alongside this was their need to maintain a balance between the far left and the far right. While noting that the dramatic solution to the economic crisis did restore the nation's finances, he emphasises the mistakes made in foreign affairs. As far as contributing to the Revolution the 'arrogance' of the regime undermined any real achievements within their grasp. Officials and soldiers during the Directory considered themselves superior to all others and entitled 'to behave according to their own rules'.

D.M.G. Sutherland

In Professor Sutherland's view (1985) the Directory did have a number of undoubted successes. These were the repression of the

Vendeans and Chouans and the Treaty of Campio Formio, which contributed to the survival of the Republic. Yet he believed these successes lacked finality. The measures taken to try and cope with the financial chaos in reality alienated the notables who it was trying to attract. According to Sutherland, the Directory fully justifies its reputation '... as one of the most chaotic periods in modern French history'.

Peter McPhee

McPhee, writing in 2002, like Sutherland, highlights the way the religious, economic, military and social policies of the Directory alienated large numbers of people. Popular response to this 'bourgeois republic' was hostile in tone. Yet McPhee does suggest that in the midst of all this upheaval the resilience of ordinary people shone through. He argues that this is clearly visible where the Catholic Church is concerned. The Directory contributed to the emergence of what he describes as a 'new Catholicism' deeply rooted in local communities. Women become the backbone of this Catholic revival, largely through bravely ignoring the hostile religious policies of the Republic.

Denis Wornoff

Wornoff (1972) believes that the achievements of the Directory were not insignificant. In spite of the political failings of its final years it was able to preserve the bourgeois revolution. He argues that it took up once again the aims of the Constituent Assembly in wanting to complete the process of reconstructing France. That they failed was due to a combination of circumstances and their own weaknesses.

Some key books in the debate

William Doyle, *The Oxford History of the French Revolution* (Oxford University Press, 1989).
Martin Lyons, *France Under the Directory* (Cambridge University Press, 1975).
Peter McPhee, *The French Revolution 1789–1799* (Oxford University Press, 2002).
D.M.G. Sutherland, *France 1789–1815 Revolution and Counter-revolution* (Fontana, 1985).
Peter Taaffe, *The Masses Arise: The Great French Revolution 1789–1815* (Fortress Books, 1989).
Denis Wornoff, *The Thermidorian Regime and the Directory 1794–1799* (Cambridge University Press, 1984).

Study Guide: AS Questions

In the style of AQA

(a) Explain why the popular risings of Germinal and Prairial 1795 failed. (12 marks)

(b) How important was the role of Napoleon in bringing about the overthrow of the Directory? (24 marks)

Exam tips

The cross-references are intended to take you straight to the material that will help you to answer the questions.

(a) Re-read pages 138–9. You need to produce a range of reasons to explain the failure of these risings, but before beginning to write you should assess the relative importance of these reasons so that you show some prioritisation and linkage between your ideas. Lack of support from the Montagnards; division within the ranks of the demonstrators; lack of leadership; inexperience and the failure of the bourgeoisie to offer support; might be cited as reasons for their weakness. However, it would be important to stress the strength of the Convention which was defended by the National Guards in April and the army in May.

(b) You will need to balance the actions of Napoleon against other factors that helped bring the downfall of the Directory in order to provide a balanced judgement. You should include:

- the loss of support for the Directory from various key supporters, notably the bourgeoisie
- Napoleon's own involvement as a compliant general who undertook repression for the Directory; suggest what he brought to the plot (pages 143–4)
- the role of Sieyès; evaluate whether he was more or less important than Napoleon
- disillusionment among the bourgeoisie at the Directory's increasing tendency to act in an undemocratic way.

In the style of OCR B

Answer **both** parts of the question.

(a) How is the Thermidorian reaction best explained?
[Explaining ideas, attitudes and beliefs.]   (25 marks)
(b) What was it about the defeat of the Prairial that made it so
significant in the course of the Revolution to 1795?
[Explaining events and circumstances.]   (25 marks)

Exam tips

Re-read the General introduction at the start of the study guide to
Chapter 1, page 24.

(a) The prompt guides you to begin your explanation in the
empathetic, starting perhaps with consideration of attitudes
among key groups as well as the wider mood of France in July
1794; the deputies of the Plain took control so their thinking
would be particularly significant in this context. You can then
shift to either a causal or intentional explanation before switching
over to the other. Given the wording of the question ('How ...
best explained?'), you need to develop a hierarchy of
explanations, worked out by assessing their relative importance.
Note also that this question is not the same one as **(b)** in
Chapter 5 but worded differently, the question here is not
focused on 1794, let alone on the overthrow of Robespierre. It is
concerned with the period 1794–5: the lifetime of the
Thermidorian reaction and why so many people wanted it.
  Don't describe what happened during the reaction. Stick to
examining and explaining the reasons for what took place. To what
extent was the reaction a move to preserve the Revolution against
the threat of monarchists on one side and the *sans-culottes* on the
other? Don't just consider the negatives: the significance of the
abolition of the Revolutionary Tribunal and the Law of Prairial.
Think equally about the purpose of the new Constitution of the
Year III, and what the religious policies of the Thermidorians tell us
about the reasons for and the thinking behind the reaction.

(b) The prompt reminds you to begin your explanation in either the
causal or the intentional mode and then switch to the other. This
question takes a very specific approach. You are asked to
consider patterns: the failure of one event in the broad
perspective of the first seven years of the Revolution: so keep
your answer focused firmly on that (*not* the Prairial itself). To
answer well you might explain first what the defeat of the Prairial
represented in the context of 1794–5 (the end of the Terror and
the Thermidorian reaction) and then develop your explanation by
broadening your assessment of its meaning to the complete
context of 1789–95. That way you will concern yourself with the
overview required and be able to determine whether the defeat
was only a change in the course of events or whether it marked
a development, an alteration with some sort of longer-term
significance.

The Prairial was not the only large popular uprising of the Revolution. Neither was it the only armed rising nor the only time the regular army was used against citizens. So ask yourself who was defeated and what was defeated in May 1795. The answers to those questions will give you important lines of thought that you can then develop. What is important about the defeat of the Prairial in the context of the Revolution is that that defeat destroyed both the political and military power of the *sans-culottes*. Workers played no further political role in the Revolution. In turn, this collapse ended the radical phase of the Revolution. Looking to the future, crushing the Prairial had another significance: it marked the start of the dependence of revolutionary politicians on the power of the army (a dependency that ended up with Napoleon Bonaparte). A moment of distinct discontinuity in the course of the Revolution, the defeat of the Prairial marked a key development in the course of the Revolution.

Study Guide: Advanced Level Question

In the style of Edexcel

'A period marked by remarkably little achievement in domestic affairs.' How far do you agree with this assessment of the government of France under the Directory 1795–9?   (30 marks)

Exam tips

The cross-references are intended to take you straight to the material that will help you to answer the question.

Before planning your answer to this question, read the Key debate (pages 160–2). It is clear that historians are divided on this issue, and the material in the section will give you scope to work up a balanced argument. You should be clear as you plan what you are going to count as achievement. Note that the question says 'remarkably little achievement' and this will enable you to argue that, given the financial crisis the Directory faced in 1795, and given the instability of the previous years, what achievements there were deserve more recognition (page 160). For example, maintaining a period of relatively settled government in spite of the weakness of the constitution (page 159) and instituting financial reform.

  The Directory's success in stabilising finances, instituting a long-lasting reform of direct taxation, improving tax collection and balancing the budget (pages 148–9) should not be underestimated especially in the light of the scale of the problems it faced (page 148). However, the limitations of its achievements in other areas, its unpopularity and abrupt overthrow (page 159) allow you to construct an argument.

7

The Impact of the Revolution

POINTS TO CONSIDER

This chapter provides you with an overview of the impact the French Revolution had on a number of key areas. These are:

- The dismantling of the *ancien régime*
- The economy
- The French army and warfare
- The territorial impact
- The ideological impact

Key dates

1790	June 19	Abolition of the nobility
	July 12	Civil Constitution of the Clergy
	November 1	Publication of *Reflections on the Revolution in France*
1791	June 14	Le Chapelier Law
	August 14	Slave revolt in Saint-Domingue
1792	August 10	Overthrow of the monarchy
1793	February 21	Convention accepts the *amalgame*
1796	March–May	Conspiracy of Equals
1802	April 18	The Concordat
1814	April 6	Restoration of the Bourbon Monarchy

1 | The Dismantling of the *Ancien Régime*

Most of the *cahiers* in 1789 were moderate and none suggested the abolition of the monarchy. Yet within a short time, beginning with the August Decrees and the Declaration of Rights, fundamental changes had taken place that swept away most of the institutions of the *ancien régime* and ultimately the monarchy itself. This prompted the American historian G.V. Taylor to comment that it was not the revolutionaries who made the Revolution but the Revolution that made the revolutionaries, as they became more confident and ambitious in their plans with each measure that was passed.

The most famous of the abandoned institutions was the Bourbon Monarchy, which was overthrown on 10 August 1792. However, this did not prove to be permanent, as the Bourbons

Key question
How radical were the changes created by the Revolution?

Key dates

Overthrow of the Monarchy: 10 August 1792

Restoration of the Bourbon Monarchy: 6 April 1814

were restored on 6 April 1814. The restored monarchy was in many ways different from that of 1789 in that its powers were limited by an elected assembly that had the right to pass laws. Assemblies during the Revolution were hardly democratic as, after the primary assemblies, voting was confined to a small minority of property-holders. An elected legislature, however, was to be one of the permanent changes brought about by the Revolution.

The reforms introduced by the Constituent Assembly (see pages 51–62) were to prove the most radical and the most lasting of the Revolution. The France of the *ancien régime* was dismembered and then reconstructed according to new principles. Most of the institutions of the old regime were abolished, never to return:

- the legal distinction between Estates disappeared
- the privileges of nobles, Church and *pays d'états* were ended
- the nobility was abolished (19 June 1790) although it returned under Napoleon
- *généralités*, *intendants*, the old courts of law and the 13 *parlements* were swept away
- the entire financial structure of the *ancien régime* was abandoned: direct taxes (the *taille*, capitation and *vingtième*); the Farmers-General; indirect taxes such as the *gabelle* and *aides*; internal customs; venal offices; the guilds and corporations all came to an end, along with other restrictive practices
- the Church was drastically transformed by the Civil Constitution of the Clergy – losing the tithe and its lands
- the sale of the *biens nationaux* was the greatest change in land ownership in France for centuries: a tenth of the land came on to the market at one time.

What replaced all that had been destroyed?

- The administrative structure of modern France with its departments, districts and communes.
- New regular courts of law for both criminal and civil cases.
- A centralised treasury with the power to tax everybody.
- The standardisation of weights and measures through metrication.
- Careers became open to talent in the bureaucracy, the army and the Church.

The three Estates of the *ancien régime* were also affected by the Revolution, though the extent to which they suffered or benefited is a matter for debate amongst historians. All this – both the destructive and constructive work – was largely achieved in two years and was to be lasting. It was a remarkable achievement.

Key question
What was the impact of the Revolution on the Church?

The Church

The Church suffered enormously during the Revolution. At an early stage it lost most of its wealth: its income from the tithe, its lands and its financial privileges, none of which were ever recovered. Later its monopoly of education was removed, as was its control of poor relief and hospitals. The clergy, in effect, became civil servants, as they were paid by the State. Many were

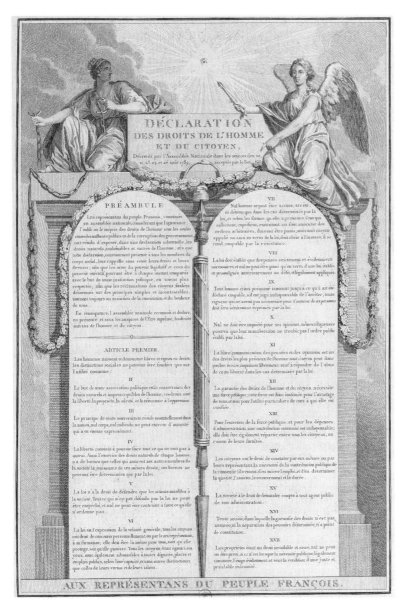

Poster showing the Declaration of the Rights of Man and the Citizen; August 1789. What do you think the government hoped to achieve by displaying the Declaration in this form throughout France?

better off, as they received higher salaries from the government than they had received from the Church. Yet the Civil Constitution of the Clergy, which was passed on 12 July 1790, produced a deep division within the Church (see pages 58–60). Those who did not accept it (about half the clergy) were persecuted as counter-revolutionaries. Over 200 were killed in the September Massacres in 1792 and over 900 became official victims of the Terror. About 25,000 (a sixth of the clergy) emigrated or were deported. Many parishes were without a priest and, during the dechristianisation campaign of Year II, most churches were closed. Even the constitutional clergy were abandoned, when the government refused to pay any clerical salaries in 1794.

In those areas where the majority of the clergy had taken the constitutional oath the result was a lowering of esteem for religion that lasted well into the nineteenth century. Many devout

Key date

Civil Constitution of the Clergy passed by the National Assembly: 12 July 1790

Catholics considered that the constitutional clergy were wrong to defy the Pope. The State was separated from the Church and was to remain so until Napoleon's Concordat with the Pope was agreed on 18 April 1802 (pages 197–8). Although the Concordat went some way to repairing and healing the divisions, in reality the relations between Church and State for most of the nineteenth century were embittered.

The nobility

Key question
How did the Revolution affect the French nobility?

Key dates

The Concordat negotiated by Napoleon restores relations between the French state and the Catholic Church: 18 April 1802

The abolition of the nobility: 19 June 1790

Nobles were amongst the early leaders of the Revolution but withdrew from participation in public affairs after 1792. It has traditionally been viewed that as individuals they were among the greatest losers from the Revolution. They lost their feudal dues and this in some areas could amount to 60 per cent of their income. 'We never recovered', wrote the Marquis de la Tour du Pin, 'from the blow to our fortune delivered on that night' (4 August 1789). They also lost their financial privileges and consequently paid more in taxation. The *vingtième* and capitation usually took about five per cent of their income: the new land tax on average took 16 per cent. They lost their venal offices, their domination of high offices in the army, Church and State and even their right to bequeath their estates undivided to their oldest son (inheritances had to be divided equally amongst sons).

On 19 June 1790 the nobility was abolished and the use of all titles was forbidden. From the beginning of the Revolution, nobles had been leaving France, and eventually at least 16,500 went abroad (seven to eight per cent of all nobles). The property of those who emigrated was confiscated and this affected between a quarter and a half of all noble land. About 1200 nobles were executed during the Terror and many were imprisoned for months as suspects. Nobles appear to have been the principal victims of the Revolution: many lost their lands and some lost their heads.

In recent years, the trend has been to revise and modify this traditional picture. It is now generally accepted that nobles who stayed in France were not extensively persecuted during the Terror. The majority retained their lands and did not lose their position of economic dominance. Napoleon's tax-lists show that nobles were still amongst the wealthiest people in France. For example, of the 30 biggest taxpayers on the Lozère in 1811, 26 were nobles. Under Napoleon many *émigré* nobles returned to France and began to buy back their lands. For example, in the Sarthe, nobles had lost 100,000 acres but had recovered them all by 1830.

Though precise statistics are not available for the whole of France, nobles overall may have recovered a quarter of the land they had lost. Members of the ruling political élite in France both before and after the Revolution were large landowners and high officials, both noble (those with titles) and bourgeois (those without titles) who came to be called **notables**. Owing to the economic disruption caused by the Revolution, they continued to invest in land rather than industry, particularly when so much

Key term

Notables
Rich powerful individuals – the élite who controlled the political and economic life of France.

land came on to the market cheaply through the sale of *biens nationaux*. The Swiss economist and historian Francis d'Ivernois (1757–1842) asked what Frenchman was mad enough:

> To risk his fortune in a business enterprise, or in competition with foreign manufacturers? He would have to be satisfied with a profit of ten, or at most twelve per cent, while the State offers him the possibility of realising a return of thirty, forty or even fifty per cent, if he places his money in one of the confiscated estates.

This group of notables governed France up to 1880 at least, and in this sense the *ancien régime* continued well into the nineteenth century.

The bourgeoisie

Since 1900 the dominant interpretation of the French Revolution has been the Marxist interpretation, although this was challenged during the second half of the twentieth century. This was most clearly expressed nearly 60 years ago by Georges Lefebvre, and later by his disciple Albert Soboul. Lefebvre regarded the French Revolution as a bourgeois revolution. The commercial and industrial bourgeoisie had been growing in importance in the eighteenth century and had become stronger economically than the nobility. However, their economic strength was not reflected in their position in society. They were kept out of positions of power by the privileged nobility and they resented their inferior position. Therefore, a class struggle developed between the rising bourgeoisie and the declining aristocracy, whose poorer members desperately clung to their privileges. The bourgeoisie were able to triumph in this struggle because the monarchy became bankrupt, and needed the financial support for which the price was a role in governing the country.

According to the Marxists, therefore, the French Revolution was a bourgeois revolution. Albert Soboul maintained that 'The French Revolution constitutes the crowning achievement of a long economic and social evolution that made the bourgeoisie the master of the world'. He argued that businessmen and **entrepreneurs** assumed the dominant role hitherto occupied by inherited wealth, mainly landowners. These men, with their willingness to take risks and their spirit of initiative, invested their capital in business ventures. In this way they contributed to the emergence of **industrial capitalism** in France.

Responses to the Marxist interpretation

The Marxist interpretation has been challenged by a number of British and American historians. They point out that the bourgeoisie continued to invest in land rather than industry, just as they had done before the Revolution. There were few representatives of trade, finance or industry in the elected assemblies: 85 out of 648 deputies in the Constituent Assembly, 83 out of 749 in the Convention. Small in numbers, they did not take the lead in political affairs. There is no doubt that laws were

Key question
How do Marxist historians view the role of the bourgeoisie in the French Revolution?

Key terms

Entrepreneurs
Individuals prepared to take risks with their capital to support business schemes which will secure high levels of profit.

Industrial capitalism
An economic system where money (capital) is invested in industry for the purpose of making a profit (the money which remains after all production costs have been met).

Key question
On what basis has the Marxist interpretation been challenged?

passed which could eventually benefit the industrialist – for example, the abolition of internal customs barriers, guilds and price controls, the prohibition of workers' associations and the introduction of a uniform system of weights and measures.

Yet it was difficult to take advantage of these new laws until transport improved sufficiently to create a national market and this had to wait for the expansion of the railways during the 1850s. Most merchants and manufacturers were worse off in 1799 than they had been in 1789. The French Revolution was not, therefore, either in its origins or its development, carried out by the mercantile and industrial bourgeoisie.

Gaining advantage from the Revolution

Key question
Why were the bourgeoisie able to prosper during the Revolution?

Over the course of the French Revolution the bourgeoisie were its main beneficiaries and provided all its leaders after 1791 (Danton, Marat, Robespierre, Carnot). Many of the reforms of the Constituent Assembly were supposed to apply to all citizens equally but only the bourgeoisie could take full advantage of them. Workers and peasants benefited little when careers became open to talent, as they were not educated. When the *biens* were put up for sale they were sold in large lots and this, too, benefited the middle classes, as it was easier for them to raise the money than it was for the peasants. By 1799 they owned between 30 and 40 per cent of French land.

The voting system also favoured the bourgeoisie, as it was limited to property owners. Consequently, nearly all the members of the various assemblies were bourgeois, as were all the ministers. Most of the revolutionary bourgeoisie were lawyers. There were 166 of them in the Constituent Assembly, and another 278 members were public officials, most of whom had a legal training. In the Convention there were 241 lawyers and 227 officials.

Lawyers were among the most prominent beneficiaries from the Revolution, as they had the training to take advantage of careers open to talent. Many were elected to new local and national offices, which paid well. The central administration employed less than 700 officials in the 1780s but by 1794, owing to the war, this number had risen to 6000. Although the bourgeoisie had always filled the lower and middle ranks of the judiciary and the administration, with the Revolution they also took over the highest posts, which previously had all been held by nobles. Their dominance of the administration was to continue throughout the nineteenth century.

However, there were many of the bourgeoisie who did not benefit from the Revolution, such as merchants of the Atlantic ports, manufacturers of luxury goods, and *rentiers*, who were paid in ultimately worthless *assignats*. In 1797 *rentiers* lost most of their investments in Ramel's 'bankruptcy of the two-thirds' (see page 148). Nevertheless, most of the bourgeoisie did well out of the Revolution and would accept only those regimes which promised to maintain their gains.

The peasantry

It is almost impossible to divide peasants into separate categories: landowners, tenant farmers, sharecroppers and labourers. Although there were usually some of each category in the villages, most peasants did not fall into any one group. The majority held some of their land freehold, rented other parts and from time to time sold their labour.

The impact of the Revolution on the peasantry was a mixture of gains and losses.

Losses

On the negative side:

- Income was lost when a depression in textile manufacturing damaged **cottage industry**.
- In many areas rents rose by as much as a quarter, when landlords were allowed to add the value of the abolished tithe to their rents.
- Conscription into military service, in 1793 and again in 1798, meant labour was lost on many holdings.
- Dechristianisation in 1793–4, which in many parts of France resulted in the Catholic Church being persecuted. Many peasants were deeply attached to the Church.
- Peasants who produced for the market were badly affected by the Maximum on the price of grain in the Year II (see page 116) and by the grain requisitions to feed the towns and the army.

The result of all these measures was a widespread, popular resistance movement, which in the Vendée flared into open revolt. In Brittany and Normandy, where the abolition of feudalism produced few benefits as most peasants rented their land, there were the pro-royalist rebels – the *chouannerie*. In the south, too, there was widespread opposition, as the Revolution seemed to benefit the rich Protestants of towns like Nîmes rather than the local Catholics. In some areas this opposition was caught up in royalist counter-revolution but peasants generally did not wish to see a return to the *ancien régime*, which might bring with it a restoration of feudal dues. Their opposition was therefore anti-revolutionary rather than counter-revolutionary. They wanted stability, their old way of life and the exclusion of 'foreigners' (officials from Paris or from outside their own district) from their affairs, rather than a restoration of the Bourbon monarchy in all its glory. Resistance produced repression and executions – nearly 60 per cent of the official victims of the Terror were peasants or workers and many more were killed when the army devastated the Vendée.

Gains

Yet most peasants benefited in one way or another from the Revolution:

Key question
To what extent did the French peasantry benefit as a consequence of the Revolution?

Cottage industry Small-scale textile production (spinning, weaving and iron work) carried out in a peasant's cottage or workshop and used to supplement income from farming.

Key term

- All gained initially from the abolition of indirect taxes and their total tax burden was reduced.
- Those who owned land benefited from the abolition of feudal dues and the tithe.
- In the north and east, where the Church owned much land, peasants were able to buy some of the *biens*, though it was usually the richer peasants who were able to do this. In the south-west even share-croppers bought *biens* and became supporters of the Revolution.
- Peasants also gained from inflation, which grew steadily between 1792 and 1797. They were able to pay off their debts with depreciating *assignats* and tenants were able to buy their land.
- Judicial and local government reforms were to the advantage of all the peasants. The abolition of seigneurial justice was a great benefit, as it was replaced by a much fairer system. The Justice of the Peace in each canton provided cheap and impartial justice.
- The right of self-government granted to local authorities favoured the peasants too, especially at the municipal level, where councils were elected and filled by peasants. Over a million people took part in these councils in 1790 and many more later. In the north and east most of these were rich peasants, though in Poitou poorer peasants, tenant farmers and share-croppers took control. Peasants looked on municipal self-government as one of their greatest gains from the Revolution. Both the self-governing commune and Justices of the Peace survived to play important roles in the nineteenth century.

Wages

The poor peasants, the landless day-labourers and share-croppers are usually regarded as among the greatest losers from the Revolution. They did not benefit from the abolition of feudal dues and they were hit hard by the inflation from 1792 to 1797, as wages failed to rise as quickly as prices. Many relied on cottage industry for survival and when the market for this collapsed, they became destitute. However, not all was loss. They did gain from the abolition of indirect taxes. From 1797 to 1799 they gained from deflation, so that by 1799 their **real wages** were higher than they had been in 1789.

The Revolution, therefore, affected the peasants in different ways but for most (as for most bourgeoisie) their gains outweighed their losses, especially for those who owned land. Peter Jones, who has researched the peasantry, concludes that: 'Those who managed to survive the dearths of the Revolution and the terrible famine of 1795, experienced a real improvement in purchasing power; the first such improvement in several generations'.

Key term
Real wages
The actual purchasing power of money.

Key question
Were workers better off as a result of the Revolution?

Urban workers

The *sans-culottes* had welcomed the Revolution and had done a great deal to ensure that it was successful. They were to be bitterly disappointed by the first fruits of the Revolution. Many became unemployed as the *parlements* were closed and nobles emigrated. The Le Chapelier Law of 14 June 1791, while opening up many trades restricted by guilds, did, on the other hand, place severe restrictions on workers' rights to organise in defence of their livelihoods. In 1793, the CPS gave in to many of their demands, such as a maximum price on bread. However, the bourgeois revolutionary leaders were not prepared in the long run to grant most of what they wanted. The urban workers disliked a free-market economy, yet this was imposed on them in 1794, with the result that prices rose dramatically. The bad harvest and harsh winter of 1794–5 reduced them to despair and contributed to the risings of Germinal and Prairial (pages 138–9), which were crushed by the government.

Following the risings of Germinal and Prairial, workers played no further political role in the Revolution. Their economic fortunes continued to decline in 1797, owing to the inflation caused by the fall of the *assignats*. Wages rose but much more slowly than prices. There was, however, a revival in the last years of the Directory from 1797 to 1799, when deflation ensured that real wages were higher than they had been for a very long time. These were also years of good harvests, when the price of bread dropped to two *sous* a pound (it had been 14 *sous* in July 1789).

The poor

The poor suffered more than most during the Revolution. In normal times about a quarter of the population of big cities relied on poor relief. This number increased with the rise in unemployment, yet at the same time their means of obtaining relief were disappearing. The main source of help for the poor had been the Church, which had paid for this out of income from the tithe. When the tithe was abolished and Church lands were nationalised, the Church could no longer pay for aid to the poor. If the poor were ill they had been cared for in hospitals provided by the Church and these were closed because of the Church's loss of income. The Constitution of 1793 said that all citizens had a right to public support but revolutionary governments were always short of money and nothing was done. As late as 1847 the number of hospitals in France was 42 per cent lower than in 1789, though the population was seven million more.

The result of the decline in the Church's role in providing poor relief and hospitals was that the poor were unable to cope with the economic crisis of 1794–5, when a bad harvest was followed by a harsh winter. Many died, either from starvation or from diseases, which the undernourished could not fight off. In Rouen the **mortality rate** doubled in 1795–6 and trebled the year after. There was also a marked rise in the number of suicides. The poor responded in the only ways they knew, by taking direct action. Some joined bands of brigands, which were to be found in many parts of France in the last years of the Directory.

Key date
Introduction of the Le Chapelier Law, which prohibited strikes and the formation of trade unions and abolished guilds: 14 June 1791

Key question
How did anti-Church policies affect the poor?

Key term
Mortality rate
The death rate, which is measured per 1000 of the population.

Summary diagram: The dismantling of the *ancien régime*

Impact on society
Who gained and who lost?

Winners? ←————————————————————————→ Losers?

| Bourgeoisie | Peasantry | Workers | Nobility | Poor | Catholic Church | Monarchy |

Key question
How did the war affect French trade?

Key date
A slave revolt breaks out in the rich French colony of Saint-Domingue in the Caribbean: 14 August 1791

Key term
Gross domestic product
The total value of goods and services produced by an economy.

2 | The Economy

Marxist historians believed that by getting rid of feudalism, ending the monopolies of the guilds and unifying the national market, the Revolution, in Soboul's words, 'marked a decisive stage in the transition from feudalism to capitalism'. Not all historians agree with this interpretation. Alfred Cobban in particular rejects this view and contends that the Revolution was '… not for but against capitalism'. Non-Marxist historians opposed to the interpretation argue that the Revolution restricted, rather than promoted, the development of capitalism in France and that it was an economic disaster.

The most rapidly expanding sector of the French economy up to 1791 was overseas trade. On 14 August 1791, a slave revolt broke out on the West Indian island of Saint-Domingue, which provided three-quarters of France's colonial trade. This was followed in 1793 by war with Britain, and the blockade of the French coast by the Royal Navy. Prosperous Atlantic seaports such as Bordeaux and Nantes suffered severely from the naval blockade imposed by Britain, as did the industries in the hinterland – sugar refineries, linen and tobacco manufacturers – which had depended on imported raw materials. In 1797 France had only 200 ocean-going vessels, a tenth of the number of 1789. French exports fell by 50 per cent in the 1790s. Foreign trade had accounted for 25 per cent of France's **gross domestic product** in 1789: by 1796 it was down to nine per cent.

War had a varied effect on French industries. Some benefited and expanded while others declined. Among those industries and sectors which benefited were:

- Iron and coal industries that expanded to meet the demand for military equipment – cannon and arms.
- The textile industry grew to meet the army's demand for uniforms and tents.
- The cotton industry gained most of all. It had been virtually ruined by English competition but with the war and French conquests it revived. English goods were kept out of territories

under French control, so that French cotton production increased four-fold between the 1780s and 1810. This, however, was a short-term gain and could not be sustained. Once the war was over in 1815 cotton was hit again by British competition and some of the largest French manufacturers went bankrupt.

- During the war there was a shift in the location of industries from along the Atlantic coast which was being blockaded by the British navy towards the Rhine. This favoured cities such as Strasbourg, which grew rich on the continental transit trade.

But other areas and industries did not do as well:

- Supplies of imported raw materials were disrupted by the war.
- Many foreign markets were lost because the Atlantic ports were blockaded by Britain.
- The linen industry in Brittany (which had exported to the West Indies and South America) saw production fall by a third, while industrial production at Marseille decreased by three-quarters.

By 1799 industrial production in France had fallen overall to two-thirds of its pre-war level. When paper money was withdrawn in 1797 industry faced other problems. There was a shortage of cash, interest rates were high and agricultural prices (and therefore the peasant market for industrial goods) collapsed.

Agriculture stagnated during the Revolution. Production kept pace with population growth but this was done by bringing more land into cultivation rather than by improving productivity, which did not rise until the 1840s. Yields remained low and old-fashioned techniques continued. Oxen were still used for pulling wooden (not metal) ploughs and the harvest was cut with sickles rather than scythes. Most peasants produced for subsistence only and plots remained small, especially when on his death, by law, a peasant's land was divided up equally amongst his sons.

Impact of the Revolution on the French economy

The Revolution held up the development of the French economy, which grew only slowly until the 1840s. **Per capita** agricultural production fell during the period with a veritable collapse occurring between 1792 and 1795. It was only by the end of the Napoleonic Empire in 1814 that French agriculture recovered to its 1789 levels, while industrial production in 1800 was still below its 1789 level.

Although France had fallen behind Britain industrially by 1789, the gap between them increased even more markedly during the Revolution. Wartime disruption and dislocation in France undoubtedly contributed towards this. The death of between 1.5 and 2 million people also had a profound affect on the economy by reducing the market and the labour force. It was not until the coming of the railways in the middle of the nineteenth century that French industrialists could take advantage of a national market. Railways lowered the cost of transport and gave a great boost to the heavy industries of coal, iron and steel. Only then did factory production become the norm. These developments,

Key question
How did the Revolution affect the French economy?

Per capita
An economic measure used to determine output, calculated by dividing the volume or value of production by the number in the population.

Key term

which occurred largely between 1830 and 1870, brought the economic *ancien régime* to an end, something the Revolution had failed to do.

3 | The French Army and Warfare

Key question
What impact did the collapse of the *ancien régime* have on the army?

It is possible to identify three areas where the impact of the Revolution was both obvious and significant in relation to the army and warfare.

Expansion and organisation of the army

Key date
The Convention accepts the *amalgame* – the merger of regular soldiers and volunteers: 21 February 1793

In 1789 the royal army was very unrepresentative of the nation. Over 90 per cent of its officers were noblemen (who comprised between 0.5 to 1.5 per cent of the population). The majority of recruits were drawn from urban areas, only a quarter were peasants (as opposed to 80 per cent of the population). The army was also disproportionately young – over half were under 25.

As the Revolution progressed, its loyalty to the Crown declined, most notably following the flight to Varennes (see page 65). Alongside the **regular army**, there emerged a new force – the National Guard. It came to symbolise the Revolution and the growing power of the bourgeoisie. On 21 February 1793 these two forces amalgamated – regular soldiers and volunteers.

Key terms

Regular army
The term used to describe the full time professional army. As events unfolded the white uniforms of the *ancien régime* were replaced by ones that reflected the colours of the Revolution: red, white and blue.

Non-Commissioned Officers (NCOs)
Soldiers with ranks such as corporal or sergeant.

When revolutionary enthusiasm was married to professional military standards a very powerful and effective force was created. Against the challenge of external enemies, the call to arms was answered by hundreds of thousands of young Frenchmen. Initially numbers of volunteers greatly exceeded expectations. By the winter of 1792 France had over 450,000 men in arms, a figure that would rise to over 750,000 by the summer of 1794. Although these figures fluctuated, largely through desertions, the sheer size of the military force was both impressive and intimidating.

The army and French society

Not only did the army increase in size, but its very nature changed as a result of the Revolution. The army came to symbolise the beliefs and values of the Revolution. In defending the Republic it was elevated in status and esteem in the eyes of the public, and assumed an influential role in society. It clearly adopted the principle of careers open to talent. Rapid and well-rewarded promotion for recruits from even the humblest of social backgrounds was an attractive possibility for ambitious career-orientated young men. If class was no longer a barrier to promotion, then neither was age. Joubert, Jourdan and Soult were all generals by the age of 30. Many an ordinary soldier would aspire to hold a field-marshal's baton, even if few would ever attain it. Almost a quarter of the generals promoted during the Revolution had been **Non-Commissioned Officers**. There was no better role model than Bonaparte himself, who rose rapidly up the ranks through talent and ability.

Successive waves of recruits, particularly the politically active *sans-culottes* from Paris and other cities, brought with them a passionate commitment to the cause and principles of 1789, and a willingness to die for *la patrie* (the fatherland). The representatives-on-mission had considerable powers to enforce the political beliefs of the Republic. A military force, enthused with revolutionary zeal, allied to a belief in the justice of its cause and bound together in the defence of its nation, had not been seen in Europe in almost two centuries. Within France the success and achievements of the army were genuinely popular with most people.

Military tactics, strategy and organisation

New methods were adopted to organise the army during the revolutionary war. In previous wars, French infantry marched into battle in line formation that enabled them to concentrate their fire on enemy positions. In 1791 new regulations were laid down on how the French army was to be deployed. Infantry could approach the battle in column, then deploy into a line to fire, and then re-form back into a column without a great loss of time and momentum. These columns subsequently developed into attack columns whose key features were shock and mobility. The use of the numerically inferior attack columns did have one important limitation – although it gave commanders much greater mobility in the field it lacked the concentrated firepower of the line. To try to compensate for this, horse artillery was introduced in 1791–2 to support them.

A new tactic, which French armies developed to great effectiveness to support the attack columns, was the use of light infantry. Light infantry were highly mobile troops, deployed in patrolling and raiding – tactics known as **skirmishing**. These soldiers needed to be loyal, self-reliant and able to operate with a measure of independence. The high level of commitment and morale within the army, particularly among the infantry, allowed officers to disperse their soldiers for operational purposes into small groups. For organisational purposes the army was divided into *ordinaires*, small groups of 14 to 16 men who lived and fought together under the command of a corporal. These operated very effectively but the tactic was only possible because of good discipline and a high level of motivation and morale among the men.

4 | The Territorial Impact of the Revolution

The French Revolution and the Revolutionary War changed the map of Europe. During the Revolutionary War (1792–1801) France annexed large amounts of territory (see map on page 150 and page 152). With the exception of the former papal territory Avignon, all these territories were lost in 1815. Among the permanent changes resulting from the Revolutionary Wars were:

- in Italy, the city states of Genoa and Venice never recovered an independent existence
- Austria lost Belgium (previously known as the Austrian Netherlands)

Key question
What developments in military organisation and tactics were introduced during the Revolution?

Skirmishing
A small group of soldiers who operate independently, fighting minor engagements and living off the land.

Key term

Key question
How did the Revolutionary War change the map of Europe?

- the Holy Roman Empire was abolished
- the process of redrawing the map of Germany was begun by amalgamating many small states.

Outside Europe, the Revolutionary Wars enabled Britain to consolidate her Empire at the expense of countries that France coerced into alliances. The most notable example was Holland, one of Britain's most important trading rivals. Britain seized the Dutch colonies of Ceylon (Sri Lanka) and the Cape of Good Hope (South Africa). Both territories were retained by Britain into the twentieth century. As well as being of strategic importance on the route to Australia, Cape Colony provided Britain with the base to expand her Empire into southern Africa, while Ceylon became an important producer of tea and timber.

Key question
What contribution did the Revolution make to political ideas?

5 | The Ideological Impact of the Revolution

The momentous and dramatic events of the period 1789–99 made an enormous impact on France in particular and Europe in general. One of the most influential legacies of the Revolution to future generations was in the field of ideas. The ideological impact of the Revolution long outlasted the structural and territorial changes created by the Republic. There are a number of areas where the ideological impact of the Revolution was significant.

Democratic republicanism

It is arguable that the most important ideological legacy of the Revolution was democratic republicanism. The French Revolution had a profound effect upon the ideas people held and therefore on the policies they pursued. The veteran radical Dr Richard Price remarked that he was thankful to have lived through such an eventful and inspirational period. He hoped that British reformers would also take the initiative. Many British writers such as the poet William Wordsworth and the radical thinker Tom Paine did react positively to the Revolution but they tended to be in a minority. Wherever French armies went in their wake they spread French ideas and methods, as they created republics, established representative government, seized Church lands and abolished privilege. These reforms and structures could be, and often were, reversed when the French withdrew. But ideas could not be eradicated so easily. Among the most influential, important and appealing of these ideas and concepts were:

- the sovereignty of the people
- equality before the law
- freedom from arbitrary arrest
- freedom of speech and association
- careers open to talent.

Conservatism

The violent and bloody birth of the First Republic did alienate many French people and a significant number of Europeans against democratic republicanism. In the eyes of many,

A painted board publicising the unity and indivisibility of the Republic. This board is a good example of the importance the Republic placed on propaganda. Note the revolutionary symbols contained within the image – the *bonnet rouge*, the national guard and the words liberty, equality and fraternity.

republicanism became synonymous with Jacobinism and Terror. The changes that occurred in France were clearly not welcomed by everyone. When so many established institutions, beliefs and practices were attacked – monarchy, religion, privilege – some writers came to their defence and the ideology of conservatism evolved. One of the first writers to mount a sustained attack on the Revolution was Edmund Burke. In his book *Reflections on the Revolution in France*, Burke defended tradition, religious faith and slow change. He argued that violent revolutions produced chaos and ultimately tyranny:

> I do not know under what description to class the present ruling authority in France. It affects to be a pure democracy, though I think it in a direct train of becoming shortly a mischievous and ignoble oligarchy [rule by a minority].

Publication of Burke's book, *Reflections on the Revolution in France*, which was critical of events in France: 1 November 1790

Key date

Burke's ideas inspired among others the Austrian statesman Metternich, who was a central figure in European affairs in the post-1815 period. Rulers who had supported reform in the 1780s now regarded it as dangerous and so there was a conservative reaction that lasted well into the nineteenth century. Conservative ideas were not the only ones produced by the French Revolution.

The definitive reply to Edmund Burke's attack on the Revolution was Thomas Paine's *The Rights of Man*, published in 1791. There were many revolutions during the first half of the nineteenth century, particularly in 1830 (France, Belgium, Italy, parts of Germany and Poland) and 1848 (France, Austria, Italy, Germany), largely because the French provided a model, which others sought to copy. Paine supported the principle of change when he commented:

> Every age and generation must be free to act for itself in all cases as the ages and generations which preceded it. The variety and presumptions of governing beyond the grave is the most ridiculous and insolent of all tyrannies.

Liberalism

The revolutionaries, following their assault on privilege and absolutism, stressed the rights and liberties of individuals. This was clearly outlined in the Declaration of the Rights of Man (see page 42). A number of these principles would, in the mid-nineteenth century, be refined and recast as liberalism. Among the core values of **liberalism** are:

- freedom of thought and conscience on all subjects (including religion) leading to freedom of expression and publication
- freedom of action and taste as long as it involves no harm to others
- freedom of individuals to unite as long as their union does not harm others.

Even within France, however, many of these ideas were ignored in practice during the Revolution – notably during the Terror. They nevertheless contributed to the **revolutionary myth**, which influenced so many people outside France, particularly middle-class liberals. Liberalism in the nineteenth century owed much to the French Revolution. The ethos of republicanism and the new networks of friendships and associations that it inspired was one way in which the Revolution left its mark on politics and political culture. In the longer term the legacy of the revolutionary struggle highlighted the possibilities for others confronted with oppression, particularly in Russia.

Jacobinism – Socialism – Marxism

Jacobinism during the Revolution is equated with revolutionary action in defence of the Republic and the rights of ordinary citizens. The debates in the Jacobin club and the speeches and writings of its principal figures proved influential to future generations of left-wing idealists and revolutionaries. Following

Key terms

Liberalism
A political belief which stresses the rights and liberties of the individual.

Revolutionary myth
The frequently misguided belief that direct revolutionary action can bring about significant material improvement for the majority of society.

Key question
What was the long-term political influence of Jacobinism?

the closure of the Jacobin Club in November 1794, disenchanted idealists who opposed the Thermidorian reaction planned an uprising. Babeuf's Conspiracy of Equals during March–May 1796 (see page 146) clearly failed in its goals yet its core values – universal suffrage, liberating the oppressed, equality for all – helped lay the foundations of one of the nineteenth century's most important political philosophies: socialism. Jacobinism also helped sustain the revolutionary ideal of direct action – the *journées* manning the barricades – a tradition that resurfaced during the French Revolutions of 1830, 1848 and 1871.

In 1848 Karl Marx published the *Communist Manifesto*. Marx owed a large debt to the Jacobin and later French socialists whose theoretical works and ideas revealed the possibilities that opened when committed individuals challenged the status quo. Marx's ideas in turn influenced the Russian revolutionaries. His analysis of economic and social change inspired a whole generation of French historians such as George Lefebvre and Albert Soboul to produce studies based on Marx's ideas. Marx interpreted history as a number of revolutionary phases leading ultimately to an **egalitarian society**. Feudalism would be replaced by bourgeois capitalism, which in turn would be replaced by socialism. For Marxist historians, the French Revolution witnessed the critical stage of the destruction of feudalism and the birth of capitalism.

Nationalism

Nationalism was another powerful force that the French Revolution unleashed. Revolutionary leaders had deliberately set out to create a unified nation, by getting rid of all provincial privileges, internal customs duties and different systems of law. Sovereignty, said the Declaration of Rights, resides in the nation. Symbols such as the *tricolore* (the new national flag of France), the *Marseillaise* and huge national festivals (the first of which was the *Fête de la Fédération* on 14 July 1790 to celebrate the fall of the Bastille), were all used to rouse patriotic fervour. Army life also helped to create loyalty to the nation. Time served in the army was often the first occasion on which peasants had been outside their own locality or had come into contact with the French language (inhabitants of Brittany for example spoke Breton).

However, the success of revolutionary leaders in uniting the nation should not be exaggerated. As late as the Third Republic (1871) peasants in the south and west still had local rather than national loyalties and looked on people from outside their area as unwelcome 'foreigners'. Yet France's success in her wars was often attributed to nationalism and the *élan* of the French soldier. Many outside France were inspired by the right to **national self-determination** that the French proclaimed. In Italy national feeling was aroused, partly by the French example, and in Germany people also began to look to the formation of a united Germany.

One of the great legacies of the French Revolution was the principle of the right to resist oppression, which was enshrined in the Constitution of 1793. Kolokotrones, a Greek bandit and patriot, said that according to his judgement:

Key term

Egalitarian society
Where citizens enjoyed equal rights and are not discriminated against on the basis of gender or social class. This is neatly summed up by the phrase most frequently linked with the Revolution – liberty, equality and fraternity.

Key question
What did the French Revolution do to inspire national identity?

Key terms

Tricolore
The symbol of the Revolution. It combined the red and blue colours of Paris with the white of the Bourbons.

Élan
Patriotic enthusiasm, commitment and identity with the revolutionary cause within the army.

National self-determination
The right of national groups such as Italians, Poles and Germans to govern themselves.

the French Revolution and the doings of Napoleon opened the eyes of the world. The nations knew nothing before and the people thought that kings were gods upon the earth and that they were bound to say that whatever they did was well done. Through this present change it is more difficult to rule the people.

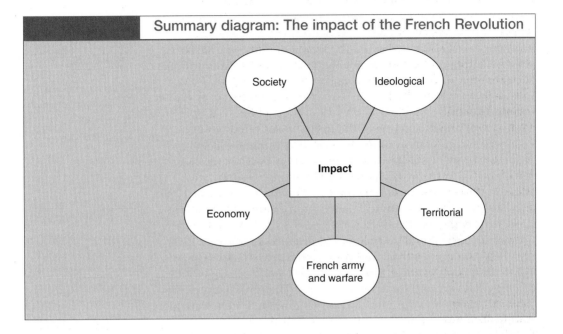

Summary diagram: The impact of the French Revolution

6 | The Key Debate

The relationship between the Revolution and the economy has produced a lively debate among both political and economic historians over the course of the last half-century. Marxist historians have sought to place the economic upheavals endured by France into their own ideological framework for interpreting history. These notions are rejected with equal commitment by other historians. A central question which scholars try and address is:

> What impact did the French Revolution have on the economy?

Jacques Solé
Professor Solé argues, that the Marxist view which calls the Revolution a decisive stage in the development of the capitalist economy and industrial society is easily belied by the stagnation of the French economy as a whole during the revolutionary period and beyond, and is essentially a myth. He believes that the ending of feudalism in France did not lead to rural capitalism.

William Doyle
Doyle suggests that it was the great left-wing historian Jean Jaurès (*Socialist History of the French Revolution*) who emphasised for the

first time the economic and social dimension of the Revolution while adding an element of Marxist analysis into the study. Marx had not written a great deal on the French Revolution, but Doyle believes that it was easy to dovetail a movement that attacked the privileged orders of the first two estates into a theory that emphasised class struggle and the conflict between capitalism and feudalism. For those subscribing to this viewpoint the French Revolution was a key moment in modern history when the capitalist bourgeoisie overthrew the feudal nobility. For Marxists, the Revolution paved the way for the emergence of capitalism in the economic development of France

Florin Aftalion

Professor Aftalion's was one of the first to focus purely on an economic interpretation of the French Revolution. He believes that the history of the Revolution is based on as many myths as facts, notably in the work of Marxist historians. According to Aftalion the decisions taken by the Constituent Assembly in 1789 inevitably led to a deepening financial and economic crisis, and to increasingly radical and disastrous policies. While noting the collapse in agricultural and industrial production between 1792 and 1795, he stresses that the existence of special factors allowed the development of some branches of the French economy such as heavy industry and the cotton industry. The unification of the national market and the introduction of a metric system were also positive benefits.

Simon Schama

Schama stresses the great contrasts that existed in pre-revolutionary France and the enormous disparities of wealth within the country. However, this was not a country with an economy 'doddering its way to the grave'. As Schama so carefully points out there were in economic terms two Frances. One, bolstered by the profits of Colonial trade, was dynamic, energetic, and prosperous. The other, in contrast, was backward, stagnant and deeply traditional. If the Revolution created a highly centralised and militarised economy, it also paved the way to its modernisation.

Some key books in the debate

Florin Aftalion, *The French Revolution: An Economic Interpretation* (Cambridge University Press, 1990).
Alfred Cobban, *The Social Interpretation of the French Revolution* (Cambridge University Press, 1964).
William Doyle, *The French Revolution: A Very Short Introduction* (Oxford University Press, 2001).
Simon Schama, *Citizens: A Chronicle of the French Revolution* (Viking, 1989).
Jacques Solé, *Questions of the French Revolution* (Pantheon Books, 1989).

---

8 Napoleon: Consulate and Empire

POINTS TO CONSIDER

After the *Coup* of Brumaire Napoleon was appointed First Consul. His enormous ambition combined with support from the military and a belief that he was fulfilling the goals of the revolution drove him to seize power for himself. He sought to establish an empire that would challenge the established powers of Europe. During the course of this attempt Europe was plunged into one of the most protracted and bloody conflicts in its history to that date. This chapter will cover four broad themes:

- The Napoleonic system in France
- The establishment of the Napoleonic Empire
- The creation of the Napoleonic Empire in Europe
- The defeat and downfall of the empire

Key dates

1799	November 10	*Coup* of Brumaire
1801	July 15	Signing of the Concordat with the Pope
1802	March 27	Peace of Amiens
1803	May 18	Start of the Napoleonic War
1804	March 21	Civil Code issued
	March 20	Murder of the Duc d'Enghien
	May 18	Napoleon declared Emperor of the French
1805	October 21	Battle of Trafalgar
1808	May 5	Forced abdication of the King of Spain
		Start of Peninsular War
1812	June 22	Napoleon invaded Russia
1815	June 18	Battle of Waterloo

1 | The Napoleonic System in France

The successful conclusion of the *coup* was only the beginning for Napoleon. He had gained political power, but needed to consolidate it if he were to make himself undisputed ruler of France. He began with the constitution.

The constitution of 1799

Late in the evening of 19 Brumaire year VIII (10 November
1799) the three newly elected provisional consuls (Napoleon,
Sieyes and Ducos) swore an oath of allegiance to the Republic.
From their base in the Luxembourg Palace in Paris the consuls set
to work on the new constitution, bypassing the two Standing
Committees that were supposed to draw up the draft plans. In a
series of long and often heated discussions Sieyes' proposed that
Napoleon should occupy the role of a figurehead in the new
constitution. Napoleon refused to countenance the idea. There
must, he argued, be a First Consul as head of state with complete
control, in peace and in war, at home and abroad; and *he* must be
that consul. The roles of the second and third consuls also caused
argument. Sieyes wanted them each to have *voix deliberative* (the
right to one of three equal votes). Napoleon, however, insisted
they should have only *voix consultative* (the right merely to express
an opinion). In all matters his decision would be final. Faced with
Napoleon's domineering personality, Sieyes was eventually forced
into the humiliating position of having to make the official
nomination of Napoleon as First Consul. After six weeks of
negotiations the government of France was transformed from one
where political responsibility was spread as widely as possible to
one where it was centralised in the hands of a single man. All
three consuls would serve initially for 10 years.

In a proclamation, Napoleon explained his reasons for seizing
power: 'To make the Republic loved by its own citizens, respected
abroad and feared by its enemies – such are the duties we have
assumed in accepting the First Consulship' and he added
reassuringly '... that the new constitution was based upon the true
principles of representative government and on the sacred rights
of property, equality and liberty. The powers it sets up will be
strong and lasting.'

The new constitution provided for 'universal suffrage', unlike
the property-based vote of the 1795 constitution, but this suffrage
was so indirect as to be of little significance in relation to the idea
of **popular sovereignty**. The references to a constitution based on
representative government were merely words. Democratic
involvement in the elections was minimal. While there was the
appearance of adult male suffrage, there were no *elections*, only
presentations of candidates suitable for appointment as deputies,
and the choice of candidates was restricted to notables. The
structure of the new constitution is shown in Figure 8.1.

The distribution of power during the Consulate

Power was firmly in the hands of one man (the First Consul), who
stood alone at the top of the political pyramid. The Senate, which
had been intended by Sieyes to act as a brake on the executive,
became under Napoleon's leadership an instrument of his
personal power. It was intended to be the guardian of the existing
constitution, but was also able to amend it by a legal procedure

Key questions
What were the main
features of the new
constitution?

Was the constitution
based on
representative
government?

Coup of Brumaire:
10 November 1799

Key date

Key term

**Popular
sovereignty**
The idea that the
people should
exercise control
over their
government, usually
by directly electing
a representative
assembly.

Key question
How was power
distributed during the
Consulate?

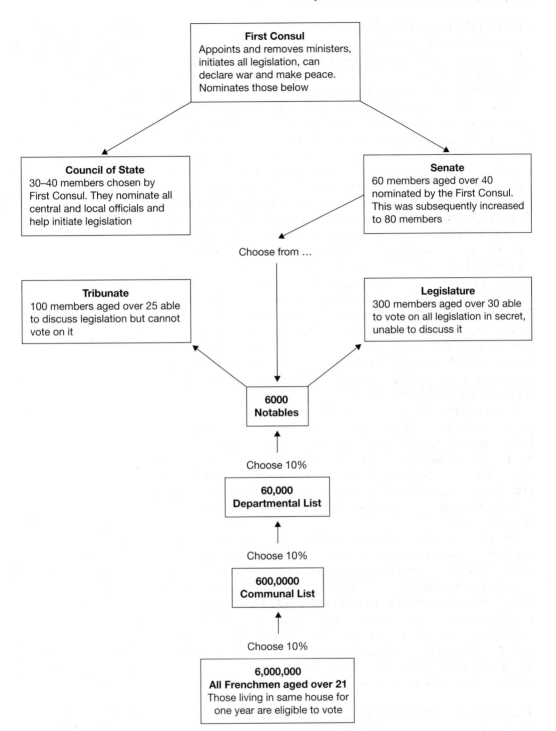

Figure 8.1: Summary of the key features of the constitution of Year VIII (1799)

known as **senatus-consultum**. It was this procedure that Napoleon used extensively from January 1801 onwards in order to block the wishes of the Tribunate and the Legislature. Senators were appointed for life, with a substantial salary, were suitably rewarded with gifts of land and money, and enjoyed considerable prestige. Membership of the Senate increased from the original 80 to about 140 by 1814, most of the addition members being Napoleon's direct nominees or 'grand signatories' of the Empire, used to fill up the Senate. As a result it developed into a largely consultative body anxious to please its benefactor and president, Napoleon.

The new constitution was submitted for approval in a plebiscite held in February 1800. Official results showed 3,011,007 voting in favour with 1562 against. A number of these plebiscites were held over the next 15 years as an attempt to seek popular approval for significant changes, as shown in Table 8.1.

Senatus-consultum
A procedure giving the Senate rights to preserve and amend the constitution and to agree major constitutional changes Napoleon wished to introduce independently of the legislative body.

Key term

Table 8.1: Plebiscites held during the Consulate and Empire 1800–15

Year	Purpose of plebiscite	Voting yes	Voting no
1800	Constitution of Year VIII	1,550,000*	1562
1802	Plebiscite on Life Consulate	3,653,000	8272
1804	Plebiscite on Empire	3,572,329	2569
1815	Plebiscite on *Acte Additionnel*	1,552,942	5740

* Revised figure.

In a number of ways the constitution established a framework for consolidating the main social changes brought about by the Revolution. Among the most important of these changes was the vast transfer of land that had taken place largely at the expense of the Catholic Church, but also from the nobility. It was necessary to bind the beneficiaries of these transfers to the new regime. This was achieved by creating a political system which favoured the well-off propertied classes. Power in the new regime was far more centralised than it had been under the Directory, in a way it was a reversion back to the Jacobin phase of the Revolution (1793–4) when France was governed by a dictatorship (see pages 106–8). By cultivating the support of notables Napoleon was seeking to incorporate and consolidate the new élite of talent and property that had emerged since 1789.

From Consul to Emperor

Napoleon only narrowly escaped assassination in December 1800, making the Senate anxiously aware of the fragile nature of a regime dependent for its continuation on one man. Partly because of this, and partly as a demonstration of gratitude to the First Consul for his achievements at home and abroad, it was decided to offer him the Consulship for life, with the right to nominate his successor. It was the first step towards the re-introduction of hereditary rule. Napoleon accepted and the decision was approved by plebiscite. (See Table 8.1 above.) While there is no evidence that the central government tampered directly with the figures, it is known that local officials often sent

◄───
Key question
Why did the Consulship give way to the Empire?

in results that they thought would be pleasing to their superiors, sometimes even recording a unanimous 'yes' vote when, in fact, no poll at all had been held.

Following the plebiscite, Napoleon's personal power increased immediately through his control of an enlarged Senate, which became responsible for everything not provided for by the constitution, and necessary to its working. This arrangement greatly reduced the power of the representative bodies, the Tribunate and the Legislature. They lost much of their importance, and met less frequently. The Tribunate was severely purged in 1802 for daring to criticise the proposed Civil Code (see page 194), and with a much reduced membership became little more than a rubber stamp for the remainder of its existence, while the Legislature's credibility was reduced by being 'packed' by Napoleon with 'safe' men who would not oppose his wishes.

Consolidating power

By 1803 Napoleon was riding in splendour around Paris and holding court in royal style. State ceremonies multiplied, etiquette was formalised, and official dress became more elaborate. The **Legion of Honour** (see page 193) had been introduced the previous year and there were hints that a nobility was to be re-established, the rumours fired by Napoleon's permission for a large number of *emigrés* to return to France. In 1804 a series of disasters, royalist plots and counter-plots culminated in the affair of the Duc d'Enghien; a member of the Bourbon royal family alleged to be involved in a plot to overthrow Napoleon by murdering him and taking over the government. The Duke was kidnapped on Napoleon's orders while on neutral territory, tried and, on rather inadequate evidence, found guilty of conspiracy. He was executed quickly in what amounted to judicial murder, justified by Napoleon on the grounds that he was entitled by the Corsican laws of vendetta to kill an enemy who threatened his personal safety.

In the wake of these events Napoleon began to prepare the people for his next step. There was widespread talk of making the Consulship hereditary within the Bonaparte family, in the hope of providing for a smooth succession and the survival of the constitution should Napoleon meet an untimely death. Then, in May 1804, a formal motion was approved by the Senate that 'Napoleon Bonaparte at present First Consul be declared Emperor of the French, and that the imperial dignity be declared hereditary in his family'. A third plebiscite held in November 1804 approved the change. Remembering that 40 per cent of the army vote two years earlier had rejected the proposal, the government took no chances this time and did not actually poll the soldiers. They simply added in approximately half a million 'yes' votes on their behalf.

To seal the transformation of the Consulship to that of a hereditary ruler, Napoleon planned a spectacular coronation to be held at Notre Dame on 2 December 1804. In the presence of the Pope, Napoleon, as previously arranged, crowned himself

Key question
How did Napoleon deal with potential rivals?

Key term

Legion of Honour
A high status organisation created by Napoleon to bind powerful men to his regime through granting them titles and rewards.

Key dates

Murder of the Duc d'Enghien: 20 March 1804

Napoleon declared Emperor: 18 May 1804

Emperor then crowned Josephine as Empress. During the next two or three years the Tribunate and the Legislature were hardly consulted at all. The Tribunate was finally abolished in 1808 and, although the Legislature survived, it was only able to do so by maintaining its subservient attitude to Napoleon's demands. Government was increasingly conducted through the Senate and the Council of State, both of which were firmly under Napoleon's personal control.

Napoleon on the Imperial Throne by Jean-Auguste-Dominique Ingres painted in 1806

All that remained to establish the Napoleonic dynasty securely was the production of a legitimate son and heir. In the years following his coronation it became increasingly obvious that an ageing Josephine was unable to provide him with an heir. Despite his continued fondness for her, Napoleon decided that a divorce was essential. He needed to persuade the Church to grant this. This was not easy, for although their original marriage had been a civil one, the Church had insisted on a second, Catholic, ceremony as a necessary preliminary to the coronation in 1804. Eventually by 1810 on the grounds of alleged irregularities in the conduct of the religious marriage, the Church unwillingly agreed to an annulment, leaving Napoleon free to remarry. A list of 18 eligible princesses was drawn up for him and later that year, at the age of 40, he married Marie Louise of Austria, a niece of Marie Antoinette. In the following year the hoped-for son and heir, Napoleon, King of Rome, was born. The succession seemed assured, the dynasty secure.

Maintaining power
Establishing financial stability

Of the many problems confronting the new government possibly the most pressing was the need to establish financial stability and secure an adequate revenue stream. There were only a few thousand **francs** available in the treasury in November 1799. Napoleon introduced a series of major financial reforms that went a considerable way to transforming the situation. As Napoleon lacked the technical skills to overhaul the financial system, he appointed a number of very able and efficient ministers to undertake this task. Among the key appointments were Gaudin as minister of finances in 1799 (a position he retained until 1814), and Barbé-Marbois at the treasury (1801–6). Both these appointments brought a measure of stability to state finances.

The early financial reforms introduced were:

- A much clearer division of roles between the ministry of finances (which oversaw collection of taxes and revenues) and the treasury (which dealt with government expenditure).
- The reorganisation of both direct and indirect tax collection.
- The first steps in establishing a public banking system.

One of Gaudin's most important reforms was to remove the assessment and collection of direct taxation from the control of local authorities and form a central organisation to undertake the task. The main source of government revenue continued to be the land tax. A much more detailed tax register detailing those eligible to pay was drawn up. More efficient land registers listing ownership helped to ensure that the amount paid was spread more evenly. Although the system was reformed and stabilised the amount raised remained fairly steady at some 250 million francs a year until 1813, which represented 29 per cent of government revenue.

A more dramatic increase in revenue came from indirect taxes. Many of these had been abolished by the Constituent Assembly.

Key questions
What measures were taken to establish financial stability? To what extent were they successful?

Key term

Franc
On 7 April 1795 the Convention introduced the silver franc as the official unit of currency replacing the *livre*.

However, faced with mounting deficits the Directory had reintroduced indirect taxes on certain goods. Napoleon centralised the collection of duties by creating a central excise office in 1804. Among the goods and services taxed were tobacco, alcohol, items made from gold and silver, playing cards and public transport. In 1806 salt was added to the list, which revived memories of the hated *gabelle* of the *ancien régime* (see page 5). Revenue from indirect taxes increased by over 400 per cent between 1806 and 1812 and was considered a much easier way of making up any shortfalls in government revenue from direct taxes. It is estimated that by 1813 revenue from all indirect taxes accounted for possibly 25 per cent of the government's revenue.

One of the most important reforms introduced by Napoleon (that still survives to this day) was the creation of the Bank of France in 1800. Although the bank was a private bank with its own shareholders, it was given a range of public functions such as the sole right to issue paper notes. A risky business venture in 1805 threatened the stability of the new bank. In order to boost state finances, a scheme aimed at importing silver from Mexico to Spain and then on to France was arranged. It even involved agreement from the British! When the scheme ended in failure, Napoleon, in order to avert a more serious crisis, imposed stricter controls on the bank.

An important indicator of the financial health of a country was the stability of its currency. The inflation linked to the *assignat* was a clear reminder to Napoleon of the problems an unstable currency could pose. On 28 March 1803 he introduced the *franc de germinal* which became the basis of his monetary system. The new gold and silver coins established a standard ratio of gold to silver at 1:15.5. Each one franc coin would weigh five grams of silver. Other denominations would be minted in strict proportion to this (e.g. a five franc coin would contain 25 grams of silver and so on). This reform gave France the soundest currency in Europe at that time. It would remain the basis of France's currency for the next 120 years.

Key question
What measures did Napoleon take to create a new currency?

The extent to which Napoleon achieved financial stability is difficult to assess. When compared with the financial chaos of previous regimes, both the Consulate and the Empire were much more successful. The currency was stabilised, public debts were honoured and the wages of public officials and the army were paid. But while greater efficiency was brought to the government's finances, greater burdens were placed on it. State expenditure increased steadily as a result of increasing military expenditure from around 700 million francs in 1806 to over 1000 million in 1813. The widening gap between the government's income and its expenditure was made up by forcing defeated countries to pay a financial penalty. The military defeats of 1813–14 removed this source of income and marked a renewed period of instability.

Key question
What measures did Napoleon take to ensure support to his regime?

Key term

Patronage
The process of distributing gifts and favours in order to build up support.

Patronage and bribery

To secure his position Napoleon sought to attract and bind to his regime as many powerful political and military figures as possible. He adopted a number of strategies which appealed to people's self-interest, vanity and desire for status. He lavished gifts of money, land, titles, honours and government appointments in order to build up a strong group of powerful individuals with a clear motive for maintaining the regime in power. The main methods used were:

- The creation of the Legion of Honour by Napoleon in 1802. This was divided into 15 cohorts (groups) each comprising 350 legionaries, 30 officers, 20 commandants and seven grand officers. Recipients received a distinctive decoration and a small annual award. In the 12 years following its establishment, 38,000 awards (only 4000 of which went to civilians) were made.
- Between 1804 and 1808, new titles were created for the officials of the new imperial court. These ranged from 'grand dignatories' such as the arch-chancellor, through 'grand officers', down to lesser dignatories such as the prefects of the palace.
- Some of these titles brought with them large estates, and were bestowed on court officials and statesmen, as well as on the 18 outstanding generals who were created Marshals of France.
- In 1808 Napoleon began the creation of a new imperial nobility. All 'grand dignatories' became princes, archbishops became counts, mayors of large towns became barons, and members of the Legion of Honour were allowed to call themselves Chevaliers. If the recipient possessed a large enough annual income – 200,000 francs in the case of a duke, for instance – the titles could be made hereditary. In all, about 3500 titles were granted between 1808 and 1814, many to military figures.
- Civilians benefited from the allocation of *senatoreries*. These were grants of large country estates to members of the Senate, together with a palatial residence and an annual income of 25,000 francs to support it. Included in the grant was appointment as *préfet* (prefect) not just of the usual department but of a whole region.
- Lesser individuals also benefited from Napoleon's personal gifts. For instance, more than 5000 presents of enough money to buy a house in Paris and to live there in comfort were made to army officers, government officials and minor members of the new nobility.

Napoleon, however, seems to have realised from the beginning that bribery as a means of control was unreliable, and was not in itself enough to maintain popular support even among the recipients. Therefore, compulsion, intimidation and indoctrination all became part of the Napoleonic system of government.

Reforms and repression

The restriction of individual liberty of thought, word and deed was an important element in Napoleon's autocratic government. By numerous measures, some more subtle than others, he built up over the years a system of supervision and control described by historian Richard Cobb as 'bureaucratic repression'.

Key question
What were the main changes Napoleon made to the judicial system?

Agents of control: police and prefects

A number of changes were made to the judiciary. Judges, instead of being elected as under the Directory, were appointed by the government for life and were kept subservient and loyal by a combination of close supervision and a system of purges. A new hierarchy of judicial tribunals was set up. The Criminal, Commercial and Penal Codes were updated in a similar way to the Civil Code. In 1810 a system of arbitrary imprisonment without trial (similar to the *lettres de cachet*, see page 33) was reintroduced, although it was never extensively used, a form of house arrest being more usual.

Key question
How did prefects and the police control opposition?

The two most important agents of control were the police and the prefects. For much of the Napoleonic era the Minister of Police was Joseph Fouché. Both police and prefects had very wide-ranging powers.

- They acted as trained spies, imposed censorship, set up surveillance of possible subversives, searched for army deserters and organised raids on areas believed to be sheltering **draft dodgers** or enemy agents.
- They were assisted in the maintenance of law and order by a well-organised body of gendarmes. In 1810 there were 18,000 stationed throughout France. Reports were submitted to Napoleon daily by Fouché on the work of his department.
- They had a prefect (*préfet*) assisted by sub-prefects (*sous-préfets*) for each department. Other local officials such as mayors and all the municipal councils were nominated by the prefect. In addition to their official duties (tax collection, conscription, etc.) prefects were expected to spread propaganda, monitor public opinion in their areas and to report on any suspicious political activity. Suspects could be placed under house arrest.

Draft dodgers
Men who avoided the call to serve in the army.

Key term

With such well-organised surveillance it is not surprising that the regime met with little serious political opposition, especially as its potential leaders, notables, intellectuals and members of the bourgeoisie, were increasingly tempted into allying themselves with the government in the hope of reward.

The Civil Code

The French legal system was extremely complex with different systems operating in different parts of France. Although the Revolution had swept away many of the complexities there was considerable scope for further reform. Napoleon took an active interest in the formulation of the new Civil Code which was issued on 21 March 1804 (in 1807 it was renamed the *Code Napoléon*). Among the most important sections of the code were those

Key question
What did the Civil Code achieve?

The Civil Code was issued, renamed in 1807 the *Code Napoléon*: 21 March 1804

Key date

relating to individual rights and property rights. The code recognised the legal rights of those who had benefited from the purchase of confiscated Church and noble land. This was an attempt to bind them in to maintaining the regime. The system of inheritance of an estate introduced during the revolution – *partage* – was confirmed. While the Civil Code maintained some of the most important gains of the revolution – the abolition of feudalism, the removal of the privileged position of the Catholic Church within the State, freedom of conscience and equality before the law – it was also illiberal and restrictive. Napoleon took a personal part in preparing those sections that dealt with family law. He was intent on strengthening the authority of the father and the husband, who could send an adulterous wife or defiant child to prison. Divorce, although permitted in theory, was made very difficult and expensive to obtain.

Among the codes, the most illiberal measures were those relating to the treatment of black people and workers. Slavery was reintroduced in the French colonies 'in accordance with the laws current in 1789'. All workmen were made subject to close police supervision through use of the *livret*, without which it was legally impossible to obtain a job. Like a number of Napoleon's achievements there were two sides to the Civil Code. While it acknowledged many of the gains made during the Revolution it also confirmed the reaction against the achievements of the Republic through a return to a more authoritarian and restrictive legal system.

Censorship and propaganda

Napoleon had clear expectations that the French press would deliver all official propaganda. He was very aware of their power to undermine his regime so in 1800 he reduced the number of political journals published in Paris from 73 to nine, and forbade the production of any new ones. These survivors were kept short of reliable news and were forbidden to discuss controversial subjects. Their editors were forced to rely for news on articles published in *Le Moniteur*, which were written by Napoleon or his ministers. In 1809 censors were appointed to each newspaper and a year later provincial papers were reduced to one per department. In 1811 all except four of the Parisian papers were suppressed and those that remained were made subject to police supervision.

In the wider cultural field up to 1810 reports on all books, plays, lectures and posters that appeared in Paris were sent, often daily, to Napoleon, and publishers were required to forward two copies of every book, prior to publication, to police headquarters. In 1810 a regular system of censors was set up, more than half the printing presses in Paris were shut down, and publishers were forced to take out a licence and to swear an oath of loyalty to the government. Booksellers were strictly controlled and severely punished, even with death, if found to be selling material considered subversive. Some authors were driven into exile for criticising the government, while dramatists were forbidden to

Key terms

Partage
An estate is divided equally among all male heirs, unlike during the *ancien régime* when the eldest male heir inherited everything.

Livret
A combined work permit and record of employment.

Le Moniteur
The official government journal.

Key question
How did Napoleon enforce censorship and propaganda?

mention any historical event that might, however indirectly, reflect adversely on the present regime. Many theatres were closed down. Others operated only under licence and were restricted to putting on a small repertory of officially sanctioned plays.

Sculptors, architects and artists got off more lightly, as Napoleon utilised their talents to project his image through paintings monuments and pillars on a grand scale. Artists such as David and Ingres (see the illustrations on pages 32 and 190) were employed by Napoleon as State propagandists, depicting him as a romantic hero-figure, or the embodiment of supreme imperial authority in classical guise, often complete with toga and laurel wreath. David as 'painter to the government' was given responsibility for supervising all paintings produced in France, with particular reference to the suitability of the subject matter.

Education

Napoleon believed that there were two main functions to an education system:

Key question
What did Napoleon consider to be the purpose of education?

- To provide the State with a ready supply of civilian officials and administrators and loyal and disciplined army officers. He intended to recruit these from among the sons of the property-owning classes.
- To bind the nation closer together: an aim that could only be fulfilled if the government took direct central control over the system.

Education for ordinary people was neglected by Napoleon as it had been during the *ancien régime* and the Revolution. All that was considered necessary was a simple 'moral education' and basic literacy and numeracy. This was provided in primary schools run by the Church, by the local community or by individuals. Napoleon often declared his belief in equal opportunities for all according to ability and irrespective of birth or wealth, what he called 'careers open to talents', but as far as education was concerned he generally failed to ensure that this was carried out in practice. He also did not consider the education of girls to be a priority. As Napoleon once said 'marriage is their destiny', and therefore they did not need to think and should not be taught to do so.

It was in the field of secondary education that Napoleon sought to make an impact. A rather ineffective system of secondary schools had been set up under the Convention: the *écoles centrales*. They lacked sufficient funding and qualified staff to make any real impact. In 1802 secondary education was brought under central government control and the *écoles centrales* were gradually replaced by *lycées*. These new schools, there would eventually be 45 in total, were staffed by instructors chosen by Napoleon himself. The State provided 6400 scholarships to these schools, of which 2400 places were for the sons of soldiers and government officials. The remaining 4000 places were to be filled by

Lycées
Selective schools introduced in 1802 for educating the sons of the privileged.

Key term

competition from pupils from the best of the remaining secondary schools. In reality, the much sought-after places were almost entirely restricted to the sons of *notables*. In this highly centralised system, the government-appointed teachers would deliver a common syllabus from identical textbooks. Conditions were strict with military discipline operating. So tightly controlled was the system, that Napoleon boasted that he knew exactly what every pupil in France was studying from the time of day. The main aim of these schools was to train for France, its future civil servants and army officers.

In 1808 the Imperial University opened. It was not a university in the ordinary sense, where learning was freely carried out. Through its tightly controlled curricula its aim was to provide loyal teachers for the State secondary schools which operated only by its permission and under its authority. Total obedience was demanded by the university from its member teachers, who had to take an oath of loyalty to their superiors. Lessons were standardised, and what was taught was dictated in accordance with the needs and demands of the government.

Religion

> **Key question**
> Why did Napoleon agree the Concordat?

Since 1789 the Catholic Church and the French State had been in conflict (see pages 58–60). During the Directory there had been a revival of Catholic public worship that no government could safely have ignored or opposed. Napoleon's motives for seeking a *rapprochement* with the Pope were those of expediency. His own attitude to religion was ambivalent. Although the Napoleonic legend was to have him die in the Catholic faith, he paid it no more than lip service during his adult life. What he appreciated was the power of religion to act as the 'social bond' cementing together a divided people, and the importance of its official re-establishment in bringing an end to the schism between clergy who had sworn allegiance to the Revolution and those who had not (see pages 58–60). Religious peace would help bring political and social peace to France as Catholicism had become identified with the royalist cause and needed instead to be identified with the people as a whole.

> **Key date**
> The signing of the Concordat: 15 July 1801

Discussions with the papacy lasted many months before the **Concordat** was finally signed on 15 July 1801. Under the agreement:

> **Key terms**
>
> *Rapprochement*
> The restoration of friendly relations between countries or people previously hostile.
>
> **Concordat**
> An agreement between Napoleon and the Pope to try and end the divisions between the Church and State.

- The separation of Church and State, which had been one of the main policies of the revolution, was to end.
- The Catholic Church recognised the Revolution and agreed that no attempt would be made to recover Church lands.
- A State-controlled Church was established, and its clergy became paid civil servants, appointed by the government and bound to it by oath.
- While it was agreed that Catholic worship, should be 'freely exercised in France', it was also agreed that there would be toleration for other faiths under the Concordat.

The Concordat was published by Napoleon in April 1802 as part of a wide-ranging ecclesiastical law on to which he tacked the so-called 'Organic Articles'. These were a series of articles limiting in every possible way Papal control over the French bishops, while at the same time increasing State control over the activities of the clergy. Tensions between Church and State however remained. Napoleon angered Pope Pius VII by ordering, without reference to him, that the Church throughout the Empire should celebrate 16 August (the day after his own birthday) as St Napoleon's Day, unceremoniously removing from the calendar of saints the existing occupant of that date. The cult of the Emperor had reached its peak. It was clear that the Church was no longer the privileged First Estate it had been under the *ancien régime* with its tax exemptions and vast, landed estates. There appeared to be very little prospect that either would ever be restored.

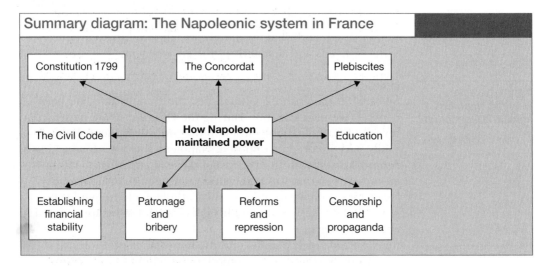

Summary diagram: The Napoleonic system in France

2 | The Establishment of the Napoleonic Empire

Although the official birth of the Empire was on 18 May 1804, when Napoleon proclaimed himself hereditary Emperor of the French, in reality it had started its unofficial life long before then, with the Revolutionary conquests and those of the Consulate (see pages 149–54). Both of these had pushed the frontiers of 'old France' (the France of 1790) out towards its 'natural frontiers' – and beyond.

The 'Empire' is often referred to as if it were a single entity embracing all French-controlled Europe. In reality it was a more complicated arrangement than that. The French Empire, properly speaking was:

- France of the natural frontiers (Rhine, Alps, Pyrenees).
- The annexed territories (*pays réunis*, ruled from Paris) of Piedmont, Parma, Tuscany, the Papal States, the Illyrian Provinces and, after 1810, the Netherlands.

Key question
What made up the Napoleonic Empire and why was it created?

- A semicircle of nominally independent satellite states (*pays conquis*) ruled by Frenchmen, usually Bonaparte relatives, which formed a buffer zone protecting the borders of the French Empire from attack. These states, combined with the French Empire proper, formed the Grand Empire. At various times these included Switzerland, the kingdoms of Spain, Naples, and Italy, the Confederation of the Rhine (which included the kingdom of Westphalia) and until 1810, the Netherlands and the Grand Duchy of Warsaw (created out of conquered Polish lands acted as a barrier to Russian expansion into central Europe, see the map on page 204). In northern Europe, Sweden came under French influence when it was compelled to operate the continental system, and accept one of Napoleon's Marshals as heir to its throne.

Of the Great Powers, Austria, Prussia and Russia, were each from time to time brought by military or diplomatic pressures into Napoleon's direct sphere of influence and each in turn became his ally, although not always willingly and only for a limited period. Only the Ottoman Empire and Britain, among the European powers, remained always outside Napoleon's control.

Napoleon's own explanation for the need to expand his territories was:

- to protect the territory of revolutionary France from attack by the 'old monarchies' of Europe
- to export the Civil Code, the Concordat and other benefits of Napoleonic rule to the oppressed peoples of neighbouring states
- to provide oppressed peoples with liberty, equality and prosperity
- to ensure the end of the old regimes in Europe
- to provide guarantees to citizens everywhere in the Empire against arbitrary government action.

Historians have argued at length over what really drove Napoleon to create the Empire. Some believe that Napoleon's conquests offered him opportunities to exploit the territories not only to secure his military domination, but also to reorganise the civil life of the annexed lands and that his imperial vision was a natural extension of his personal dynastic ambition. He was also determined to place as many of his close family and allies either on the thrones of newly conquered countries or to administer them (see page 214). Napoleon hoped that this would ensure complete loyalty to him. In the case of Spain this policy proved disastrous (see pages 203–6).

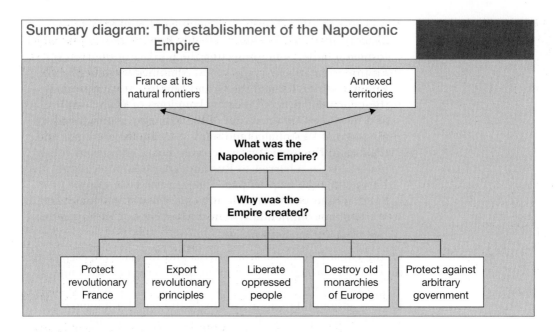

Summary diagram: The establishment of the Napoleonic Empire

France at its natural frontiers

Annexed territories

What was the Napoleonic Empire?

Why was the Empire created?

| Protect revolutionary France | Export revolutionary principles | Liberate oppressed people | Destroy old monarchies of Europe | Protect against arbitrary government |

3 | The Creation of the Napoleonic Empire in Europe

Key question
How successful militarily was Napoleon following his *coup d'état*?

For many, the most memorable of Napoleon's achievements were his military conquests, which laid the basis of his empire in Europe. His early military successes in Italy have been noted in Chapter 6 (page 151). Following these he had taken an army to Egypt to try to disrupt British power in the eastern Mediterranean. The campaign was a failure and he returned to France and joined in the plot to overthrow the Directory (pages 156–60). The need for an early victory and a quick peace after the *coup d'état* of November 1799 in order to strengthen his own position as First Consul led Napoleon back to Italy. There in June 1800, after a march across the Alps, he inflicted a decisive defeat on the Austrians at Marengo. A further French victory at Hohenlinden in Bavaria six months later brought about the peace of Luneville. It recognised French possession of Belgium (the Austrian Netherlands) as well as the left bank of the Rhine and the gains in Italy. Austria lost control of all northern Italy, except Venetia, and its influence in Germany was reduced. With the collapse of the Second Coalition Britain agreed to the Peace of Amiens (27 March 1802), by which France withdrew from the Papal States and Naples, and Britain returned most of its conquests including Egypt, which was restored to the Ottoman Empire.

Key date
The Peace of Amiens, which marked the end of the Revolutionary War, 1792–1802: 27 March 1802

The start of the Napoleonic War

Key question
Why did the war resume in 1803 and what was the outcome of Napoleon's plan to invade Britain?

The peace settlement proved to be unstable, in effect nothing more than a truce in a war that had already been going on for almost a decade. After a period of increasingly acrimonious relations between France and Britain the war resumed once again on 18 May 1803. While France was the dominant power on land,

Start of the
Napoleonic War:
18 May 1803

Battle of Trafalgar:
21 October 1805

Key questions
How significant were
the victories of
1805–7?

What was the extent
of Napoleon's
achievement by
1807?

Continental system
The attempt by
Napoleon to bring
economic chaos to
Britain by
preventing its
exports entering
Europe.

Satellite state
A state that is
subservient to
another, and cannot
act independently.

Britain was in clear control of the sea. Neither in itself was
sufficient for victory. Napoleon tried to remedy this by planning
an invasion of Britain. A large army was to be transported across
the English Channel by a combined Franco-Spanish fleet. The
plan failed when the Royal Navy under Nelson won a great sea
battle off Trafalgar on 21 October 1805. Even before this disaster,
Napoleon had gathered up his Army of England and marched
south to the Danube to confront Austria, who had declared war
on France during the summer.

The campaigns of 1805–7

The campaigns of 1805–7 that followed Napoleon's departure
from Boulogne showed him at his military best, winning a series
of crushing victories against the armies of Austria, Prussia and
Russia. The Austrians were outmanoeuvred and forced to
surrender at Ulm in October 1805. The defeat of an Austro-
Russian army at Austerlitz in December caused Russia to retreat
rapidly out of Napoleon's reach and Austria to agree to the Treaty
of Pressburg, which recognised French supremacy in northern
Italy and the loss of Austrian authority in Germany. Complicated
negotiations between Napoleon and Prussia, involving Prussia's
acquisition of Hanover in return for adherence to Napoleon's
continental system, led to a breakdown of relations and then to
war between the two countries.

In a remarkable one-week campaign Napoleon destroyed
Prussia at the twin battles of Jena and Auerstadt (October 1806).
In February 1807 Napoleon marched through Poland to attack
Russia, his remaining continental enemy, winning a technical
victory over the Russians in the bitter battle of Eylau. A major
defeat at Friedland in June convinced the Russians of the need to
make peace. This was done in July 1807 at Tilsit in a personal
meeting between Napoleon and Tsar Alexander I that took place
initially on a raft in the middle of the River Niemen, which
marked the Russian frontier.

In two years (1805–7) and a series of short campaigns,
Napoleon had in turn defeated three of his four opponents. In
November 1806 he established the continental blockade to deal
with the remaining one, Britain, who had taken no active part in
the war, restricting itself to supplying allies with subsidies.
Napoleon's achievements were:

- French domination in Germany by defeating Austria and
  abolishing the Holy Roman Empire.
- The creation of the Confederation of the Rhine as a French
  satellite state.
- The destruction of Prussian power in Poland, which was
  converted into the Grand Duchy of Warsaw.
- Prussia's lands in the west created into the new satellite
  kingdom of Westphalia.
- Napoleon crowned himself King of Italy, and added Parma and
  Tuscany to the existing French possessions of Piedmont and
  Lombardy.

- Naples becoming a French satellite.
- Russia was forced to concede peace in 1807, and Tsar Alexander was compelled to make a formal alliance with France.

By the end of 1807 Napoleon controlled directly or indirectly the greater part of Europe. The 'Grand Empire' had come into being.

Military and strategic developments

During the years 1805–7 Napoleon created in essence what became the Grand Empire. On the battlefields of Europe his forces were triumphant. His victories were gained as the consequence of a number of inter-related factors. Among these were circumstances that related to him personally and those concerned with the changing nature of warfare and the opponents he faced. The most important were:

Key question
What factors contributed to Napoleon's military success between 1803 and 1807?

- Napoleon's leadership qualities. He was a great general who achieved important conquests in a relatively short space of time, but also knew how to exploit his victories, to extract the maximum advantage from those he defeated. French domination therefore relied on diplomatic success as well as military achievements, and the great achievement of French diplomacy was to keep the coalition powers divided.
- Through the issue of daily bulletins Napoleon formed a special bond between himself and the army. He played on the ideas of military glory, of patriotism and of comradeship, while giving at the same time the impression that he had a deep paternal concern for his men.
- Napoleon's army was a product of the Revolution which had brought into existence a mass army forged in the belief that they were spreading revolutionary ideals. His army was based on the strength of the whole nation.
- Between 1801 and 1805 Napoleon created what became the *Grande Armée*. The whole army was divided into corps of about 25,000–30,000 men each composed of two or three divisions, infantry and cavalry; some of the cavalry were kept separate, as were the reserve artillery and several élite groups, the most important of which was the Imperial Guard. He controlled the army directly, which allowed unity of command and flexibility in action. Each corps was given a particular role on a campaign march, but this role could, if necessary, be changed quickly.
- New tactics were developed which emphasised troop mobility (infantrymen were required to march 12–15 miles a day) and living off the land instead of relying on military food supplies. Although senior officers were committed to the idea of the offensive and forcing the enemy to fight, this was only resorted to after they had been outmanoeuvred.
- From 1805 onwards he developed the use of war as *une bonne affaire* ('a good thing') financially. Peace treaties imposed on defeated countries not only provided for maintaining of Napoleon's troops on their territory (food and shelter), but included the payment of massive indemnities: Prussia was

Key term

Grande Armée
Napoleon's renamed army after 1805. At its largest in 1812 it numbered over 600,000 men, among them Poles, Italians, Swiss and Bavarians.

forced to find 311 million francs after being defeated at Jena in 1806. War had become satisfactorily self-financing.

- The only consistent theme running through the years from 1800 to 1815 was his hatred for Britain. Following the defeat of his invasion plan in 1805, Napoleon adopted another strategy to try to defeat Britain. He planned to destabilise the British economy by means of the continental system. This system envisaged blockading British trade by denying it access to European markets. The continental system had an important consequence for the war since it meant the need for further conquests to try to close mainland Europe to British exports.
- The weakness of Napoleon's enemies – Britain, Russia, Austria and later Prussia – formed a series of anti-French alliances with each other, but these were continually undermined by their mutual suspicions and jealousy. Only Britain remained opposed to France for the whole period. The other three powers were tempted away from time to time by Napoleon's offers of territory.

4 | The Defeat and Downfall of the Empire

From the height of his power in Europe in early 1810, Napoleon and his Empire collapsed in spectacular fashion. Two events in particular played a crucial role in contributing to Napoleon's downfall: the Peninsular War (1808–14) and the invasion of Russia in 1812.

The Peninsular War

Key question
Why and with what consequences did Napoleon become involved in the Peninsular War?

Iberian peninsula
Spain and Portugal combined.

Key term

Forced abdication of the King of Spain and the beginning of the Peninsular War: 5 May 1808

Key date

To try to secure the defeat of Britain Napoleon decided to enforce the continental system (see page 201) much more rigorously. In 1808 he invaded and occupied the Papal States in an attempt to force the Pope to impose this strategy. However, British goods were continuing to enter Europe via their long-standing ally, Portugal. The value of British exports entering Europe through Portuguese ports actually doubled between 1808 and 1809 to nearly £1 million, and by 1811 the annual total had increased to more than £6 million. Portugal's more powerful neighbour Spain, was a country very much in decline whose government and vast overseas empire in the Americas were ruled very inefficiently. To ensure the continental system was fully enforced, and to stop British imports entering the **Iberian peninsula**, Napoleon on 5 May 1808 deposed the Spanish king and his heir, and placed his own brother Joseph on the throne. There were a number of consequences to this decision:

- Large numbers of ordinary Spanish people rose in revolt against French rule.
- Maintaining garrisons in Spain proved to be a significant drain on French military resources.
- The Franco-Spanish attack on Portugal prompted Britain to commit military forces to defend its ally.

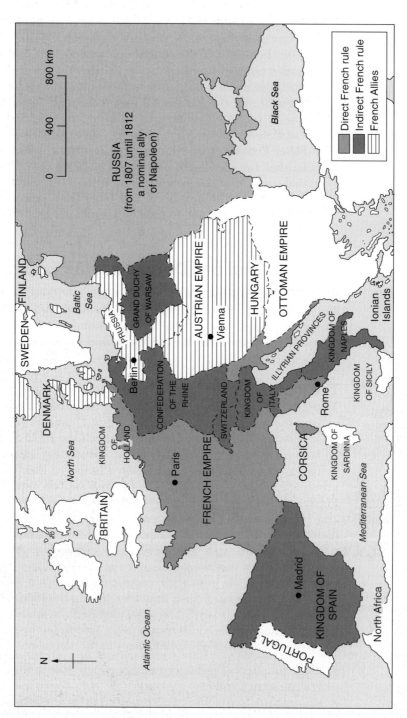

Map showing Europe in 1810 when Napoleon's Grand Empire was at its height

- Napoleon's inability to resolve the situation cast doubts on his military and political judgement.

As soon as Joseph arrived in Spain in May 1808 he was confronted by a revolt in Madrid which was put down by the French with great ferocity. A hundred Spaniards were executed in retaliation for the killing of 31 Frenchmen. The artist Goya's horrific images helped rouse the whole population to patriotic anger against the French occupying forces (see below). Local resistance committees (*juntas*) were set up, coordinated by the clergy and members of the nobility, to raise guerrilla fighters and regular soldiers. A small and comparatively inexperienced French army was defeated at Baylen by a force of Spanish regular troops. The sensation created by this defeat brought Napoleon himself to Spain with 100,000 veterans of the *Grande Armée*. A British expeditionary force was dispatched to the peninsula in answer to a Spanish request for help and quickly drove the French out of Portugal.

The campaign fought in the Iberian Peninsula over the next six years was a brutal guerrilla war (see page 97). In 1812 it was estimated that there were between 33,000 and 50,000 Spanish irregular forces engaged in the campaign against Napoleon. The arrival of the Duke of Wellington in Portugal in 1808 provided a

The Disasters of War: Heroic feat! Against the dead! created by Francisco Goya in the period 1810–14. Goya was the first modern artist to use the power of visual images to depict the horrific reality of war and to bring this to a large audience.

substantial boost to the anti-French campaign. Wellington's army
numbered some 35,000 men and, because they lacked both
artillery and cavalry, they relied heavily on guerrilla forces. He
proved to be a formidable opponent, and although a cautious
commander he was able to exploit French weaknesses regarding
lack of supplies while at the same time fully utilising British naval
supremacy to re-supply and reinforce his own forces. In 1810–11
Marshal Massena attacked Lisbon, failed in his objective and
suffered 25,000 casualties in the process. As Wellington shrewdly
observed in 1811, there were 353,000 French troops in Spain and
yet they had no authority beyond the spot where they stood.

Wellington made little impact on the general European
conflict. Britain was unable to prevent the defeat of Austria in
1809 or the invasion of Russia in 1812. In the wake of France's
military commitment and disasters in Russia however, Wellington
moved on the offensive. In 1812 he captured Ciudad Rodrigo
and Badajoz. Following the defeat of Marmont at Salamanca he
entered Madrid. Northern Spain was liberated in 1813 following
his victory at Vittoria. French forces were driven back across the
Pyrenees and finally defeated at Toulouse in 1814. The war in
Spain was never popular in France. French military prestige was
eroded during the long drawn out campaign against guerrillas,
which was both expensive and demoralising. It is aptly called the
'**Spanish ulcer**'.

Spanish ulcer
Used by Napoleon
as a term for a
wound that weakens
the victim without
ever being fatal.

Key term

The invasion of Russia 1812

The improved relations between France and Russia that the treaty
of Tilsit in 1807 brought about proved to be difficult to maintain,
and both sides felt uncomfortable about the relationship. A
number of issues caused friction between the two countries and
led to a resumption of hostilities. The main factors that led to
conflict were:

Key question
Why did Napoleon
invade Russia in
1812?

- Mutual distrust of each other's hostile expansionist aims in the
  Baltic, central Europe and the Balkans.
- Napoleon's refusal to support the Tsar's ambitions to seize
  Istanbul.
- Alexander attacked Sweden with French encouragement, but
  without French agreement seized and annexed Swedish
  Finland.
- There were arguments over the future of the Grand Duchy of
  Warsaw.
- The main disagreement arose over the Tsar's virtual withdrawal
  from the continental blockade. On the last day of 1810 he
  introduced a new trade tariff that discriminated against France
  and in favour of Britain.

Of these factors the determination to enforce the continental
blockade was essential. The army Napoleon gathered to invade
Russia was the largest he had ever assembled. It was also one of
the most cosmopolitan forces created since the time of the
crusades in the twelfth century. The *Grande Armée* of 600,000
consisted of Germans, Swiss, Spanish, Portuguese, Italians, Poles

and Lithuanians. Only about 270,000 of the total were Frenchmen. Napoleon had never before commanded such a large force, over such a vast area. During the course of the campaign he was inexplicably indecisive and lethargic at critical moments.

On 22 June 1812, without any declaration of war, Napoleon crossed the River Niemen. He was unable to use his usual strategy of luring the enemy towards him, and forcing a decisive battle early in the campaign. The much smaller Russian armies continually retreated before him destroying food supplies as they went. Napoleon was therefore drawn ever deeper into Russia, extending his supply lines and increasing the difficulties for his large, slow-moving force of catching up with the enemy. The Russian army's **scorched earth** tactic meant that Napoleon found it difficult to feed his men and horses. By the time Napoleon reached the outskirts of Moscow on 7 September the Russians decided to stand and fight. In a day-long battle of enormous ferocity, Napoleon won a victory of sorts, after a prolonged artillery duel, but at great cost in men and guns. The French lost 30,000 men, and the Russians 50,000. On 14 September Napoleon's advance guard rode into a largely deserted and burning Moscow. The Tsar refused to negotiate despite the loss of Moscow.

The retreat from Moscow

The unusually mild autumn tempted Napoleon to linger in Moscow for over a month. He ignored the warnings of bad weather to come, and only the eventual realisation that the *Grande Armée* would starve to death if he stayed longer in the ruined and empty city caused him to order a return home. Laden with loot and slowed down by their wounded, the army began the retreat on 19 October, which became one of the greatest military disasters of Napoleon's career. Sickness and skirmishes, famine and exhaustion took their toll, and the onset of the severe Russian winter made any problems significantly worse. The *Grande Armée* was effectively destroyed. Only 25,000 survived to reach Germany by the end of 1812. The fragility of the imperial government was exposed by the Malet affair (22–3 October 1812) when a plot by a former general almost succeeded in persuading some key officials that the Emperor was dead and a provisional government needed to be formed. But the ruse failed to convince everyone and the plotters were arrested and quickly executed.

There were a number of factors which help explain Napoleon's defeat in Russia. The *Grande Armée* was lost through a combination of bad management, poor supply arrangements, lack of local knowledge, and over-confidence. Napoleon had allowed himself nine weeks to defeat Russia and return in triumph to Germany. His army had only summer clothing and enough food for three weeks (he intended to be comfortably ensconced in Moscow as Emperor of the East by then). Many supplies proved inadequate or non-existent. There was no fodder for the horses, nor frost nails for their shoes, no maps covering more than a few miles inside the Russian border, and no

Key date

Napoleon invaded Russia: 22 June 1812

Key term

Scorched earth
A policy of destroying all food and shelter in front of an invading army to deny them essential supplies.

Key question
What were the consequences of the retreat from Moscow?

bandages for the wounded. There was unusual confusion in the French army command, too. General Caulincourt wrote after leaving Moscow, 'Never was a retreat worse planned, or carried out with less discipline; never did convoys march so badly … To lack of forethought we owed a great part of our disaster.'

The final campaigns 1813–15

The Russian disaster encouraged Napoleon's enemies to construct a new anti-French coalition. Although this was not a formal alliance, by late summer 1813, for the first time *all* the Great Powers, Britain, Russia, Prussia and Austria, were at war with Napoleon. In October the numerical superiority of the combined armies of Austria, Prussia and Russia enabled them to win a decisive but expensive victory at Leipzig in the three-day 'Battle of the Nations'. Outnumbered, Napoleon was heavily defeated and forced back to the Rhine. His influence in Germany gone, the Grand Empire was starting to unravel. The members of the fourth coalition agreed a formal alliance through the Treaty of Chaumont in March 1814. This treaty, which converted the coalition into a Quadruple Alliance, committed each of the four powers not to conclude a separate peace but to fight on until Napoleon was defeated.

In France there was discontent and opposition to the war as preparations began in bitter winter weather for a new campaign. Napoleon set to work to raise yet another army and to find the money to equip it. The financial situation was desperate, and the burden of conscription had become intolerable in a country that had been at war for 20 years. Despite the fact that for the first time since 1792 France was facing invasion by the 'kings' of old Europe, the country was war weary and there was no real enthusiasm for continuing the struggle. Despite a series of small victories Napoleon was unable to prevent his enemies from entering Paris in March 1814. He abdicated in favour of his young son, but the allies restored the Bourbons with Louis XVIII becoming the new king. The terms of Napoleon's future were settled by the Treaty of Fontainbleau. Napoleon was granted the sovereignty of the Island of Elba and a pension.

The Hundred Days

Following Napoleon's abdication the future of France and its Empire was discussed at Vienna. Differences between the victorious allies emerged regarding the post-war settlement. Napoleon, sensing an opportunity to split the allies and recover his throne, left Elba and landed in France to launch a new campaign which lasted 100 days. He immediately gathered together an army of former soldiers. His immediate targets were the two allied armies in Belgium under Wellington and the Prussian General, Blucher. Napoleon hoped to defeat them before they could combine with significant numbers of Austrian and Russian forces heading towards France. On 18 June 1815 one of the decisive battles in European history was fought near the Belgian village of Waterloo. Napoleon had a slight numerical

Key question
Why did Napoleon's invasion of Russia fail?

Key question
How was Napoleon finally defeated?

Battle of Waterloo: 18 June 1815

Key date

advantage over Wellington, 72,000 men to 68,000. The outcome of this evenly balanced struggle was ultimately determined in favour of the allies by the arrival of the Prussians. As Wellington said the next day 'it was a damned close thing – the nearest run thing you ever saw in your life'. Napoleon's hopes of continuing the campaign were dashed when he failed to secure further support. Without political or popular support he had no option but to agree to demands for his second abdication. On 8 July Louis XVIII made his second entry into Paris. After Napoleon's final abdication and exile in June, the second Treaty of Paris (November 1815) reduced the frontiers of France beyond the proposals of the previous year, to those of 1790. The First Empire was finally at an end.

Key question
To what extent did Napoleon preserve the Revolution?

Assessing Napoleon's impact on France

There is a measure of agreement that France changed less in the Napoleonic period than during the shorter Revolutionary one. In many ways aspects of his regime resembled the *ancien régime*:

- Governmental and administrative reforms replaced the popular sovereignty of the Revolution (loosely controlled, devolved government based on a system of elections) with a centralised autocratic rule not unlike that of the *ancien régime*, especially after the establishment of the Empire in 1804.
- Legal and judicial reforms were based on the authoritarianism of Roman law.
- The suppression of freedom of expression and his extension of police powers smacked more of the Bourbon monarchy than of the Revolution (with the exception of the Jacobin dictatorship).
- Opposition was vigorously rooted out. Life was geared to the service of the State and its ruler in a way never previously seen in France, even in the time of Louis XIV.
- By the Concordat the Catholic Church was restored to a position of power and influence in the state with few exceptions as it had been during the *ancien régime*.
- Although for administrative purposes the departments of the revolution were retained, he reintroduced the 40,000 pre-1789 communes as the basic territorial and 'electoral' unit.
- A central role in local government during the Napoleonic era was the prefect, who although he resembled the *intendent* of the *ancien régime*, had in reality far more power.
- During the Revolution the nobility and all ranks and status had been abolished, but under Napoleon a new imperial nobility was created and the Legion of Honour recreated a hierarchy of ranks.

Despite the authoritarian nature of his regime, Napoleon *did* maintain the great gains of the Revolution. He confirmed in the constitution and the Civil Code, the end of feudalism in France and the equality of Frenchmen before the law, and in the Concordat the irrevocability of the sale of the *biens nationaux* (see page 55).

In a number of areas the Napoleonic era did not significantly transform France, although the country did change. The most notable feature of Napoleon's rule was the almost continuous period of war: unbroken after 1803 until his overthrow in 1815. This had a profound impact on the country in a number of areas:

Key question
To what extent had Napoleon transformed France by 1815?

- *Society*. The wars had a dramatic effect on French population. The 916,000 killed (out of two million in the army) between 1800 and 1814 represented about 7 per cent of the total population of France. They were, however, mostly young men of marriageable age – a devastating 38 per cent of men born in the years 1790–5 were killed, the majority of them between 1812 and 1814. To the extent that this must have left many young women without husbands, and have reduced further the already declining birth rate, Napoleon's wars must accept some responsibility for the slow growth of the population in nineteenth-century France.
- *The economy*. Behind the protection of the continental system, French industry did expand slowly during Napoleon's rule albeit from a rather low base. Textile production increased as did the iron and coal industry. Trade with continental Europe certainly expanded. Across industry as a whole there is little evidence that by 1815 France was on the verge of an industrial revolution of the kind experienced in Britain.
- *Culture*. Even allowing for the stifling effect of his policies of propaganda and indoctrination, Napoleon was not much concerned with the arts, literature, sculpture, painting or drama, except in so far as they glorified himself. He closed down most of the theatres in Paris. Paris itself changed little under Napoleon. Apart from the addition of a number of triumphal monuments in classical style – the Arc de Triomphe itself, and the column in the Place Vendôme that bears a statue of Napoleon in a toga. The style of the years 1800–15, was known as 'Empire' (perhaps to emphasise the importance of official art), and is seen at its most distinctive in the context of interior decoration where it directly reflects Napoleon's own interests, inspired from the classical world of Greece and Rome or from Egypt.
- *The frontiers of France*. At the height of the Empire in 1811 Napoleon controlled, either directly or through his allies and satellites, most of mainland Europe. The prestige of having the largest European empire since that of Rome counted for little when the first Treaty of Paris (1814) pushed the frontiers of France back to those of 1792, the second Treaty of Paris pushed them back to 1790. There was nothing left of the imperial possessions. Even the 'natural frontiers' were lost. In territorial terms no trace of the Empire survived.

Some key books on Napoleon

R.S. Alexander, *Napoleon* (Arnold, 2001).
Geoffrey Ellis, *Napoleon* (Longman, 1997).
Martyn Lyons, *Napoleon Bonaparte and the Legacy of the French Revolution* (Macmillan, 1994).

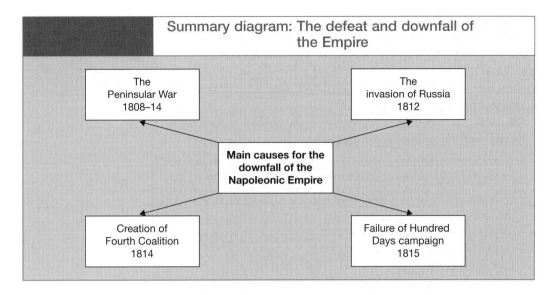

Summary diagram: The defeat and downfall of the Empire

The Peninsular War 1808–14

The invasion of Russia 1812

Main causes for the downfall of the Napoleonic Empire

Creation of Fourth Coalition 1814

Failure of Hundred Days campaign 1815

Study Guide: AS Questions

In the style of AQA

(a) Explain why Napoleon established the Legion of Honour in 1802. (12 marks)

(b) How important was the Concordat of 1801 for the consolidation of Napoleonic rule in France? (24 marks)

> *Exam tips*
>
> *The cross-references are intended to take you straight to the material that will help you to answer the questions.*
>
> **(a)** Try to think of long- and short-term or general and specific factors here so as to show the relative importance of the different reasons you may offer. To explain the general or long-term position you would need to refer back to the demise of the traditional nobility in the revolution that had left the way open for a new system of rewards. More specific short-term Napoleonic concerns might include a love of pageantry, a need to bind men to Napoleon's regime in order preserve it, a concern for reward: both civilian and military and a wish to bring ex-*émigrés* back into the new regime to strengthen and legitimise it.
>
> **(b)** You will need to show the opportunities that the Concordat provided for Napoleon and balance these against other factors that enabled him to consolidate his rule. Re-read pages 197–8. The importance of Church–State conflict in the revolutionary period will need to be addressed and the advantages of religious peace and Church support explained. Rather than listing the terms of the Concordat, try to assess their importance in bolstering the cult of Napoleon and providing the government control he sought. Other factors that also helped the consolidation of Napoleonic rule must include political measures, establishing financial stability, and Napoleonic reforms and repression. Remember to decide your argument before you begin and try to provide a supported judgement in your answer.

In the style of OCR A

'The *main* effect of Napoleon's reforms during the Consulate was to bring order and stability to France.' How far do you agree with this view? (50 marks)

Exam tips
The cross-references are intended to take you straight to the material that will help you to answer the question.

In this evaluative question, you first need to provide an argument that supports the view. Some of the following points may be referred to:

- constitutional reforms that brought about a more ordered and efficient government (pages 186–8)
- stable finances and economy (pages 191–2)
- law, order and the police (pages 194–5)
- religious toleration, the Concordat (pages 197–8)
- reforms to the Civil Code (pages 194–5)
- educational developments (pages 196–7).

A counter-view should then be given that might include the following:

- Napoleon's centralisation of power (pages 186–8 and 189–90)
- the lack of personal freedom (pages 194–5)
- educational benefits (pages 196–7)
- codification of the law (page 194–5).

'Napoleon was successful in Europe between 1803 and 1809 because his enemies were incompetent and divided.' How far do you agree with this view? (50 marks)

Exam tips
The cross-references are intended to take you straight to the material that will help you to answer the question.

This question requires you to give a balanced response that evaluates a range of factors. Arguments in favour of the view are:

- poorly constructed second and third coalitions and coalitions that never included all the great powers (page 203)
- Austrians in 1805 at Ulm (page 201)
- Prussians in 1806 at Jena-Auerstadt (page 201)
- divisions between generals and rulers at Austerlitz
- separate peace treaties (pages 201–2)
- slow troop movements.

Against these points, more positive reasons may be given:

- the size, tactics and organisation of the French army (pages 202–3)
- the quality of conscription and morale of the army
- Napoleon's generalship and diplomacy
- the unity of command
- available resources.

Reach a judgement based on your main lines of argument.

Study Guide: Advanced Level Question

In the style of Edexcel

'The years 1799–1804 in France were marked primarily by Napoleon's establishment of a personal dictatorship.' How far do you agree with this judgement?   (30 marks)

Exam tips

The cross-references are intended to take you straight to the material that will help you to answer the question.

In planning your answer, you should be clear what measures Napoleon took to increase his control, consider whether these constituted a dictatorship, and whether there were other developments of significance within France in the period. Napoleon's increased control can be shown by an analysis of its nature in 1799 (page 186) and its growth in the period: Consul for life; the purging of the Tribunate and Legislative Assembly in 1802; becoming Emperor of the French (pages 188–90); and increasing control of the press (page 195).

   To assess whether this constituted a dictatorship you should assess what constraints there were on his exercise of power (page 186). You will need to be careful to respect the chronological timeframe of the question, but you could draw selectively on the material (pages 186–9) to show that the measures Napoleon took to strengthen the regime after 1804 would suggest that a dictatorship was not securely in place by then. The period clearly saw a dramatic increase in the control Napoleon was able to exercise, but you should consider other matters before coming to an overall judgement. There were key reforms: the creation of the Bank of France and reform of finances (pages 191–2); the Concordat (page 197); the development of the *code civile* (page 194); educational reforms (page 196). These would enable you to argue that it was a period marked by significant domestic reform and change in France.

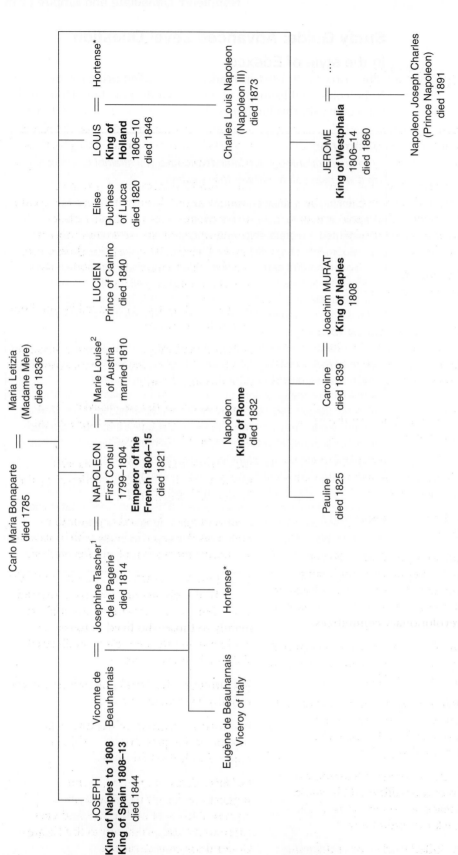

Napoleonic family tree. Note how Napoleon sought to place close members of his family on the thrones of countries he was seeking to control.
[1] Josephine was Napoleon's first wife. [2] Marie Louise was Napoleon's second wife. * Hortense was Josephine's daughter from her first marriage, and married Napoleon's brother, Louis.

Glossary

Active citizens Citizens who, depending on the amount of taxes paid, could vote and stand as deputies

Agents nationaux National agents appointed by, and responsible to, the central government. Their role was to monitor the enforcement of all revolutionary laws.

'Altar of the fatherland' A large memorial to commemorate the Revolution.

Ancien régime An expression that was commonly used during the 1790s to describe the French system of government laws and institutions before the Revolution of 1789.

Annates Payments made by the French Church to the Pope.

Annex To incorporate foreign territory into a state – usually forcibly and against the will of the local people.

Anti-clericalism Opposition to the Catholic Church.

Anti-republican opposition Forces opposed to the Republic. Comprising former members of the nobility, refractory priests and monarchists. Sometimes known simply as revolutionary committees.

Appel nominal Each deputy was required to declare publicly his decision on the guilt or innocence of Louis XVI.

'Armée révolutionnaire' *Sans-culottes* sent to the provinces to confront counter-revolutionary forces and ensure the movement of food supplies.

Armistice An agreement between two countries to end hostilities. This would precede a peace settlement that would formally mark the end of a war.

Artisan A skilled worker or craftsman.

Assignat Bonds backed up by the sale of Church land that circulated as a form of paper currency.

'Austrian Committee' A group of influential politicians and close confidants who gathered around Marie Antoinette, the daughter of the Austrian Empress Maria Theresa. They kept in close secret contact with Vienna, the capital of the Austrian/Habsburg Empire.

Avignon Territory controlled by the Pope in southern France.

Balance the budget To create a situation in which the government's expenditure is equal to its income.

'Bankruptcy of the two-thirds' The government wrote off two-thirds of the debt it owed its creditors.

Biens nationaux The nationalised property of the Church as ordered by the decree of 2 November 1789.

Bonnet rouge The red cap popularly known as the cap of liberty, which became an important symbol of the Revolution.

Bourgeoisie Usually translated as middle class. In the eighteenth century it carried a much less precise meaning and applied mainly to those who lived in towns and made a living through their intellectual skills or business practices.

Brigandage Outbreaks of lawlessness and violence by groups of bandits.

Brissotins A group of deputies who supported Jacques Brissot and later merged with the Girondins.

Cahiers Lists of grievances and suggestions for reform drawn up by representatives of each estate and each community and presented to the Estates-General for consideration.

Canton An administrative subdivision of a department.

Centralisation Direct central control of the various parts of government, with less power to the regions.

Centre Those who sat facing the speaker favouring neither left nor right.

'Certificates of citizenship' Proof of good citizenship and support for the Republic, without which no-one could be employed.

Checks and balances Ensuring that the power given to the executive was balanced by the power granted to the legislature.

Chouan Guerrilla groups operating in the Vendée between 1794 and 1796.

Citizens' militia A bourgeois defence force set up to protect the interests of property owners in Paris. After the storming of the Bastille it became the National Guard.

Collective bargaining Where a trade union negotiates with employers on behalf of workers who are members.

Comités de surveillance Surveillance or watch committees.

Committee of General Security Had overall responsibility for police security, surveillance and spying.

Committee of Public Safety Effectively, the government of France during 1793–4 and one of the twin pillars of the Terror along with the CGS.

Commune The smallest administrative unit in France.

Communist A follower of the political belief that centres on social and economic equality as outlined Karl Marx.

Concordat An agreement between Napoleon and the Pope to try and end the divisions between the Church and State.

Conscription Compulsory military service.

Conservatives Those who did not want any reforms. They were deeply suspicious and sceptical of the need for any social or political change.

Conspiracy of Equals Babeuf's theory of how to organise a revolution – using a small group of committed revolutionaries rather than a mass movement.

Constitution The establishment of structures for governing a country. Among the most important of these are the making of laws, forming governments, conduct of elections, division of powers. The detail relating to these structures would be presented in the form of a written document.

Constitutional monarchists Supporters of Louis who welcomed the granting of limited democratic rights to the French people.

Constitutional monarchy Where the powers of the Crown are limited by a constitution. Also known as a limited monarchy.

Consulate The system of government that replaced the Directory. It took its name from the three Consuls of whom Napoleon was the most important as first Consul. They formed the executive in the new constitution of 1799.

Continental system The attempt by Napoleon to bring economic chaos to Britain by preventing its exports entering Europe.

Conventionnels Members of the Convention between 1792 and 1975.

Corvée Unpaid labour service to maintain roads, in many places money replaced the service.

Cottage industry Small-scale textile production (spinning, weaving and iron work) carried out in a peasant's cottage or workshop and used to supplement income from farming.

Counter-revolutionaries Those groups and individuals who were hostile to the

Revolution and the changes it imposed, and wished to reverse them at the earliest opportunity.

Coup of Thermidor The overthrow of Robespierre and his closest supporters, which marked the end of the Terror.

Cult of the Supreme Being Robespierre's alternative civic religion to the Catholic faith.

Decentralisation Where decision making is devolved from the centre to the regions of a country.

Dechristianisation Ruthless anti-religious policies conducted by some Jacobin supporters against the Church – aimed at destroying its influence.

Decree of Fraternity Set out the intention of the Convention to support those in any state who wished to overthrow their rulers and establish a democratic political system.

Deficit When expenditure is greater than income it results in a deficit.

Deflation A fall in prices as demand for goods and services falls.

Departments On 26 February 1790, 83 new divisions for local administration in France were created to replace the old divisions of the *ancien régime*.

Diocese An area served by a bishop. It is made up of a large number of parishes.

Disenfranchised Stripped of the right to vote.

Draft dodgers Men who avoided the call to serve in the army.

Egalitarian society Where citizens enjoyed equal rights and are not discriminated against on the basis of gender or social class. This is neatly summed up by the phrase most frequently linked with the Revolution – liberty, equality and fraternity.

Egalitarianism Derived from 'equality' – the aim to have all citizens equal, with no disparities in wealth status, or opportunity.

Élan Patriotic enthusiasm, commitment and identity with the revolutionary cause within the army.

Émigrés People, mainly aristocrats, who fled France during the Revolution. Many *émigrés* joined foreign opponents of the Revolution.

Entrepreneurs Individuals prepared to take risks with their capital to support business schemes which will secure high levels of profit.

Estates-General A body that, in 1789, contained 939 representatives of all three estates of the realm – Church, nobility and Third Estate. It was only summoned in times of extreme national crisis, and last met in 1614.

Executive power The power to make decisions relating to the government of a country.

Federalism A rejection of the central authority of the State in favour of regional authority.

Fédérés Mainly national guardsmen sent from the provinces to display national unity during the Fête de la Fédération that commemorated the fall of the Bastille.

Feudal dues Either financial or work obligations imposed on the peasantry by landowners.

Feuillants Constitutional monarchists, among them Lafayette, who split from the Jacobin Club following the flight to Varennes.

First coalition A loose anti-French alliance created by Britain and consisting of Holland, Spain, Piedmont, Naples, Prussia, Russia, Austria and Portugal. Russia refused to commit soldiers to the coalition when Britain did not send money to support her armies.

Forced loan A measure compelling the wealthy to loan money to the government.

Franc On 7 April 1795 the Convention introduced the silver franc as the official unit of currency replacing the *livre*.

Free market   A trading system with no artificial price controls. Prices are determined solely by supply and demand.

Free trade   Trade without the imposition of taxes and duties on the goods.

Gardes-françaises   A royal infantry regiment, many of whom deserted to opponents of the King in July 1789. They helped capture the Bastille.

General Maximum   Tables that fix the prices of a wide range of foods and commodities.

Généralités   34 areas into which France was divided for the purpose of collecting taxes and other administrative functions, and under the control of an intendant.

Germinal   Popular demonstration on 1 April 1795 in Paris. Named after a month in the new revolutionary calendar.

Girondins   A small group of deputies from the Gironde and their associates – notably Brissot.

Grande Armée   Napoleon's renamed army after 1805. At its largest in 1812 it numbered over 600,000 men, among them Poles, Italians, Swiss and Bavarians.

Great Powers   Countries that were more powerful than others on the basis of their military, economic and territorial strength – the major ones were Austria, Prussia, Russia, Great Britain and France.

Gross domestic product   The total value of goods and services produced by an economy.

Guerrilla warfare   Military action by irregular bands avoiding direct confrontation with the larger opposing forces. They did not wear uniforms in order to blend in with civilians.

Guild   An organisation that tightly controlled entry into a trade.

Guillotine   A machine introduced in 1792 for decapitating victims in a relatively painless way. It became synonymous with the Terror.

Habsburg Empire   Territory that roughly corresponds to modern-day Austria, Hungary, the Czech Republic and Slovakia. The empire also considered itself to be the leading German state.

Hoarders   Those who bought up supplies of food, keeping them until prices rose and then selling them at a large profit.

Iberian peninsula   Spain and Portugal combined.

Indulgents   The name given to Danton, Desmoulins and their supporters who wished to see a relaxation of the Terror.

Industrial capitalism   An economic system where money (capital) is invested in industry for the purpose of making a profit (the money which remains after all production costs have been met).

Inflation   A decline in the value of money, which leads to an increase in the price of goods.

Insurrection   An uprising of ordinary people, predominantly *sans-culottes*.

Intendants   Officials appointed by and answerable to the Crown. They were responsible for police, justice and finance. They were also responsible for public works, communications, commerce and industry.

Irish Nationalists   Irish who were staunchly anti-British and wished to be free from what they considered foreign rule. During the Revolution they approached the republicans for support.

Jeunesse dorée (**gilded youth**)   Young men who dressed extravagantly as a reaction to the restrictions of the Terror. They were also known as muscadins.

Journée   Day of popular action and disturbance linked to great political change.

La Marseillaise   The rousing song composed by Rouget de l'Isle in 1792 and adopted as the anthem of the Republic on 14 July 1795.

La patrie en danger   'The fatherland is in danger' became a rallying cry to ordinary people to help save the country.

Laboureurs   The upper level of the peasantry who owned a plough and hired labour to work their land.

Laissez-faire   Non-interference in economic matters, so that trade and industry should be free from state interference.

Law of Hostages   Laid down that the relatives of any French citizens challenging the authority of the Republic would be imprisoned at their own expense and their property seized to pay for damage done by anti-government rebels.

Law of Prairial   The most severe of the laws passed by the revolutionary government. The purpose of the law was to reform the Revolutionary Tribunal in order to secure more convictions. The law paved the way for the Great Terror.

Law of Suspects   Anyone suspected of counter-revolutionary activity and undermining the Republic could be arrested and held without trial indefinitely.

Laws of Ventose   Property of those recognised as enemies of the Revolution could be seized and distributed among the poor.

Left   Those seated on the left of the speaker favouring extreme policies such as removing the King and having a republic.

Legion of Honour   A high status organisation created by Napoleon to bind powerful men to his regime through granting them titles and rewards.

Legislative assembly   Came into existence in October 1791 and was the second elected Assembly to rule during the Revolution. It differed from the National/Constituent Assembly in that members were directly elected.

Legislative power   The power to make laws. In an absolute system this power belongs solely to the Crown. In a democracy legislative power rests with an elected parliament.

Le Moniteur   The official government journal.

Lettres de cachet   Sealed instructions from the Crown allowing detention without trial of a named individual.

Levée en masse   Compelled citizens to perform duties to defend the Republic – military service for single men, married men to move supplies, women to manufacture uniforms. Buildings and horses were taken over for military use.

Levy   An assessment to raise an agreed number of conscripts.

Liberals   Deputies who were far more tolerant of differing political views and who supported a measure of cautious reform.

Liberalism   A political belief which stresses the rights and liberties of the individual.

Livres   The currency of France during the *ancien régime*. One livre was made up of 20 *sous*.

Livret   A combined work permit and record of employment.

Lycées   Selective schools introduced in 1802 for educating the sons of the privileged.

Man of party   A phrase used by Napoleon to indicate he was not tied to any particular group, such as the monarchists or Jacobins, and that he was acting in the best interests of France.

Mandats territoriaux   The new paper currency issued by the Directory in March 1796 and withdrawn in February 1797, when worth only 1 per cent of face value.

Martial law   When there is severe rioting or public disorder, the authorities can declare martial law which would impose restrictions on movement and may suspend civil liberties.

Marxist interpretations   The interpretation of the Revolution as part of Karl Marx's analysis of history as a series of class-based struggles, resulting in the triumph of the proletariat.

Menu peuple   Used to describe ordinary people living in towns.

Militants   Those who differed from ordinary sans-culottes in that they adopted an extreme political position such as arguing for a republic, greater democracy and the destruction of privilege.

Mobilising   Calling up part-time soldiers or national guardsmen for military service.

Monarchist   Active supporters of the Bourbon monarchy.

Montagnards   The Mountain – the name given to Jacobin deputies who occupied the upper seats in the tiered chamber of the National Assembly.

Mortality rate   The death rate, which is measured per 1000 of the population.

National debt   Money borrowed by the government from its own people, on which it has to pay interest. This debt increased during the Revolution and the war.

National self-determination   The right of national groups such as Italians, Poles and Germans to govern themselves.

National synod   An assembly of representatives of the entire Church.

Natural frontiers   A barrier, such as a river, mountain range, the sea, etc., that separates countries.

Non-Commissioned Officers (NCOs)   Soldiers with ranks such as corporal or sergeant.

Non-juror   Those members of the clergy who refused to take the new oath of allegiance to the Civil Constitution.

Notables   Rich powerful individuals – the élite who controlled the political and economic life of France.

'Organiser of victory'   Description given to Carnot for his help in securing victory in Belgium and reversing the tide of defeat.

Paris Sections   Paris divided into 48 sections to replace the 60 electoral districts of 1789 – the section became the power base of the *sans-culottes*.

Parlementaire   Judges who held hereditary positions on one of the 13 parlements.

Parlements   Consisted of 13 high courts of appeal. All edicts handed down by the Crown could not be enforced until registered by the parlements.

Passive citizens   Approximately 2.7 million citizens who enjoyed the civic rights provided by the Declaration of the Rights of Man, but paid insufficient taxes to qualify for a vote.

Patriot party   A loose group of progressive reformers, mainly nobles and bourgeoisie who wanted changes to the political structure – a reduction in royal power in order to enhance their own positions.

Patronage   The process of distributing gifts and favours in order to build up support.

Partage   An estate is divided equally among all male heirs, unlike during the *ancien régime* when the eldest male heir inherited everything.

Pays d'états   Areas that had local representative assemblies of the three estates that contributed to the assessment and collection of royal taxes.

Penal code   A list of the laws of France and the punishments for breaking those laws.

Per capita   An economic measure used to determine output, calculated by dividing the volume or value of production by the number in the population.

Philosophes   A group of writers and thinkers who formed the core of the French Enlightenment.

Physiocrats   A group of French intellectuals who believed that land was the only source of wealth and that landowners should therefore pay the bulk of taxes.

Picketing   The practice used by strikers of trying to get others to join in.

Plain   The majority of deputies in the Convention who sat on the lower seats of the tiered assembly hall.

Plebiscite   A popular vote on a single issue.

Plurality   The holding of more than one bishopric or parish by an individual.

Politicisation   A process when people who were previously unconcerned with politics take an active interest in political issues which affect their daily lives.

Popular movement   Crowds of ordinary Parisians who became politically active as a consequence of the economic crisis. They demanded a political role as a means of improving their living standards.

Popular sovereignty   The idea that the people should exercise control over their government, usually by directly electing a representative assembly.

Prairial   A large popular uprising in Paris on 20–1 May 1795. It was named after a month in the new revolutionary calendar.

Prefect   Centrally appointed government official whose task was to administer a department and ensure government policy was carried out.

Primary assemblies   Meeting places for voters.

Purge   Forced removal of political opponents.

Rapprochement   The restoration of friendly relations between countries or people previously hostile.

Real wages   The actual purchasing power of money.

Refractory priests   Those who refused to take the oath.

Regicides   Those involved in the trial and execution of Louis XVI.

Regular army   The term used to describe the full time professional army. As events unfolded the white uniforms of the *ancien régime* were replaced by ones that reflected the colours of the Revolution: red, white and blue.

Representatives-on-mission   Mainly Jacobin deputies from the Convention who were sent to reassert government authority.

Republic   A political system which does not have a hereditary head of state and where the supremacy of the people is recognised through mass democracy.

Requisitioning   Compulsory purchase by the government of supplies of food and horses paid for in *assignats* – the new paper currency.

Revisionist historians   Historians who reject the Marxist analysis of the French Revolution and provide a revised interpretation.

Revolutionary myth   The frequently misguided belief that direct revolutionary action can bring about significant material improvement for the majority of society.

Revolutionary Tribunal   A court specialising in trying those accused of counter-revolutionary activities.

Revolutionary War   Fought by France against other European powers between 1792 and 1802.

Right   Those seated on the right of the speaker and supporting a limited monarchy.

Saint-Cloud   A former royal palace in the suburbs of Paris away from the influence of the Parisian populace, where the plotters believed that Jacobinism was still a powerful force.

Sans-culottes   Literally those who wear trousers (workers) and not knee-breeches (bourgeoisie) and has implications regarding social class. Used as a label to identify the more extreme urban revolutionaries of 1792–5.

Satellite republics   States that had the appearance of being independent but were in reality under French control.

Satellite state   A state that is subservient to another, and cannot act independently.

Scorched earth   A policy of destroying all food and shelter in front of an invading army to deny them essential supplies.

Séance royale   Session of the Estates-General in the presence of the monarch.

Second Coalition   Formed in 1799 and consisting of Britain, Russia, Austria, Turkey, Portugal and Naples.

Self-denying ordinance   Approved by the Constituent Assembly to ensure that none of its members could belong to the new assembly.

Senatus-consultum   A procedure giving the Senate rights to preserve and amend the constitution and to agree major constitutional changes Napoleon wished to introduce independently of the legislative body.

Separation of Church and State   The Republic was legally committed to religious neutrality. In order to serve their parishioners, priests were required to follow French law as opposed to Church law.

Separation of powers   The division of executive and legislative powers in order that the government could not make laws without the support of the legislature.

Serfdom   Part of the feudal system where the inhabitants of the land are the property of the landowner.

Skirmishing   A small group of soldiers who operate independently, fighting minor engagements and living off the land.

Social interpretations   The emphasis on changes in society – population trends, social class – as having a significant impact upon the Revolution.

Spanish ulcer   Used by Napoleon as a term for a wound that weakens the victim without ever being fatal.

State monopoly   A system whereby the State exercises total control over an industry and can set whatever price it wishes.

Summary execution decree   From 19 March 1793, any rebels captured with arms were to be executed immediately.

Suspensive veto   The right to reject a measure proposed by the assembly.

Tax farming   A system where the government agrees a tax assessment figure for an area, which is then collected by a company that bids for the right to collect it.

Tax rolls   Lists of citizens who had to pay taxes to the State.

Terror   The period roughly covering March 1793–August 1794 when the Jacobin government used execution and brutal repression to maintain the survival of the Republic against both its internal and external enemies.

Terrorist   An active supporter of the policies of the Terror.

Thermidor   A month in the new revolutionary calendar equivalent to 19 July–17 August.

Thermidorians   Those individuals and groups who had helped overthrow Robespierre.

Total war   All aspects of the State – population, economy, buildings – were used by the government to try and ensure victory.

Tricolore   The symbol of the Revolution. It combined the red and blue colours of Paris with the white of the Bourbons.

United Provinces   Present-day Holland ruled at the time by the House of Orange.

Universal male suffrage   A vote for every man over a certain age.

Venality   A system whereby certain jobs could be bought and transferred on to descendants.

Verona Declaration   A reactionary statement issued by the new heir to the throne promising to reverse many of the gains made during the Revolution.

Versailles   The vast and splendid palace built outside Paris by Louis XIV. Within the grounds Marie Antoinette had a small rural village built where she could pretend to be a simple peasant.

Vertu   'Virtue' – meaning moral excellence.

Voting by head   Decisions taken by the Estates-General would be agreed by a simple vote with a majority sufficient to agree any policy. This favoured the Third Estate, which had the most deputies.

Voting by order   Each estate votes separately on any issue. Any two estates together would outvote the third.

Index